SCIENCE PREP
PREPARATION FOR THE FLORIDA 8TH GRADE SCIENCE FCAT 2.0

2ND EDITION

Contact Information:

For comments, bulk purchase order requests, or related issues:

Email: **PrepCatPurchaseOrder@gmail.com**

CreateSpace eStore: **https://www.createspace.com/3658878**

Please accept our humble apologies for any errors that may have occurred during the publication process. It was never our intention : (

Contents

ABOUT THE NEW SCIENCE FCAT 2.0

The new FCAT 2.0 is a test that you will hopefully breeze through with the help of the **SCIENCE PREP CAT 2nd EDITION**. FCAT 2.0 science items are all multiple choice, focusing on content specific information that you have learned from 6th grade through 8th grade. However, because of the immense gap of time between testing, this book is a **must** for review purposes. Why, you ask? It is simple. The content of the book is formatted just like the FCAT 2.0. It is broken down into four areas; *Life Science*, *Earth and Space Science*, *Physical Science*, and the *Nature of Science* **(Scientific Thinking)**. Each area is written to specific Next Generation FCAT 2.0 standards encompassing 5th through 8th grade content (the 5th grade standards are thrown in for good measure!)

As for the FCAT 2.0 test, you should expect three types of questions; **low, moderate,** and **high complexity**. For low complexity questions you should expect mostly identification, retrieval, recognition, and even some calculations. For moderate complexity questions, you are going to have to apply your scientific knowledge, describe using examples, predict, compare, and choose the best responses. Lastly, high complexity questions require that you construct, explain, design, analyze, interpret, and even generalize based on the background knowledge you already possess. You should expect about 10-20 percent low complexity questions (roughly 8 to 10 questions), 60-70 percent moderate complexity questions (35-40 questions), and 10-20 percent high complexity questions (roughly 8-10 questions).

The ultimate goal of the FCAT 2.0 test is not only to test your knowledge of science content but to test your scientific understanding as well. If you diligently study the **SCIENCE PREP CAT 2nd EDITION** and give yourself ample time to allow the information to absorb into your mind, not only will you master exam content but you will also develop an understanding of science that leads to a greater appreciation of the discipline.

HOW TO USE THIS BOOK

1. Begin your study by organizing a good study schedule. Depending on when the upcoming exam will be administered, create a plan that will enable you to study the complete book in its entirety over time and which will allow you to chunk the contents into manageable amounts.

2. Remember that studying has four components; ***reading***, ***memorization***, ***practicing***, and ***teaching***. You should start your studies by reading each chapter, paragraph by paragraph, repetitively until you form a basic understanding of the concepts. Then you will move on to memorization. Certain concepts have to be consciously memorized, while others will automatically be committed to memory each time you engage in reading and re-reading for understanding. Once you have memorized a concept you should test your memory.

This is where practicing comes in. You can practice your memory by writing down everything you remember about a topic on a blank sheet of paper. Then use your notes to fill in gaps in your knowledge. The final component of studying involves teaching the material to someone else. This special someone can be a family member, friend, study group, or even a pretend class full of pretend students. If you can teach the material to another and do so with confidence and skillful ability than you have mastered the content and should then move on to the next concept. Obviously, this process requires time so you should make a solid commitment to engage in studying months before the exam. Your brain is a muscle that expands with exercise. Studying is the exercise of the brain!

3. Start studying your weakest content area first and save your most knowledgeable areas for last. Areas you struggle with will take more time to master.

4. Answer the sample review questions included at the end of each chapter and then check your answers. Go back and review the chapter content for questions answered incorrectly. The review questions are merely suggested sample questions. You can get further practice answering FCAT questions at the FL DOE website, by using your school-issued textbook, or by asking your teacher for additional resources. You should even make up your own questions and incorporate them into your studies.

5. When all four chapters are completed take and grade the *Final Exam*. You should aim for 80% proficiency or higher on the final exam. Continue to browse through all content periodically until a few days before the science FCAT. This will serve as a refresher for you.

6. The glossary contains vocabulary commonly found on the FCAT. You may not necessarily need to memorize each vocabulary word but you do need to understand what each word means. Familiar methods of studying vocabulary include; flashcards, graphic organizers, picture maps, etc.   As a challenge see if you can verbally define each term using three words or less in your definition. For example; "**abiotic**= nonliving"

7. Remember the *SCIENCE PREP CAT 2nd EDITION* is a study aid to be used along with any other resource you choose (class textbook, class notes, etc). It works great as a content stand-alone too! It is a workbook. Write in it. Highlight it. Use sticky notes. Read a little. Read a lot. Take it with you to the beach. Make it a constant companion!

8. You will do well to treat your brain like a computer. Without an operating system the computer could not function. *Science Prep Cat* is that operating system that will enable your computer (your brain) to function by assimilating information (thinking) in order to perform tasks (FCAT testing). So, the more work you do with this book the better you will be able to think about and explain science concepts—skills necessary to achieve a higher FCAT score. *IT'S THAT SIMPLE!!*

9. The night before the test do no studying. At this point it will only be considered cramming. Get a good night's sleep, a healthy breakfast the day of the exam and go into the test with the confidence that advanced preparation creates.

"High school is only one step away…prepare yourself properly so you can master your own FCAT scores and begin your high school career with excellence!!"

Best regards,
Dr. Matthew Phillips, Author

GLOSSARY OF SCIENCE TERMS

abiotic - describes the nonliving part of an ecosystem including water, rocks, light, and temperature.

absorption - the taking up and storing of energy, such as radiation, light, or sound, without being returned or transmitted.

acceleration - the rate at which velocity changes over time; an object accelerates if its speed, direction, or both change; usually expressed in meters per second squared (m/s^2).

acid - a substance that increases the hydrogen (H^+) concentration when added to a water solution.

activation energy - the least quantity of energy required to start a chemical reaction.

adaptation – a behavior or characteristic of an organism, such as fur color or speed that increases its chance of survival in its environment.

air resistance- "air friction". The force that opposes the motion of objects through air.

allele - one of the alternative forms of a gene that governs a characteristic, such as hair color.

amino acid – an organic molecule containing an amino group and a carboxyl group from which proteins are created; the building blocks of proteins.

amphibian - a cold-blooded, smooth-skinned vertebrate, which characteristically hatches as an aquatic larva with gills, then converts into an adult having air-breathing lungs.

amplitude – the maximum distance the particles of a wave travels from their rest position; the height of a wave.

anaerobic - occurring in the absence of oxygen or not requiring oxygen to live.

anatomy - the study of the parts of an organism (i.e.; organs and other structures).

angiosperm – flower producing plants.

antibiotic - a drug, often derived from fungi, used to kill bacteria and other microorganisms.

aquatic - taking place in or on water.

arthropod – invertebrate (lacking a backbone) animal characterized by a hard exoskeleton made of chitin and a segmented body to which jointed appendages move in pairs.

asexual reproduction - a form of reproduction that doesn't involve sex cells (gametes) and results in the offspring being genetically identical to the parent cell.

asteroid - small, often irregularly shaped rocky bodies that orbit the Sun primarily in the asteroid belt (a region between the inner and outer planets).

atmosphere - the layers of gas that surround Earth and other planets.

atom - the smallest unit of an element that has the same chemical properties of that element and is made up of a nucleus, protons, electrons, and neutrons.

axial skeleton - the bones constituting the head and trunk of a vertebrate's body.

axis - the imaginary line on which a planet rotates.

bacteria - a large group of single-celled organisms that lack a cell nucleus; reproduce by fission or by forming spores; and in some cases cause disease or death.

barometric pressure - the pressure of the atmosphere usually expressed in terms of the height of a column of mercury.

base - a substance that increases the hydroxide (OH^-) concentration of a solution.

Big Bang Theory - a theory of the origin of the universe stating that the universe formed approximately 20 billion years ago from the violent explosion of matter leading to the creation of stars, planets, and cosmic bodies.

biodiversity- having variety or diversity in the number and types of organisms living in a specific area.

biosphere - the part of Earth in which living organisms exist and that is capable of supporting life.

biotechnology -the manipulation of living organisms or their components to produce useful, usually commercial or medical products.

biotic - describes the living part of an ecosystem, including humans, plants, animals, etc.

boil -to change from a liquid to a vapor by the addition of heat.

black hole - a region of space from which nothing, including light, can escape. It is the result of a supernova when the mass of the star increases causing it to cave in on itself.

calorie - the amount of energy needed to raise the temperature of 1 g of water 1°C at 1 standard atmosphere.

carbohydrate - a group of organic compounds that includes sugars, starches, celluloses, and gums and serves as a major energy source in the diet of animals.

catalyst - a substance that speeds up or slows down the rate of a reaction without being consumed or altered.

cell - the smallest unit of structure and function of living things. May contain membrane bound organelle.

chemical change – a reaction or change in a substance that changes its identity and result in the formation of a new substance. Rusting and combustion result in chemical changes.

chemical weathering - the process by which rocks and other objects break down as a result of chemical reactions.

chemotroph- an organism that is capable of using carbon dioxide and other inorganic compounds as its primary energy source.

chloroplast – a chlorophyll containing organelle in the cells of green plants and algae that creates glucose and oxygen through the process of photosynthesis.

chromosome - a structure in all living cells that consists of a single molecule of DNA bonded to various proteins and that carries the genes determining heredity.

circuit - an interconnection of electrical elements forming a complete path for the flow of current.

clone –a cell or organism that is grown from a single cell and is thus genetically identical to that cell.

coagulation - the process of changing from a liquid to a gel or solid state by a series of chemical reactions, especially the process that results in the formation of a blood clot.

codominant - relating to two alleles of a gene pair in a heterozygote that are both fully expressed. When alleles for both white and red petal color are present in a carnation, for example, the result is a pink carnation since both alleles are expressed together.

comet - a celestial body made up primarily of ice and rocky dust particles and which orbits the Sun. It's often referred to as a "dirty snowball".

compound - a substance made up of at least two different elements held together by chemical bonds.

concentration - the relative amount of a particular substance, a solute, or mixture.

condensation - the process of changing from a gas to a liquid.

conduction - the transfer of sound, heat or electricity through a stationary system.

conductivity - the ability or power to conduct or transmit heat, electricity, or sound.

conductor - a material or an object that conducts heat, electricity, light, or sound.

connective tissue - tissue that connects, supports, binds, or encloses the structures of the body.

conservation of mass - the principle that mass cannot be created or destroyed (also conservation of matter).

consumer - an organism that feeds on other organisms for food.

convection - heat transfer in a gas or liquid by the circulation of currents from one region to another.

crest - the highest point of a wave.

crust - the thin and solid outermost layer of Earth above the mantle.

current - the amount of electric charge flowing past a specified circuit point per unit time. The circulation of water due to temperature and density differences.

cytoplasm - the jellylike material that makes up much of the inside of a cell.

decomposer - any organism that feeds or obtains nutrients by breaking down organic matter from dead organisms.

deforestation - the wide scale cutting down and removal of trees in a forested area.

delta - a usually triangular mass of sediment, especially silt and sand, deposited at the mouth of a river.

density – the concentration (mass per unit volume) of a substance. Density = mass/volume

dependent variable - factor being measured or observed in an experiment.

deposition - the process by which sediment carried by forces such as wind accumulates in a particular area.

desertification - the transformation of arable or habitable land to desert as a result of destructive land use or climate change.

diffraction - a change in the direction (i.e.; bending) of a wave when it meets an obstacle. Waves also tend to spread out as they pass through an opening.

diploid - having two sets of chromosomes or double the number of haploid chromosomes.

disaccharide - any of a class of sugars, including lactose and sucrose that are composed of two monosaccharides.

dissolve - to make into a solution.

DNA - deoxyribonucleic acid; a nucleic acid that carries genetic information.

dominance - tendency of certain alleles to mask the expression of their corresponding alleles.

dune - a hill or ridge of sand piled up by the wind.

ductile – a property of metals that shows that they are able to be shaped into long thin or tube-like extensions of wire.

earthquake - the shaking of the ground caused by a sudden release of energy in Earth's crust.

eclipse - the partial or total blocking of light of one celestial object by another. An eclipse of the Sun or Moon occurs when the Earth, Moon, and Sun are aligned.

ecosystem – the interactions between the biotic (living) and abiotic (nonliving) factors in an environment.

efficiency - a quantity, usually expressed as a percentage that measures the ratio of work output to work input.

electric field - a region associated with a distribution of electric charge or a varying magnetic field in which forces due to that charge or field act upon other electric charges.

electric potential - a measure of the work required by an electric field to move electric charges.

electricity - the physical phenomena arising from the presence and flow of electric charges.

electromagnetic force - the fundamental force that is associated with electric and magnetic fields and is accountable for atomic structure, chemical reactions, and the attractive and repulsive forces.

electromagnetic radiation - the emission and propagation of energy waves originating in the Sun.

electromagnetic spectrum - the entire range of electromagnetic radiation. The spectrum ranges from very short wavelength gamma rays to very long wavelength radio waves.

electron - a negatively charged particle that makes up an atom.

electrophoresis - the migration of electrically charged molecules through a fluid or gel under the influence of an electric field.

embryology - the branch of biology that deals with the formation, early growth, and development of living organisms.

endothermic reaction - a chemical reaction that absorbs heat.

energy - the capacity to do work.

entropy - a measure of the unavailable energy in a closed thermodynamic system that is also usually considered to be a measure of the system's randomness or disorder.

environment - the sum of conditions affecting an organism, including all living and nonliving things in an area. It is made up of plants, animals, water, soil, weather, landforms, air, etc.

enzyme – proteins produced by living cells that catalyze (speed up) chemical reactions within the organism.

epithelial tissue - membranous tissue covering internal organs and other internal surfaces of the body.

equator - an imaginary circle around Earth's surface that is equal distance from the North and South Poles and divides Earth into a northern and southern hemisphere. Its plane is perpendicular to the Earth's axis of rotation.

erosion - the wearing away of earth's surface by the breakdown and transportation of rock and soil.

eukaryote - an organism whose cells contain a nucleus surrounded by a membrane and whose DNA is bound together by proteins into chromosomes. Eukaryotes have membrane bound organelles.

evaporation - the process by which a liquid is converted to a gas by heating the liquid.

evolution - a theory that the various types of animals and plants have their origin in other preexisting types or organisms.

exoskeleton - a hard outer structure, such as the shell of an insect or crustacean, that provides protection or support for an organism.

exothermic reaction - a chemical reaction that releases heat.

experiment - a procedure that is carried out and repeated under controlled conditions in order to test a hypothesis and investigate a question.

fatty acid - organic acids found in animal and vegetable fats and oils.

fertilization – the union of the nuclei of a sperm and egg cell to form a zygote.

fission – the splitting of an atom's nucleus producing a large amount of energy.

food chain - transfer of energy from one organism to another as a result of the feeding patterns of eating and being eaten.

force -- a push or a pull

forensic - relating to the use of science or technology in the investigation and establishment of facts or evidence in a court of law.

fossil – the remains of a prehistoric plant or animal typically preserved in rock.

fossil fuel - a nonrenewable energy resource formed from the remains of organisms that lived long ago; includes natural gas, oil, and coal.

freeze - to change from a liquid to a solid by the loss of heat.

frequency – how many times a wave passes a given point in a specific amount of time; a cycle.

friction- the force of contact that opposes motion.

fungus – a eukaryotic organism that reproduces by spores; including mushrooms, mold, yeast, and mildew.

fusion - the combination of the nuclei of two atoms that releases a great amount of energy.

galaxy - the more than billions of stars and cosmic bodies bound together by gravitational forces in the universe.

gamete – a sex cell (egg or sperm).

gas – a state of matter in which molecules have greater kinetic energy to move around and do not have a fixed volume or shape.

gene – segment of genetic instructions (DNA) for a trait located on chromosomes.

genetic - determined by the inheritance of genes.

genotype - the genetic makeup of an organism; the type of alleles present.

geocentric – theory that erroneously stated that Earth was the center of the universe and the Sun revolved around it.

geosphere - the part of Earth that includes the Earth's internal structures, landforms, rocks and minerals.

germination - the beginning of growth of a seed, spore, or bud in response to warmth and moisture.

glacier - a huge mass of ice slowly flowing over a land mass.

gravity - the force of attraction between any two objects.

greenhouse - a structure, primarily of glass, in which temperature and humidity can be controlled for the growing of plants.

greenhouse effect – natural event that is responsible for the normal heating of the Earth's surface and atmosphere.

gymnosperm - a plant, such as a cycad or conifer, whose seeds are not enclosed within an ovary.

habitat - a place in an ecosystem where an organism lives.

haploid - having a single set of each chromosome in a cell or cell nucleus

heat - the transfer of energy from a warmer object to a cooler object.

heliocentric - theory that identifies the Sun as the center of the universe having Earth and the other planets revolving around it.

heterozygous – having two different alleles for a trait.

histology - the study of plant and animal tissues.

homeostasis - ability of an organism to maintain internal stability in spite of disturbances that may disrupt its normal condition.

hominid – extinct primates characterized by opposable thumbs, increased brain size and intelligence, a flattened face, an upright pace and smaller teeth and jaw.

homozygous - having identical alleles for a trait on a set of chromosomes.

hormone - a substance produced by one tissue that has a metabolic effect on another tissue. Hormones are transported in the blood.

humidity - the amount of water vapor in the atmosphere.

hydrosphere - all of the Earth's water including oceans, groundwater, surface water, and water vapor.

hypothesis – an educated guess. A possible explanation for a scientific problem that can be tested by an experiment.

igneous - a type of rock that forms from molten (melted) or partly molten material that cools and hardens.

inclined plane - a simple machine made up of a slanting surface which connects a high level to a low level.

independent variable - the variable that is tested or manipulated. The factor that is changed in an experiment in order to study changes in the dependent variable.

inertia - the tendency of an object, as a result of its mass, to resist being moved or, if the object is moving, to resist a change in speed or direction until an outside force acts on the object. This is Newton's first law of motion.

inference – a conclusion arrived at by observation.

infrared - relating to the invisible part of the electromagnetic spectrum with wavelengths longer than those of visible red light but shorter than those of microwaves.

insulator - a material or an object that does not conduct heat, light, electricity or sound well. It does not easily allow these forms of energy to pass through.

invertebrate - an animal that has no backbone or spinal column. Most animals are invertebrates.

investigation - a procedure that is carried out in order to observe a response caused by a stimulus; not a complete experiment.

kinetic energy - the energy of motion.

kinetic friction – the force opposing objects in motion.

latitude - a measure of relative position north or south of the equator on the Earth's surface.

law - an accepted theory.

lever- a simple machine made up of a rigid bar that sits on a fulcrum and is used to lift or move loads; it multiplies mechanical force.

life cycle - the entire sequence of events in an organism's growth and development.

light - electromagnetic radiation that can be seen with the naked eye.

liquid – a state of matter in which molecules have more kinetic energy than a solid but less than a gas and which has a definite volume but no definite shape.

lithosphere - the outer part of the solid earth composed of rock; makes up the crust and outermost layer of the mantle. It sits on top of the asthenosphere.

lunar eclipse – an eclipse that occurs when the Earth passes between the Moon and the Sun and blocks the Sun's rays from striking the Moon. The Moon appears dark.

magnet - an object that is surrounded by a magnetic field and can attract iron or steel.

magnetic – the force of attraction within a magnetic field.

magnetic field - the region where magnetic force exists around magnets or electric currents.

malleable- the ability of a metal to be hammered into thin sheets.

mammal- warm-blooded vertebrate animals with hair covering that are able to nourish their young via milk production in the females.

mass - the amount of matter an object contains.

matter – anything that has mass and takes up space.

meiosis – form of sexual reproduction in which the number of chromosomes is reduced by half.

melt - to change from a solid to a liquid especially by the application of heat.

membrane - a thin layer of tissue that surrounds or lines a cell or cavity.

metal – elements, such as gold and silver that are good conductors of heat and electricity, and are characterized by a shiny surface, malleability, and ductility.

metamorphic - a type of rock that forms from existing rock because of extreme changes caused by heat, pressure, or chemical environments.

metamorphosis – growth and developmental changes during the life cycle of some animals.

microscope – an instrument used to see small or microscopic objects.

microwave - an electromagnetic wave with a wavelength between that of infrared and radio waves.

Milky Way galaxy - the spiral galaxy in which the Sun and Solar System is located.

mineral – a solid inorganic substance occurring in nature and having a definite chemical composition, crystalline structure, color, and hardness.

mitochondria – the organelle responsible for making energy in the cell through cellular respiration; the "powerhouse" of the cell.

mitosis – a form of asexual reproduction in which the nucleus of a cell divides forming two identical cells.

model - a representation of an object or concept that can be organized in different ways including visual and mathematical.

molecule - a single atom or a group of atoms bonded together.

momentum - the motion of an object equal to the product of its mass and velocity.

monosaccharide – the building blocks of sugars. Carbohydrates that cannot be broken down to simpler sugars.

moon - a natural satellite that revolves around a planet.

motion - the act or process of changing position or place.

mutation - a change in DNA sequence or a structural change in the chromosome.

natural resource – resources found in nature that serve useful purposes for organisms. Natural resources includes trees, water, the Sun, mineral deposits, etc.

natural selection –"survival of the fittest". The theory created by Charles Darwin stating that organisms having genetic variations that offer them an advantage towards survival in their environment, tend to be the ones that live long enough to reproduce and pass on their genetic traits. They are better adapted for survival in their environment.

neap tide –a low height tide that occurs midway between spring tides.

nebula – a cloud of gas and dust from which new stars are formed.

neutral - lacking a net charge.

neutron - a subatomic particle found in the nucleus of an atom and having zero charge.

nonrenewable resource - a resource that can only be replenished over millions of years. Includes fossil fuels (coal, natural gas, oil, etc).

nuclear reaction – a reaction occurring in the nucleus of an atom that releases a tremendous amount of energy. Examples include fission and fusion.

nucleus – in atoms, it is the center region where protons and neutrons are located. In eukaryotic cells, it is considered the "brain of the cell". It is the organelle that contains the cell's genetic material (DNA).

observation – information gathered from the five senses (seeing, hearing, tasting, touching and smelling).

ocean basin - the area of Earth that is covered by oceans.

offspring - the product of reproduction.

orbit – the path of an object around another object such as the circular path of a planet around the Sun.

organ - a structure made up of tissues that are organized to carry out a specific function of the body (e.g., liver, lungs, brain, etc).

organelle – the structures within a cell, such the ribosome or endoplasmic reticulum that performs a specific function.

organism - any living thing that carries out the various life functions (i.e.; respiration) necessary for life.

parasite - an organism that lives off of another organism while contributing nothing to the survival of its host.

periodic table – a table for the pattern-like arrangement of elements according to their chemical properties.

pH - the measure of the acidity or alkalinity of a solution.

phenotype - the physical expression of genes (i.e., eye color). The appearance or other observable characteristic of an organism resulting from the interaction of its genetic makeup and its environment.

photosynthesis – the process by which plants trap light energy to convert carbon dioxide and water into carbohydrates (sugars). It occurs in the chloroplast.

physical change - a change in matter that doesn't change the identity of the matter (i.e., ripping paper).

planet - large cosmic bodies that orbit a star and does not produce light of its own.

plasma – the liquid portion of blood in which the blood cells and platelets are normally suspended. Also the fourth state of matter; a high energy state of a gas such as lightening.

plate tectonics - the theory that explains how large pieces of Earth's outermost layer, called tectonic plates, move and change shape which results in seismic activity where the plates meet.

pole - the northern and southernmost areas on Earth (the North or South Pole); either of the points at which the earth's axis of rotation intersects the earth's surface.

pollen – a substance produced by plants that contain the male reproductive cells.

pollination - the transfer of pollen from the male reproductive structure of plants to the female reproductive structure.

pollution – a harmful change in an environment that is harmful to living things and often caused by human activity (i.e., water pollution).

polysaccharide - long chain carbohydrates, such as starch and cellulose, consisting of more than two monosaccharide units.

potential energy - energy stored in an object due to its position.

power - the rate at which work is done. It is expressed as the amount of work per unit time and is measured in units such as the Watt and horsepower.

precipitate - a solid that forms in a solution during a chemical reaction.

precipitation - any form of water that falls to the Earth's surface. Includes rain, snow, sleet and hail.

pressure - the amount of force exerted per unit area of a surface.

prism - an object used to separates white light into its colors (wavelengths).

products – substances that are produced at the end of a chemical reaction.

producer - an organism that makes its own food from the environment; usually a green plant.

prokaryote - single-celled organisms (i.e., bacteria) that lack membrane bound organelles and a nucleus and that are considered the most primitive form of life.

proton - a positively charged subatomic particle found inside the nucleus of an atom.

pulley – a simple machine consisting of rope and wheels with a grooved rim used to raise, lower, and move loads.

pulsar – a rotating or spinning neutron star.

punnett square - a graphic used to predict the results of a genetic cross.

quasar - the most radiant, potent, and energetic objects known in the universe.

radiant energy - energy in the form of waves, especially electromagnetic waves. Radio waves, X-rays, and visible light are all forms of radiant energy.

radiation - emission of energy in the form of rays or waves.

radioactive dating - measurement of the amount of radioactive material that an object contains that is used to estimate the age of the object.

radioactivity - the property possessed by some elements (i.e., uranium) or isotopes (i.e., carbon 14) of spontaneously emitting energetic particles.

rate of reaction - the speed at which reactants are consumed and products are formed in a chemical reaction.

reactants – the starting substances in a chemical reaction.

recessive - an allele for a trait that is masked or hidden. A recessive trait is expressed only if two copies of the gene is present (homozygous).

recycling - the collection and often reprocessing of discarded materials for reuse.

reflection - the bouncing off or turning back of light, sound, or heat from a surface.

renewable resource - a resource that is naturally replaced or restored as it is used. It includes (wind, water, and solar energy).

replication – the repeating of an experiment in scientific research to confirm findings or to increase accuracy.

reproduction – producing new individuals.

repulsion - the tendency of particles or bodies of the same electric charge or magnetic polarity to separate.

resistance - the opposition of a body or substance to current passing through it, resulting in a change of electrical energy into heat or another form of energy.

scientific method - a system or plan of investigation that scientist use to solve problems.

scientist - a person having expert knowledge of one or more sciences.

screw- a simple machine consisting of an inclined plane wrapped around a pole that is used to lift things or hold things together.

season – a change in climate due to the Earth's revolution around the Sun and the tilt of the Earth's axis.

sedimentary - rock formed from layers of sediment that overlay and squeeze together or are chemically combined.

semiconductor - having electrical conductivity greater than insulators but less than good conductors. These are typically metalloids.

sexual reproduction - reproduction involving the union of male and female gametes producing an offspring with traits from both parents.

solar eclipse – when the moon passes between the Sun and the Earth and blocks the view of the Sun from a location on Earth.

solar system - a star and all the planets and other bodies that orbit it; the region in space where these bodies move.

solid -a state of matter having a definite shape and a definite volume and to which the molecules are tightly packed inside the object with only room for slight movement (vibrating).

solubility - the ability or tendency of one substance to dissolve in another at a given temperature and pressure.

sound wave - longitudinal pressure waves that require a medium (solid, liquid or gas) to travel.

space - the region of the universe beyond Earth's atmosphere.

spectroscope - an instrument used to study the properties of light.

speed - the rate of change of an object's position; distance traveled divided by time of travel.

spring tide – a bimonthly tide occurring at the new and full moons.

sun - the closest star to Earth and the center of our solar system. The Sun is an average sized yellow star.

superposition - the principle that in a group of undisturbed layered sedimentary rocks the lowest layer is the earliest deposited and therefore the oldest.

synapse – a small junction across which a nerve impulse passes from one nerve cell to another nerve, muscle, or gland cell.

telescope - an optical instrument for viewing distant objects in space.

theory – a widely accepted explanation of a principle or phenomena often based on repeated tests.

thermal energy - the kinetic energy of randomly moving molecules inside an object; depends on temperature and amount.

thermometer - an instrument for measuring temperature. Some contain a liquid, typically mercury or colored alcohol that expand and rise in the tube as the temperature increases.

tide - the regular rise and fall in the surface level of the Earth's oceans, seas, and bays caused by the gravitational attraction of the moon and to a lesser extent of the Sun.

tissue - similar cells that act together to perform a specific function. Four basic types of tissue are muscle, connective, nerve, and epithelial.

triglyceride – the main component of fats and oils.

tropism - growth of all or part of an organism in response to an external stimulus, such as light.

trough - the lowest point of a wave.

ultraviolet - relating to electromagnetic radiation; having frequencies higher than those of visible light but lower than those of x-rays.

vaccine - a preparation of a weakened or killed pathogen, such as a virus, and that stimulates immune cells to recognize and attack it.

vacuole – a small cavity in the cytoplasm of a cell, bound by a single membrane and containing water, food, or metabolic waste.

vacuum - a space empty of matter.

variable – factors affecting an experiment which must be tested or controlled.

velocity - the rate of change of an object's displacement; measured as distance divided by time.

vertebrate - any of a large group of chordates, characterized by having a backbone.

vibration - a repetitive movement around an equilibrium point.

virus - a non-cellular, disease-causing particle that uses the genetic material from its host to reproduce.

voltage - a measure of the difference in electric potential between two points in space, a material, or an electric circuit; expressed in volts.

volume - a measure of the amount of space an object takes up; also the loudness of a sound or signal.

water cycle - the path water takes as it is being cycled through the environment. It involves condensation, evaporation, transpiration, precipitation, groundwater and runoff.

wavelength - the distance from any point on a wave to an identical point on the next wave (for example, from one crest to the next crest).

wedge - a simple machine that is made up of two inclined planes and that moves; often used for cutting.

weight - the force with which a body is attracted to Earth and is equal to the object's mass times the acceleration of gravity.

wheel and axle - a simple machine consisting of a wheel with a rod (axle) through its center that is used to lift or move loads.

x-ray - a high-energy stream of electromagnetic radiation having a frequency higher than that of ultraviolet light but less than that of a gamma ray.

CHAPTER 1 Nature of Science

In this section you will explore the many facets of science and its impact on the world. You will participate in scientific inquiry as you learn how to design investigable questions, construct and carry out scientific investigations and to evaluate data in order to develop scientific recommendations. Good science thinking skills are needed to solve problems, validate results and provide explanations.

PART I THE PRACTICE OF SCIENCE

Standards: SC.5.N.1.1, SC.5.N.1.2, SC.5.N.1.3, SC.5.N.1.4, SC.5.N.1.5, SC.5.N.1.6,
SC.5.N.2.1 SC.6.N.1.1, SC.6.N.1.2, SC.6.N.1.3, SC.6.N.1.4, SC.6.N.1.5, SC.7.N.1.1,
SC.7.N.1.2, SC.7.N.1.3, SC.7.N.1.4, SC.7.N.1.5, SC.7.N.1.6, SC.7.N.1.7, SC.8.N.1.1,
SC.8.N.1.2, SC.8.N.1.3, SC.8.N.1.4, SC.8.N.1.5, SC.8.N.1.6

This section of the **Science Prep Cat 2nd Edition** outlines many of the science process skills you will need to perform scientific investigations and to communicate scientific knowledge. These skills include the following:

a. classifying

b. observing

c. predicting/hypothesizing

d. inferring

e. identifying and controlling variables

f. making and using models

g. collecting data

h. interpreting data

i. investigating and experimenting

j. communicating

k. concluding

l. estimating and measuring

m. forming questions

A mastery of these skills will heighten your science experiences and make them more productive and enjoyable. These skills will be referred to throughout the chapter.

The practice of science always begins with a question. As scientist work to answer their questions new and interesting discoveries are made. Scientific study is based on **_scientific methods_**. These are procedures scientist use to answer questions and to solve scientific problems. There exists a variety of scientific methods. Some may even differ from the traditional idea of the "scientific method" you may have learned in elementary school. For the most part they all include some variations of the procedures outlined below. Scientist may use all of the steps or just a few in any order that works best for their investigation. Having a structured procedure to follow greatly organizes your study and helps you arrive at logical conclusions for the investigations you carry out at school or home.

1. Start investigating your topic by doing research on the Internet or in the library. Your research proceeds after making **_observations_** of something. An observation is information gathered by use of your senses (seeing, hearing, tasting, touching, and smelling).

2. Create a scientifically investigable question ("identify the **_problem"_**). This type of question requires an investigation to arrive at the solution. The answer should not be obvious or require explanations beyond your realm of control (i.e., "Why is outer space so big?")

3. Create a **_hypothesis_**, which is a possible solution to the problem or question posed. A good hypothesis is testable or investigable. You should be able to conduct an experiment to confirm or disprove your hypothesis.

4. Construct an investigation into your question ("design an **_experiment_** "). The purpose of the experiment is to test your hypothesis. It puts you one step closer to answering your question.

5. Collect and evaluate your data ("analyze **_data_**"). This will tell you if your investigation supports your hypothesis. Data can be better analyzed by organizing it using graphs, charts, and tables. Mathematical calculations are often involved.

6. Draw a ***conclusion*** at the end of your investigation. Here you state the final answer to the problem or question originally asked. The conclusion will acknowledge whether your hypothesis should be supported or rejected based on the results of the investigation.

7. ***Repeat*** the process again (steps 4-6) to make sure your results are ***accurate*** (correct) and ***valid*** (true or reliable).

8. ***Communicate*** the results of your experiment to the scientific community (such as your classmates). Make appropriate recommendations based on the evaluation of your results.

The type and complexity of the question you ask will determine the method you use to solve the problem. Some investigations may require you to conduct an experiment to which the method described above may suffice. Another type may be a simple investigation requiring only the recording of observations. Further yet, some investigations may warrant the construction and study of a ***model*** (a representation of an object or system). It all really depends.

Sample Problem Showing the Usage of Scientific Methods Involving a Controlled Experiment

Standards: SC.5.N.1.1, SC.5.N.1.3, SC.5.N.1.4, SC.5.N.1.6, SC.5.N.2.2, SC.6.N.1.1, SC.6.N.1.2, SC.6.N.1.4, SC.6.N.1.5, SC.7.N.1, SC.7.N.1.2, SC.7.N.1.4, SC.7.N.1.7, SC.8.N.1.1, SC.8.N.1.2, SC.8.N.1.3, SC.8.N.1.4

Let's design a simple ***controlled*** experiment to see how you can think like a scientist and use a scientific method to solve a problem. A controlled experiment involves the usage of a comparison group (known as the ***control group***) to compare with the results of an experimental group.

> **Step 1—Investigate your topic**

You are interested in growing plants and are curious whether or not they need sunlight to grow. You start your inquiry by investigating online the topic of plant growth. You use reference materials to gather good information.

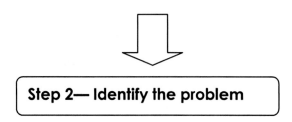

Step 2— Identify the problem

When investigating your topic you use appropriate reference materials to support your scientific understanding of plant growth. After some time of making careful observations you decide to ask a research question. The question you will investigate is; "Do plants grow more in light or under dark conditions? This process is called "defining the problem."

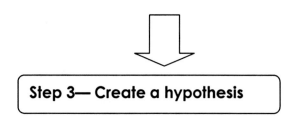

Step 3— Create a hypothesis

You create a hypothesis, which is a statement that proposes a possible explanation to your problem. A sample hypothesis could be:

"If plants are exposed to sunlight they will experience more growth than if grown in the dark."

You evaluate your hypothesis to be well written in that it meets the following criteria: it is testable, it shows a relationship between the variables, and is written in an acceptable form (such as an "If...then" form).

At this point a smart idea would be to conduct a literature review of your hypothesis to review what is already known about it. This could help you to fine tune your experiment or to confirm a prior experiment conducted by another scientist to see if you could obtain similar results.

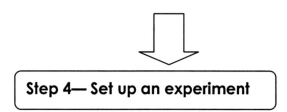

Step 4— Set up an experiment

You must now set up an experiment to prove your hypothesis. You do this by first identifying your **_variables_**. Variables are those things that can affect your experiment. These include the **_independent variable_** (the one that is tested), the **_dependent variable_** (the one that is measured and the one that depends on the independent variable) and your **_constants_** (all the things that must be kept the same between your experimental and control group to prevent inaccurate data).

In this experiment your *independent variable* will be light (because that's what you are testing). Your *dependent variable* will be plant growth (because that's what you are measuring). You will set up two groups of plants having a large sample size (perhaps with 100 plants per group). One group will be called the **_experimental group_** and the other the **_control group_**. The experimental group receives the independent variable, which in this case is light. Thus, it will be placed in the light. The control group will be placed in a dark area. It will not receive the independent variable. Its purpose is to serve as a comparison group.

You will be measuring growth in both groups. To ensure the accuracy of your data you have to make sure all the other factors that could affect the experiment are controlled for. Both groups must have the exact same growing conditions with the exception of the presence of light. These growing conditions are your **constants**. For example, each group must have the same type of plant, the same type of soil, the same amount of water, the same amount of growing time, etc.

Remember, all conditions have to be the same for both groups *EXCEPT* the experimental group will get the light and the control group will not. In a controlled experiment you should test only one variable at a time. All others are "controlled" (kept the same). An experiment that tests more than one variable would prove to be inaccurate and confusing. You would not know which variable involved produced the test results.

Changing one variable could change the outcome of the experiment. In this experiment if you are testing the effect of light on plant growth you cannot set up your experiment by putting one plant in sandy soil in the light and another plant in regular soil in the dark. If you did that how would you know which variable caused the change? Was it the amount of light or type of soil? This is the reason you test only one variable at a time.

Getting back to the experiment, you decide to grow the plants for 12 days and measure the growth in centimeters using a metric ruler. In order to obtain good results it will be important for you to follow correct experimental procedures.

Step 5— Record and analyze data

Each time you collect data by measuring plant growth you must record it. This can be organized neatly in a **_data table_**. It is important that you make careful observations and keep accurate records of your data. This will help you to properly explain your results.

You could analyze your data by creating a **graph** of your results. The graph should clearly show you which group had the most amount of growth. In this section you will also record your observations of the experiment. **_Comparing_** (how they are the same) and **_contrasting_** (how they are different) observations and results are valuable skills for any scientist to have. This skill requires the ability to classify or put things into groups for better interpretation. Looking for patterns or trends in the data is a valuable skill as well. Organizing your data in charts, tables, graphs, and diagrams greatly facilitates the interpretation of your results.

Plant grown with sunlight   Plant grown without sunlight

Plant Growth (in cm)

Data
Table

	Light	Dark
Day 1	1	0
Day 2	2	1
Day 3	7	2
Day 4	10	5

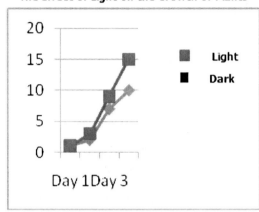

Graph

An important note on recording observations and analyzing data is that they must be done as objectively as possible. You need to report the _facts_ and not skew the results with your personal opinions. Your opinion is a belief you may hold to be true but it may differ significantly from verified observation. Opinions are often wrong and could negatively affect the interpretation of scientific investigations, including yours.

Objective scientific research seeks to minimize the influence of bias or prejudice in the experimenter when testing a hypothesis. The experimenter should not prefer one outcome over another. Sometimes you are influenced to prematurely determine the outcome of the experiment based on prior personal experience. An example of this would be ruling out or ignoring data that does not support the hypothesis. This should not be the case. Unbiased methods and logical reasoning should take precedence over personal opinions. Try to stick to the facts. Ultimately in the end you will have to create explanations that fit the evidence and not your opinions.

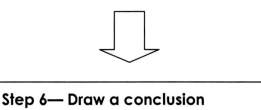

Step 6— Draw a conclusion

After analyzing your data you should be able to now go back to the original problem/question and answer it with the support of your empirical evidence. Your conclusion may very well be that plants grown in the light do grow taller. You may however discover something surprisingly different.   Your experimental tests would lead either to a confirmation of the hypothesis if your prediction agreed with your results or a rejection of it if your hypothesis is incompatible with your data.   In your conclusion you would discuss whether or not your data/results supported your hypothesis. Your results however, would serve as support of your claim and not absolute proof.

Whether your hypothesis is supported by the data or fails to be supported, it is valuable still and should not be simply discarded because of unfavorable results. Rejected hypotheses can be modified and often lead to further investigations.   For this reason the process of science remains a reflective process involving a depth of analytical thought and creativity. It is a field which effectively creates explanations that fit evidence.

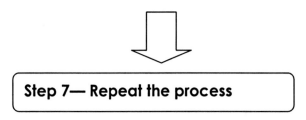

Step 7— Repeat the process

It is important to conduct multiple trials (**repetition**) of your experiment to increase the validity of the results.   If you **_replicate_** (repeat) the experiment and get the same results chances are your experiment was correctly done and your results are valid. When scientific investigations are carried out the evidence produced by those investigations should be replicable by others.

If on the other hand you repeat the same process and get different results this could lead to further investigation to determine if the difference is statistically significant. There is therefore a need for repeated experimental trials.

Step 8— Communicate your results

In science one hardly ever conducts experiments and keep the results a secret. Knowledge eventually becomes available to everyone. Scientists from all backgrounds and ***disciplines*** (fields of science) come together often to share their knowledge with one another. They present their findings at meetings or in scientific publications. They communicate their written and recorded findings in order to transmit their ideas and so that others will find them to be credible (believable). By publically communicating their work they are exposing their ideas to criticism by other scientist and are keeping informed of scientific developments worldwide. They make it possible for other scientist to be able to follow their same procedures (***replication***) to determine if similar results can be obtained. To do so brings validity to their study.

If on the other hand the investigation is replicated and scientists obtain different results they must then determine if the difference is significant and if the body of knowledge must be changed. Scientific communication and argumentation plays an important role in the generation and validation of scientific knowledge. Important benefits of active experimentation and open communication among members of the scientific community are the reduction of bias and the promotion of the idea that science be based solely on observation and evidence.

When your experiment has been concluded your teacher may ask you to document your experiences in a written lab report. Presenting your research findings to your class is an excellent way to share the value of your scientific knowledge with all.

Many students believe the practice of science only involves performing experiments. Much of what occurs in the scientific world does not involve actual experiments at all. Some forms of investigative work in science involve making observations and reviewing the works of other scientist. In these cases the process you would follow to solve the problem would not exactly follow the traditional scientific method.

A scientific study could involve surveying groups of people over a period of time to investigate an unknown behavior or gather opinions. Notwithstanding, it could even involve conducting online research from a body of established works. Again, not all scientific knowledge is derived from experimentation. Nevertheless, a large proportion of our understanding of science is based on empirical evidence (experiments).

The controlled experiment that we outlined in the sample problem is but one example of an investigation. Depending on the topic and scope of your investigation a controlled experiment may be impossible. For example, in earth science class you may be asked by your teacher to investigate moon phases. It would be impossible for you to set up a controlled experiment because you would have no control over the phases of the moon. In this case you would conduct an observational investigation involving nothing more than paper and pencil and your powers of observation. You could observe the appearance of the moon for 30 days and draw and describe the phase visible each night.

The type of investigation you perform might vary depending on the nature of the discipline. For example, in physics your investigation might involve carrying out complex mathematical calculations of theoretical concepts. Geological studies could lend themselves to a chemical assay of earth materials (i.e., soil), while life science may incorporate the building of a model of the heart to better understand the functioning of the circulatory system. These are all types of investigations a scientist could employ to obtain answers to their questions.

Tools of Measurement

The **_tools of measurement_** are the tools that are used to make observations and collect data for an experiment. Sophisticated scientific instruments include such things as computers, microscopes, telescopes, spectrophotometers, centrifuges, etc. In an 8th grade lab you would expect to see some basic tools such as those listed in **Table 1-1** on the following page.

Table 1-1 Tools of Measurement

Measurement Tool	Picture	Usage	Standard Metric Units
Graduated Cylinder		Measures volume of liquids	Liters (L) 1 milliliter (ml) = 0.001 liter
Triple Beam Balance		Measures mass	Gram (g) 1 milligram (mg) = 0.001 grams
Ruler		Measures length	Meter (m) 1 millimeters (mm) = 0.001 meters
Thermometer		Measures temperature	degrees Celsius (°C) boiling point of water (at sea level) = 100 °C freezing point of water (at sea level) = 0 °C
Stopwatch		Measures time	1 minute = 60 seconds 1 hour = 60 minutes 1 day = 24 hours 1 week = 7 days 1 year = 365 ¼ days
Electronic Balance		Measures mass	Gram (g) 1 milligram (mg) = 0.001 grams
Beaker		Measures volume	Liters (L) 1 milliliter (ml) = 0.001 liter
Spring Scale		Measures weight (force)	Newton (N)

Safety in the Science Lab

As peanut butter is to jelly, safety and science just belong together. Whenever you are conducting experiments you have to think of how to protect yourself as well as others around you. Safety is your personal responsibility. Your teacher will give you a set of safety rules to follow (and a contract to sign with consequences for breaking the rules). In general, to remain safe in the science laboratory just remember a few simple things:

1. No eating, running, horse-playing or tasting of the chemicals is allowed in the lab.
2. Pay attention to your teacher, follow directions and report accidents immediately.
3. Safety gear such as goggles and aprons help protect your eyes and clothing and should be worn whenever necessary.
4. Familiarize yourself with the safety symbols found in your science textbook and be aware of the cautions they alert to.
5. When conducting experiments involving animals be sure to handle them carefully. You should practice good safety around animals by not handling them when they are feeding or by not making sudden moves around them.

PART II THE CHARACTERISTICS OF SCIENTIFIC KNOWLEDGE

Standards: SC.5.N.1.6, SC.5.N.2.1, SC.5.N.2.2, SC.6.N.2.1, SC.6.N.2.2, SC.6.N.2.3, SC.7.N.2.1, SC.8.N.2.1, SC.8.N.2.2

Scientific knowledge is based on systematic study and is organized by general principles. Much of our scientific knowledge is based on a combination of observation and inference. An observation is the collection of information based on the senses (i.e., seeing, hearing, tasting, etc). Noting that at a specific temperature ice will undergo a phase change and change in properties is an observation. To expand and enhance their senses scientist routinely use technology such as computers and microscopes.

An ***inference*** on the other hand, is an explanation or conclusion based on observation. Stepping outside your home to find the ground wet may lead you to make the inference that while you were in the house it rained outside. Inferences often involve entities that are not directly observable.

The nature of scientific knowledge is grounded in observations of the real world and revolves around natural phenomena. Certain elements characterize scientific knowledge and its methods.   These include the following;

1. **Scientific knowledge** is the result of accurate recordkeeping, openness, and replication in conjunction with critical review (debate and confirmation) of one's work within the science community.

2. **Scientific knowledge** is derived primarily from logic and reasoning, and is based on evidence that is verifiable by experience or experiment (empirical). This evidence is supported by quantitative and/or qualitative data and it is testable.

3. **Scientific knowledge** is based on careful observations of phenomena.

4. **Scientific knowledge** is tentative (subject to change) in light of new evidence and new ways of thinking and as new observations challenge prevailing theories. Although many ideas in science have remained largely unchanged for hundreds of years all scientific knowledge is subject to change as new discoveries are made. For example, the long-held erroneous geocentric theory (Earth being the center of the Solar System) remained virtually unchanged until the mid-1500s when Copernicus, the astronomer, introduced the heliocentric theory (the Sun being the center of the Solar System). With the presentation of new evidence the old theory was changed and the new one adopted.

5. **Scientific knowledge** is durable and robust once generally accepted. It strives for objectivity.   Nevertheless, it is not uncommon for human nature, societal values, personal beliefs and intuition to influence how scientist view data.

6. **Scientific knowledge** is helpful in understanding how the natural world works but it is not based on absolute truths. It cannot provide complete answers to all questions. Outside the realm of science it provides limited explanations of other ways of knowing, such as religion, art and philosophy. Things such as personal belief in the supernatural are not science based and as such cannot be proved or disproved using scientific methods.   Mainly, scientific knowledge is distinguished from other activities involving thought in its reliance on empirical evidence and careful observations.

7. **Scientific knowledge** is cumulative.   It increases or grows by accumulation of large bodies of evidence and observations.

8. **Scientific knowledge** is explanatory. Scientists construct explanations to try to make sense of observations of natural phenomena. Presuming that the natural world is composed of consistent patterns, scientist use scientific knowledge to make it all comprehensible through careful, systematic study.

9. **Scientific knowledge** is based on creativity, which is a source of innovation in science. Scientist use creative insight and imagination to come up with hypotheses and theories and in their investigations. Creativity is used to imagine how the word works and in questions and explanations.

10. **Scientific knowledge** is distinguishable from pseudoscientific ideas, which are loosely science based but not truly scientific. For example, the study of astronomy is an acceptable discipline in science. However, astrology, which is somewhat derived from astronomy, is not a generally accepted scientific discipline.

PART III THE ROLE OF THEORIES, LAWS, HYPOTHESES AND MODELS

Standards: SC.6.N.3.1,   SC.6.N.3.2, SC.6.N.3.3,   SC.6.N.3.4,   SC.7.N.3.1, SC.7.N.3.2, SC.8.N.3.1,   SC.8.N.3.2

Scientific knowledge is constantly modified as new experiments are conducted and new ideas are generated. Scientific knowledge is described in terms of theories, laws, hypothesis and models which each represent a different stage in the acceptance of knowledge.

We have already dealt with **_hypotheses_** earlier on in this chapter. It does suffice to say that a hypothesis can form the basis of a theory. In its initial proposal a hypothesis may be nothing more than guesswork regarding cause and effect in specific situations. At this point it refers to an early state of knowledge before experiments and investigations are conducted. It is only when the hypothesis is tested and replicated, and reviewed and argued that it wins general acceptance in the scientific community. After such time it could develop into a theory.

Models are based on scientific facts and are very helpful tools in visualizing and understanding concepts and for explaining how things work. A model is a representation of an object or system. The Bohr model of an atom and the double helix model of DNA are examples. Models uses something familiar to help you better understand something that is unfamiliar. Though very helpful, models do have their limitations in that they are idealized and not true representations of how something really functions. They are never exactly like the objects they represent. Nevertheless, despite their limitations scientist actively engage in building, testing, comparing and revising models. They can be invaluable in studying hard to conceptualize concepts such as tiny atoms or the expanding universe.

There are three types of scientific models. These are ***physical***, ***mathematical*** and ***conceptual*** models. Physical models are ones that you can touch. A model of the solar system made with Styrofoam balls is a physical model. Physical models of cars and planes, for example, help improve product design and safety before the real object is produced. This saves time and money later on. Mathematical models involve equations and calculations and are often complex. They sometimes require the use of computers to design and solve. Mathematical models can be used to determine the speed of Earth's rotation. Finally, conceptual models are ones that are based on hypotheses and theories and serve to explain ideas. The Atomic Theory that all matter is made up of atoms is a conceptual model.

A ***theory*** represents a hypothesis or group of related hypotheses, which has been confirmed through repeated experimental tests. It is a way scientist attempt to describe, predict, or explain the way the world works. It is an explanation that may originate from a hypothesis and subsequent investigation. A theory is well-supported by evidence and widely accepted among scientist. The word theory denotes an altogether different usage in science than in everyday life, which often likens it to a prediction posed by an individual. In order to validate a theory careful observation and much evidence is required. The Big Bang Theory of the origin of the universe (see chapter 4), the Cell Theory (see chapter 3), and the Theory of Plate Tectonics (see chapter 4) are all examples of theories.

History has proven that an accepted theory may be proven incorrect. In this case, the theory may be modified, replaced, or altogether discarded. Lamarck's theory of heredity, (the inheritance of acquired characteristics), was one such theory found to be incorrect. His discredited theory stated that characteristics or traits obtained during the lifetime of a parent, such as an increase in muscle mass, could be passed on to its offspring. His theory was ultimately replaced by Darwin's Theory of Natural Selection (see chapter 3).

Scientific theories should not be confused with scientific **_laws_**. Whereas theories are explanations, laws describe relationships under certain conditions in the natural world. A law is more like a statement of fact that describes a specific situation. It is generally accepted to be true and is universal. In contrast to theories that are well supported and validated by observation and evidence, laws are simple statements of truth that are consistently observed in nature and that describes the behavior of something that occurs. They don't require the same amount of in depth proofs necessary to validate theories (although they do require some evidence).

Laws are often associated with mathematical equations, such as Newton's Second Law of Motion (F=ma) or *Newton's Law of Universal Gravitation. Other examples of laws are the Law of Conservation of Mass, the Law of Conservation of Energy, and the Law of Conservation of Momentum (see chapter 2).

$$F = G\frac{m_1 m_2}{r^2}$$

* Newton's Law of Universal
Gravitation

PART IV SCIENCE AND SOCIETY

**Standards: SC.8.N.4.1, SC.8.N.4.2**

Science is a body of objective knowledge individuals everywhere use to solve problems. Scientific knowledge touches every citizen in all parts of the world. Its practice and application involves men and women of all ethnic, national and social backgrounds. Needless to say, science is a public entity that empowers people toward better health, longevity, preservation of resources, understanding of natural and technological disasters, ecological accountability and much more.

Because of the public nature of science it is widely used as a platform to inform individuals and influence matters of public concern. Scientist are often called upon in court trials as expert witnesses relating to issues of DNA evidence and other science-based issues. Their expertise serves to lend credence and support to testimony.

The issue of global warming is another instance demonstrating the impact of science on public policy. Not too long ago global warming as a matter of public concern was widely dismissed. Many scientists themselves doubted the certainty of claims of destructive climatic changes without solid evidence. Its hypothetical nature precluded it from forming the basis of policy decisions. However, in time, with extensive scientific research and the collection of enormous amounts of evidence in support of global warming, the issue was embraced by the scientific community and catapulted to the forefront of public, political, economic and societal concern. The insight brought about by scientist has caused a major shift in the collective thoughts and practices of people concerning global warming. They have changed their practices and modified previous beliefs all in an effort to reduce their carbon footprint and preserve our remaining earthly resources. This emphasis would not have been possible without the impactful influence of science. In the United States alone global warming laws concerning the reduction of carbon emission from motor vehicles have made it as far as the steps of the highest court of the land, the Supreme Court.

The study of science is ever so empowering. Like a quiet storm, it is motivating young people around the globe to responsibly accept the charge of leaders of tomorrow and cultivators of new ways in thinking about our planet. To handle this enormous responsibility they are educating themselves about the issues that affect society. Furthermore, they are embracing science as a solution towards improving and resolving these issues. Once problems are studied in depth it is then time to apply scientific methods towards fixing them. The way this is done is by interjecting sound scientific inquiry methods in areas where science can provide answers to these societal problems. Investigable questions are constructed along with investigations of those questions. Data is collected and evaluated. Based on their findings scientific recommendations are developed and shared as public policy.

SECTION REVIEW

CHAPTER 1 SAMPLE QUESTIONS

1) Safety in the science lab is as critical as any form of scientific inquiry. It is something every student, teacher, or scientist should follow each time an investigation is conducted. Which of the following situations demonstrates proper science lab safety?
   a. A student wearing goggles on his head, and not over his eyes, during the lab activity.
   b. A teacher eating lunch during a dissection with student participants.
   c. Listening only to the first five minutes of your teacher's instructions and then rushing into the lab activity.
   d. Thoroughly reviewing safety symbols so that you can understand them while doing the lab activity.

2) The statement that best summarizes scientific knowledge is
   a. Scientific knowledge is based on absolute truths.
   b. Scientific knowledge is based on contemporary theories only and totally disregards theories of the past.
   c. Scientific knowledge is tentative (subject to change) in light of new evidence and new ways of thinking and as new observations challenge prevailing theories.
   d. Scientific knowledge makes no distinction between pseudoscientific ideas, such as astrology.

3) Sarah has just finished her experiment on onion root tip cells but did not get the results she expected. Her hypothesis was not supported by her data. According to logical scientific methods what should Sarah do next?
   a. Sarah should repeat the experiment to determine if she conducted the procedures for the experiment correctly and to verify her results.
   b. Sarah should immediately change her hypothesis without repeating the experiment.
   c. Sarah should immediately report the results to the scientific community through email or scientific publications without repeating the experiment.
   d. Sarah should focus on changing her results so that they fit with her original hypothesis.

4) Tyrone would like to determine the density of three irregularly shaped rocks. Which of the following tools could he use to accurately perform his measurements?
   a. Ruler and a Triple Beam Balance
   b. Graduated Cylinder and Ruler
   c. Electronic Balance and a Beaker
   d. Triple Beam Balance and a Graduated Cylinder

5) Scientific knowledge is based on systematic study and is organized by general principles. A good example of scientific knowledge concerning the structure of the Earth is
   a. The Earth has four main atmospheric layers that all play a role in the existence of life on Earth.
   b. The concept of global warming is a mere marketing ploy to get consumers to purchase hybrid cars.
   c. Earth is composed of mostly water, which has little use because most of this water is fresh water.
   d. The thermosphere is the coldest layer of Earth's atmosphere.

6) Keiko has recently become interested in gardening as a hobby. She is curious to know how the pH of soil affects the height of garden peas. She seeks to answer this question by using a scientific method. Keiko must first identify the independent variable and dependent variable before designing her experiment but she is confused. Which of the following correctly identifies the independent and dependent variables in her experiment?
    a. Independent variable – soil pH / dependent variable – plant height
    b. Independent variable – soil depth / dependent variable – plant germination
    c. Independent variable – sunlight / dependent variable – amount of water
    d. Independent variable – soil texture / dependent variable – plant color

7) Below are four statements written in response to the problem statement; "Does solar radiation affect bacterial growth on a glass dish?" The statement that serves as the best hypothesis for the problem statement is
    a. "If bacteria grows then the Sun will shine"
    b. "I think that solar radiation will improve the cleanliness of the dish".
    c. "If you increase the amount of solar radiation then the amount of bacterial growth will decrease."
    d. "I think that solar radiation definitely kills bacteria".

8) How can society benefit from the advancement of scientific knowledge?
    a. Scientific knowledge is widely used as a platform to inform individuals and influence matters of public concern.
    b. Scientific knowledge can be used as a means of explaining and supporting problems like global warming.
    c. Through the application of scientific knowledge important investigable questions are constructed and investigated.
    d. All of the above statements demonstrate how society can benefit from enhancing its scientific knowledge.

9) Models, which are representations of objects or systems, are used to explain the role that hypotheses play in scientific investigations. All of the following statements about models are true **Except**
    a. Models use something familiar to help you better understand something that is unfamiliar.
    b. Models have their limitations in that they are idealized and not true representations of how something really functions.
    c. Conceptual models are ones that are based on hypotheses and theories and serve to explain ideas.
    d. Physical models involve equations and calculations and are often complex. They sometimes require the use of a computer to design and solve.

10) Lamarck's theory of heredity, (the inheritance of acquired characteristics) stated that characteristics or traits obtained during the lifetime of a parent, such as an increase in muscle mass, could be passed on to its offspring. His theory was discredited and ultimately replaced by Darwin's Theory of Natural Selection. Which statement below concerning scientific knowledge is best supported by this occurrence?

a. Scientific knowledge provides complete answers to all questions.
b. Scientific knowledge is progressive and is based on pseudoscientific ideas.
c. Scientific knowledge is cumulative. It increases or grows by accumulation of large bodies of evidence and observations.
d. How scientist view data is never influenced by human nature, societal values, personal beliefs and intuition.

11) Which instrument is used to measure the average kinetic energy of a substance?

a. Stopwatch
b. Thermometer
c. Triple beam balance
d. Spring scale

12) The graph below represents the result that Tywana received from an experiment done in her own yard. Which of the following conclusions can be made based on the interpretation of the graph of her results?

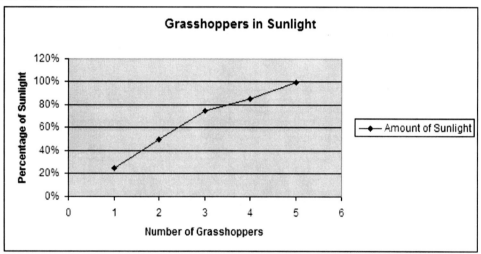

a. The number of grasshoppers increases with the decrease in sunlight
b. The number of grasshoppers decreases with the increase in sunlight.
c. The number of grasshoppers is the highest at full sunlight exposure.
d. The number of grasshoppers cannot be determined from the graph.

13) Evidence of good safety practices when working with laboratory animals include all of the following **Except**

a. Allowing lab animals to run freely around the lab while you clean out its cage
b. Not making sudden moves around lab animals
c. Handling lab animals carefully
d. Not handling lab animals when they are feeding

14) Because of the public nature of science it is widely used as a platform to inform individuals and influence matters of public concern. Which of the following situations is an example of how scientific knowledge has influenced public policy?

    a. The scientific link between lung cancer and tobacco has resulted in the tobacco industry having to print health warning labels on cigarette cartons.

    b. Enhanced scientific research on women's health issues has influenced public health practice, policy, and program development for women.

    c. The government cuts funding on a nuclear waste storage site because of public safety issues.

    d. All of the above

    e. Choice (a) and (c) only

CHAPTER 2 PHYSICAL SCIENCE

Prep Cat

The physical science section of the FCAT measures your ability to apply physical and chemical concepts. Remember, before you can *apply* concepts you must first *learn* them thoroughly. Study the concepts and work through the study questions until the information becomes second nature to you. Spend quality time with the material for greater mastery.

PART 1 PROPERTIES OF MATTER

Standards: SC.5.P.8.1, SC.5.P.8.2, SC.5.P.8.3, SC.5.P.8.4, SC.8.P.8.1, SC.8.P.8.2, SC.8.P.8.3 , SC.8.P.8.4, SC.8.P.8.5, SC.8.P.8.6, SC.8.P.8.7, SC.8.P.8.8, SC.8.P.8.9

Matter is anything that has mass and takes up space. These are the two fundamental properties of matter. All objects and substances in the world are made of matter. You are matter. Your shoe is matter. Even air is matter because it has mass and takes up space. Try inflating a balloon and weighing it to prove this. Everything in the universe is matter.

Matter is made up of small particles called **_atoms._** Just as bricks are the building blocks of a house, atoms are the building blocks of matter. Atoms combine in so many different ways to make up matter. When groups of atoms combine it is called a **_molecule_**. A pure substance is made up of only one type of atom or molecule. The compound water and any of the elements found on the periodic table, such as gold, are examples of **_pure substances_**. Pure substances can't be broken down into simpler substances by physical or chemical means. Each substance has its own characteristic properties that are different from the set of properties of any other substance.

Mixtures

Standards: SC.5.P.8.3, SC.8.P.8.8, SC.8.P.8.9

You can think of a **_mixture_** as the opposite of a pure substance. Mixtures are two or more substances that are **NOT** chemically combined. They can be broken down into simpler substances. For example, if you take two pure substances such as salt and water and combine them you will have a salt-water mixture. However, you can separate the salt from the water again by simply evaporating off the water. What remains will be the salt. Apple juice is another example of a mixture of apples, sugar, water, and acids.

Homogeneous mixtures have a uniform composition (they look the same throughout) but can be separated by physical means (dissolution, centrifuge, gravimetric filtering, etc,). Examples include air, blood, vinegar and corn oil. Components retain their characteristic properties and may be separated into pure substances by physical methods. Mixtures of different compositions may have widely different properties

Heterogeneous mixtures contain more than one pure substance and more than one phase. It is one which does not have a uniform composition. It may have localized regions with different properties. Examples include an oil and water combination, milk, pizza, chocolate, chicken soup and smoke. Beach sand is heterogeneous since you can visibly distinguish different colored particles. A mixture of sand and iron filings is heterogeneous and can be separated mechanically by using a magnet to attract the iron filings and lift them away.

Mixtures are classified as **_solutions_**, **_suspensions_**, or **_colloids_**. A mixture is called a solution when the particles are very small and appear to be one substance (such as apple juice). These mixtures are created when something is completely dissolved in water. Therefore, they are easily separated by physical means such as distillation or evaporation.

Mixtures are called suspensions when the particle size are large and can be separated into layers (such as a sand and water suspension). These are mixtures of solids and liquids in which the solids do not dissolve in the liquid. The particles are visible and will settle out upon standing. Clay in water is another example of a suspension.

A heterogeneous mixture is called a colloid when the particles are in a size range between the size of those found in a suspension and a solution and are dispersed in a gas, liquid or solid medium. The particles do not settle out. They can be described as a substance trapped inside another substance. They are identified by their characteristic scattering of light. Two examples of colloids include dust, which contains solid particles suspended in air, and clouds, which contains ice or water droplets dispersed in air. Other examples include milk, fog, and Jell-O.

For the FCAT you should know that mixtures of solids can be separated based on observable properties of their parts such as particle size, shape, color, and magnetic attraction. They can be separated by mechanical means such as heat, centrifugation, and filtration. For example, a centrifuge, which is an instrument that rotates at high speed and separates substances of different densities, can be used to mechanically separate blood into various layers consisting of liquid plasma and solid blood cells.

Also for the FCAT you should be able to identify basic examples of and be able to compare and classify the properties of compounds, including acids, bases, and salts. Scientists group compounds based on the type of **_chemical bonds_** (how atoms or ions are held together) they form. This has been summarized in **Table 2-1** on the next page.

Table 2-1 Examples of Common Compounds and Their Properties

Type of Compound	Examples	Properties
Covalent Compounds	Sugar Oil Water Ammonia Carbon tetrachloride Carbon-based organic compounds (proteins, carbohydrates, lipids, nucleic acids).	Formed when a group of atoms share electrons (covalent bonds). Made up of molecules. Weaker attractive forces hold atoms together. Low solubility (does not dissolve well in water). Low melting points (due to weak attractive force). Most do not have electrical conductivity (will not conduct an electric current).
Ionic Compounds	Table Salt (sodium chloride) and other salts Magnesium oxide Nickel (II) oxide Potassium dichromate Sodium oxide	Formed by the transfer of electrons from one atom to another. The chemical bond is formed between oppositely charged ions. Formed between metals and nonmetals. Strong attractive forces. High melting points (due to strong attractive forces). High solubility (dissolves well in water). Brittleness (breaks apart when hit). Have electrical conductivity (will conduct an electric current).
Acids	Vinegar Lemon juice Hydrochloric acid (harmful)	Solutions that contain the element hydrogen and can dissolve in water to release hydrogen ions into solution. Sour taste. Causes color changes. Corrosive to metals. Turns litmus (an indicator) red. Have electrical conductivity.
Bases	Baking soda Sodium hydroxide Drain cleaner Antacids	Opposite of an acid. Solutions that have an excess of OH- ions. Feels slippery. Change litmus (an indicator) blue. Have electric conductivity.

Note: Please refer to your school-issued textbook for more information on compounds.

Solubility

Solubility refers to the relative ability of a solute (solid, liquid or gaseous substance) to be dissolved in a solvent (solid, liquid or gaseous substance) under normal conditions. A substance that is highly soluble in water, for example, will form a homogeneous solution when it mixes with the water. Solubility depends on the nature of the substances being mixed (solute and solvent), temperature and pressure. At standard temperature and pressure water usually exist as a liquid. Because water is used to create so many solutions it is considered a "universal solvent".

Since solubility is mentioned in **Table 2-1** (pg. 50) we will take a second to identify materials that will dissolve in water as well as identify the conditions that will speed up or slow down the dissolving process. In general, whether something dissolves in water or not depends on its chemical properties. Water is a **polar** molecule. This means that one end of the water molecule has a slightly positive charge and the other end has a slightly negative charge. Ionic substances tend to dissolve well in water because water molecules will attract the positive and negative charged ions of this type of compound and pull the ions away from one another. This is what is called "dissolving".

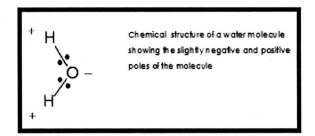

Chemical structure of a water molecule showing the slightly negative and positive poles of the molecule

Substances that dissolve well in water are classified as **hydrophilic** (water-loving). These include sugars, acids, carbon dioxide, oxygen, and salts. Hydrophobic (water-fearing) substances do not mix well with water. Oils and fats are hydrophobic. These substances tend to be covalent compounds. These types of compounds form chemical bonds with other substances by sharing electrons between atoms. As a result, no net charge is created. Because they typically do not possess a charge they do not attract the charged water molecule.

Physical and Chemical Properties

Standards: SC.8.P.8.4,   SC.8.P.9.2

Matter can be identified by its **_physical properties_** and its **_chemical properties_**. A physical property is one that can be measured or observed without taking something apart or changing it chemically. We will explore physical properties first. These include such properties as volume, density, mass, weight, boiling point, freezing point, ductility and malleability (for metals).

You can compare one type of matter with another by comparing their physical or chemical properties. For instance, you could calculate the densities of two objects and surprisingly discover that the one with the larger density was not necessarily the largest in size. You could also compare two equal volumes of liquids and discover that they have different masses altogether.

Some physical properties are independent of the amount of the sample. They can be used to identify substances (**_intensive properties_**). You can identify water, for example, by its density. The physical properties of sodium metal can be observed or measured. It is a soft, lustrous, silver-colored metal with a relatively low melting point and low density.

For the FCAT you should be able to compare different types of matter by comparing their physical properties. **Table 2-2** on the following page lists some common physical properties of matter. You should know that these properties are independent of the amount of the sample. An ounce of a substance will have the same melting point as a gallon of that same substance.

Table 2-2 Physical Properties of Matter

Property	Description	Example
Electrical conductivity	Ability to carry electricity	Copper is a good electrical conductor, so it is used in wiring.
Heat conductivity	Ability to transfer energy as heat	Aluminum is a good heat conductor, so it is used to make posts and pans.
Density	Mass-to-volume ratio of a substance; measure of how tightly matter is "packed"	Lead is a very dense material, so it is used to make sinkers for fishing line.
Melting point	Temperature at which a solid changes state to become a liquid.	Ice melts to liquid water at the melting point of water.
Boiling point	Temperature at which a liquid boils and changes state to become a gas at a given pressure.	Liquid water becomes water vapor at the boiling point of water.
Index of refraction	Extent to which a given material bends light passing through it.	The index of refraction of water tells you how much light slows and bends as it pass through water.
Malleability	Ability to be hammered or beaten into thin sheets.	Silver is quite malleable, so it is used to make jewelry.
Ductility	Ability to be drawn into a thin wire.	Tantalum is a ductile metal, so it is used to make fine dental tools.

Density

Standards: SC.8.P.8.3

Density is the ratio of the mass of a substance compared to its volume. Mass is how much matter or "stuff" is in an object or substance. Volume is the amount of space that the object or substance occupies. The scientific formula for calculating density is **D = mass/volume**. That is, density is equal to the mass of an object divided by its volume. It is expressed in units of mass per volume (i.e., grams/cm ^{3}).

Remember, objects float when their density is less than the material they are placed in and sink when their density is greater than the material they are placed in. Be aware that different

Table 2-3 Densities of Various Materials

Material	Density (g/cm³)
Water	1.00
Brick	1.84
Air	0.0013
Feathers	0.0025
Ice	0.92
Aluminum	2.70
Wood	0.6 - 0.9
Steel	7.80
Gold	19.30
Silver	10.50

materials have different densities and that density is not always related to size. The density of a small object could be greater than the density of a larger object. Smaller objects can weigh more than bigger objects because of density. The density of a small cube made of iron is greater than the density of a large piece of Styrofoam. Therefore, the cube would weigh more than the Styrofoam. Also remember that when different materials are mixed together (like oil and water) it is their densities that will determine how they order themselves. In the example of an oil and water mixture, when settled, oil will form a layer on top of the water since it has a density less than water.

From **Table 2-3** you can compare densities of various materials. Ice will float in water because it has a density less than water. Likewise, a brick will sink when placed in water because it has a density greater than water.

Chemical properties are based on the ability of matter to react chemically with other substances and to form new substances as well. Examples of chemical properties include rusting, oxidation, reactivity and flammability (burning). One of the chemical properties of alkali metals such as sodium and potassium is that they react with water. To determine this we would have to combine an alkali metal with water and observe what happens. In other words, we have to define chemical properties of a substance by the chemical changes it undergoes.

PART II CHANGES IN MATTER
Standards: SC.5.P.9.1,   SC.8.P.9.2,   SC.8.P.9.3

Matter can be characterized, described and compared based on their physical and chemical properties. This means you can tell what the matter is and how it is the same or different from another type of matter based on things such as its density, volume, melting point, or flammability, to name a few. All sections of a pure sample will have the same physical and chemical properties. For example, if you divide a wood beam into smaller sections each section would have the same physical properties (i.e., density) and the same chemical properties (i.e., flammability).

Matter can undergo many changes. These changes can be physical or chemical in nature. If you can understand physical and chemical properties it will be very easy to understand **_physical changes_** and **_chemical changes_**. A physical change is any type of change that does not alter the identity of matter. On the other hand, a chemical change does change the identity of the substance. It forms new substances.

If you rip a sheet of paper in half this is a physical change. Ripping the paper does not change the paper into a different material. It may change its form but it is still paper. The density of the ripped paper, for example will be identical to that of the whole sheet. However, if you burn the paper it will change the physical properties of the paper when it turns to ash. The ash formed is a new substance. Burning, therefore, is a chemical change because it *does* change the identity of the paper and results in the formation of a new substance (ash)

Many physical changes are reversible. Ice can be melted to form water again. In general no changes occur in the structure of the atoms or molecules composing the matter. However, chemical changes are often not reversible (irreversible) because new products with different characteristics are formed. In chemical changes there is a rearrangement of bonds between the atoms which results in a new substance with new properties. Cooking an egg results in a chemical change. The application of heat to the egg changes its chemical properties in an irreversible way. The protein of the egg yolk becomes damaged (denatured) by heat and it becomes white (i.e., when boiled or fried). Temperature thus influences chemical changes. When heat is added to cake batter it becomes cake. However, the cake cannot reform cake batter once the heat is removed.

Temperature also influences physical changes. These changes are reversible however. Adding heat energy to liquid water causes it to change in form to water vapor (it evaporates). Nevertheless, this water vapor can cool and condense to form liquid water again. Removing heat from liquid water causes it to freeze (form solid water). The properties of the water generally do not change (although due to the unique nature of water the density of ice is slightly below that of liquid water).

Some signs that a chemical reaction has occurred include an odor forming, a color change, energy being given off (heat, light or electricity), bubbling, fizzling, or the formation of a precipitate (a solid substance formed in the test tube). Any or all of these signs can accompany a chemical change. The bottom line is that chemical changes make new products.

You can demonstrate a chemical change by writing a ***chemical equation***. Chemical equations describe in words a chemical reaction. An example is provided below.

Chemical Equation:

$$4Al + 3O_2 \longrightarrow 2Al_2O_3$$

reactants   products

In this chemical reaction aluminum atoms combine with oxygen atoms to form the product aluminum oxide. You can see that this is a balanced equation. The numbers of each atom on both sides of the arrow are equal. This is the Law of Conservation of Mass at work!! Atoms are not created or destroyed; just rearranged to form new products. [**NOTE:** Please refer to your school- issued science textbook for more information on chemical equations, chemical compounds, chemical bonding, and balancing equations].

The Law of Conservation of Mass

Standards: SC.8.P.9.1

The Law of Conservation of Mass is simple to understand. It states that the quantity of mass is unchanged when substances undergo physical and chemical changes. Thus, mass is "*conserved*" (it stays the same). Basically, the amount of matter you begin with before a chemical or physical reaction will be the same amount of matter you end up with after the reaction. There is no observable change in the quantity of matter during chemical or physical reactions.

Let's take another look at the ripped paper illustration again. Say you measured the mass of the sheet of paper before ripping it and found it to be 2 grams. Then, after ripping the paper you collected and measured the mass of all the little pieces of paper together. They would still add up to 2 grams. This is because mass is "conserved" or stays the same before or after doing something to the matter. Scientist word this by saying that mass is not created nor destroyed by natural, physical or chemical means.   This is even true if you burn the paper (a chemical reaction). The mass of the unburned paper would equal the combined mass of the new products formed from burning the paper (specifically, the ash, carbon dioxide and water).

The States of Matter

Standards: SC.5.P.8.1, SC.7.P.11.1, SC.8.P.8.1, SC.8.P.9.1

Matter exists in four states or physical forms; **_solid_**, **_liquid_**, **_gas_**, and **_plasma._**   The state of matter depends on the amount of energy and motion of the atoms that make up the matter. Remember, particles in matter have kinetic energy, which is the energy of motion. These particles are always moving.   The measure of kinetic energy is temperature. Substances with a lot of kinetic energy will have a high temperature. With the study of states of matter you can easily observe that when heat is added or taken away, a temperature change occurs.   This temperature change may possibly result in a change of state. Let's first deal with the first three states of matter, solid, liquid and gas. We'll save plasma for last.

In the solid state of matter the atoms that make up matter are packed very tightly together and there is very little movement between them. They have a strong attraction for each other. The atoms have very little energy or movement but they do vibrate and rotate around a fixed position. Solids maintain their fixed, rigid shape. They have definite shape and volume.

In the liquid state, atoms and molecules have more space between them as compared to the solid state, but less than in the gas state (i.e., it is more "fluid".) Atoms have room to move around. Because molecules in a liquid have more energy than in a solid they tend to move around more and have less attraction for each other.   Liquids take on the shape of their container. They lack a definite shape but they do have a definite volume.

In the gas state molecules are moving in random patterns with varying amounts of distance between the particles. Atoms tend to move around freely. These particles have the most energy and movement.   They can spread out because they gain the right amount of energy to escape their attraction for each other. Gases have no definite shape or volume. Examples of substances in the gaseous state are smoke and steam.

Plasma is a gas but is no ordinary type of gas. It is a gas in which the particles develop an electric charge and can conduct an electric current. It responds strongly to an electromagnetic field. Like a regular gas, plasma has no definite shape or volume. Apart from this similarity, plasma has distinct properties that make it different from a solid, liquid or gas. It is the most common form of matter. Plasma makes up over 99% of the visible universe and perhaps most of that which is not visible. Common examples of plasma include lightening, stars, the Sun, neon lights and a flame.

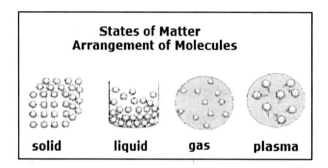

Matter can change in physical form from one state to another. Predictably, this concept is called a ***change of state***. An object in the solid state can change to the liquid state by absorbing enough heat energy to break the attraction of the molecules for each other. The atoms will then have enough energy to move around more freely. This is called ***melting***. This same liquid can absorb more heat energy to further break the attraction of the molecules for each other so that they can escape into the gaseous state. This is called **vaporization** or ***evaporation***. Furthermore, the gas can lose energy, cool down and re-form a liquid. This is called ***condensation***. A solid can undergo a phase change directly to become a gas without passing through an intermediary liquid phase. This is called **sublimation**. **Freezing** is going from the liquid state to the solid state. Plasmas are formed when gas molecules becomes charged or ionized. This is called **ionization**.

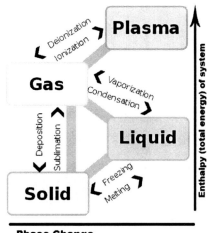

Phase Change

During a phase change the temperature of the substance does not change until all molecules have gained/lost enough energy to escape/attract the other molecules.   At this point the transition to the next phase occurs. This fact can be demonstrated by the shape of the phase change graph for water shown on below. The horizontal line representing an area of uniform temperature along with the steep slope vertical line representing a temperature change.

The actual point when a change of state occurs is called the phase transition point (for instance, the **melting point**, **_freezing point/crystallization_**, and **_boiling point_**).   The melting point of a solid is the temperature at which it changes state from solid to liquid. The freezing point/crystallization point of a liquid is the temperature at which it changes from liquid to solid. At the boiling point a liquid becomes a gas.

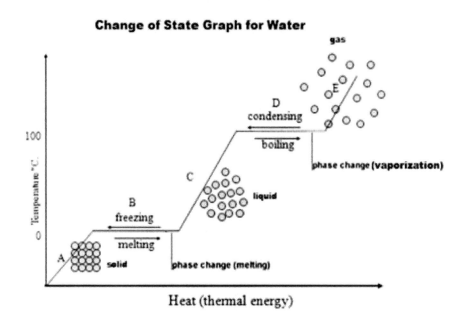

Change of State Graph for Water

Atomic Theory (Scientific Theory of the Atom)

Matter is made of small particles called **_atoms_**.   Atoms are the smallest unit of a substance that retains the properties of that substance. These particles are too small to be seen without magnification. Since atoms are thousands of times smaller than the size of a wavelength of light (400–700 nm) they cannot be viewed using an optical microscope.   You can however observe atoms using a scanning tunneling microscope.

Atoms are responsible for the physical and chemical properties of matter. This is the main idea of the **_atomic theory_**.   In chemical reactions, atoms are rearranged, combined, or separated.

Modern Atomic Theory

1. Elements are composed of atoms.
2. All atoms of a given element have the same chemical properties and contain the same number of protons.
3. Compounds are formed by the chemical combination of two or more different kinds of atoms.
4. Atoms are rearranged during chemical reactions.

Atoms are made up of smaller subatomic particles known as **_protons_**, **_electrons_**, and **_neutrons_**. They consist of a positively charged **_nucleus_** with negatively charged electrons orbiting it. Inside the nucleus are protons, and neutrons. A breakdown of each subatomic particle is located in **Table 2-4** on the following page. Protons have a positive charge while neutrons have no charge at all. They are neutral (whenever you think "neutron" think "neutral").

Bohr Model of the Atom

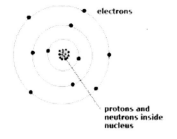

Electron Cloud Model of the Atom

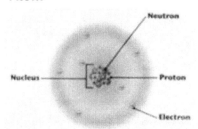

Since the electrons are on the outside of the atom they are the ones that determine its chemical reactivity or the ease at which it participates in chemical reactions. These are called **valence electrons**. They participate in chemical and electrical processes by combining with other atoms. When atoms combine to form new substances they develop properties that are different from their original **element**. An element is a substance that is made entirely from one type of atom. It is a pure substance.

The **periodic table** is a chart which classifies and organizes all the known elements. Examples of elements include gold, silver, copper, oxygen, carbon, hydrogen, nitrogen, iron, and helium. Atoms of the same element have the same number of protons, called the **atomic number**. The sum of the protons and neutrons is the **mass number.**

The process of atoms joining together is called **chemical bonding**. The number of valence electrons will determine whether or not atoms form chemical bonds. Electrons can be gained, lost or shared. There are special names for these chemical bonds. When atoms form chemical bonds by transferring electrons this is called an **ionic bond**. When bonds are formed by sharing electrons this is called a **covalent** bond. An atom is classified according to the number of protons and neutrons in its nucleus. The number of protons determines the chemical element and the number of neutrons determines the **isotope** of the element. Isotopes are different versions of an element. All isotopes of a particular element have the same number of protons but different number of neutrons.

Table 2-4 Subatomic Particles of Atoms

Particles	Charge	Size	Symbol	Location
Protons	Positive charge (+)	$2.5 \times 10{-}15$ m	p^+	Found in the nucleus
Neutrons	Neutral (no) charge (0)	$2.5 \times 10{-}15$ m	N^0	Found in the nucleus
Electrons	Negative charge (-)	Size too small to be measured	e^-	Found orbiting the nucleus

Atoms are in constant motion. This is the **_Kinetic Theory of Matter_**. In solids, atoms are tightly packed and confined as crystalline structures. They move around by spinning or vibrating. Atoms of liquids and gases are able to move around more freely. In a liquid the atoms are close together with no regular arrangement. They vibrate, move about, and slide past each other. However, in a gas atoms are well separated. They vibrate and move freely at high speeds.

Behavior of Atoms in a Solid, Liquid and Gas

Solid   Liquid   Gas

When atoms collide with each other they transfer energy. These collisions with atoms of other elements often lead to chemical and physical reactions. A chemical reaction occurs when the colliding of atoms, the transfer of energy and the breaking (and remaking) of chemical bonds lead to the formation of new substances. A physical change occurs when the transfer of energy lead to a rearrangement of the molecules, as in the melting of ice.

Atoms are naturally neutral particles unless they gain or lose electrons. When this happens we call them **_ions_**. When atoms gain electrons they develop a negative charge (remember electrons are negative so if you gain more of them then it becomes even more negative). When atoms lose electrons they become positive (losing a negative makes it more positive). A positive ion is called a **_cation_**. A negative ion is called an **_anion_**.

The History of the Atomic Theory
Standards: SC.5.P.8.4, SC.8.P.8.1, SC.8.P.8.7

Many decades ago groups of male and female scientists from diverse backgrounds performed such innovative research in the nature and structure of the atom that it radically changed the face of science and medicine. Likewise, our understanding of the function of matter also greatly expanded. They contributed to the development of the atomic theory. The evolution of the atomic theory is presented here in the form of a chart. You should familiarize yourself with each scientist. You need not memorize them. What you should take from this section is that scientific knowledge is modified as new information becomes available. It builds upon itself. You should also understand that diversity in the many scientists' background, talent, and ethnicity, helped to successfully build atomic theory and other scientific knowledge.

Table 2-5 Development of the Atomic Theory

DEVELOPMENT OF THE ATOMIC THEORY		
Name of Scientist	Contribution	Year
Democritus	The Greek philosopher who said atoms were particles that couldn't be divided any further and were in constant motion. He was the first to begin the study of the atom. His theory was ignored for centuries.	~ 400 B.C.
Aristotle	Another Greek philosopher. He did not agree with Democritus' theory.	
John Dalton	Created the first modern atomic theory. He said that all matter is composed of atoms. All atoms of an element are identical yet different from those of other elements and that atoms can be rearranged chemically to make different compounds.	1804
Dmitri Mendeleev	Created the first periodic table of the elements which organized them in a chart and predicted their chemical properties.	1869
Marie and Pierre Curie	First to discover radioactivity as an atomic property of matter. Marie Curie later died from exposure to the radioactivity.	1896-1899
J.J. Thomson	Found flaws in Dalton's theory. Thomson conducted a cathode-ray tube experiment that showed that atoms could be divided into even smaller parts. He discovered the electron. Thomson created the "plum-pudding" model of the atom's structure. He thought electrons were imbedded throughout the atom like plums in pudding.	1897
Ernest Rutherford	Discovered the structure of the atom. He proved J.J. Thomson's theory wrong. He discovered through his gold-foil experiment that the atom was not a solid mass of positive and negative charges. He found that atoms were mostly made up of empty space surrounding a central core called a nucleus. He also confirmed the presence of the proton and alluded to the presence of the neutron.	1911 and 1919
Niels Bohr	He described how electrons travel in definite paths around the nucleus in energy levels. According to his theory electrons can jump between energy levels.	1913
H. Moseley	Determined that each nucleus had an atomic number equal to the number of positive charges. This led to the rearrangement of the periodic table by atomic number.	1913
J. Chadwick	Confirmed the presence of the neutron.	1932
Erwin Schrodinger and Werner Heisenberg	Contributed to the modern atomic theory by proposing the "electron-cloud model" of the atom. Contrary to Bohr's theory, The modern theory stated that electrons are not found in definite locations around the nucleus but in electron clouds which are locations around the nucleus where electrons are likely to be found.	After the late 1920's

The Organization of the Periodic Table

Standards: SC.8.P.8.5, SC.8.P.8.6, SC.8.P.8.7

Periodic Table of Elements

1 1 H																		0 2 He
2 3 Li	4 Be											5 B	6 C	7 N	8 O	9 F	10 Ne	
3 11 Na	12 Mg											13 Al	14 Si	15 P	16 S	17 Cl	18 Ar	
4 19 K	20 Ca	21 Sc	22 Ti	23 V	24 Cr	25 Mn	26 Fe	27 Co	28 Ni	29 Cu	30 Zn	31 Ga	32 Ge	33 As	34 Se	35 Br	36 Kr	
5 37 Rb	38 Sr	39 Y	40 Zr	41 Nb	42 Mo	43 Tc	44 Ru	45 Rh	46 Pd	47 Ag	48 Cd	49 In	50 Sn	51 Sb	52 Te	53 I	54 Xe	
6 55 Cs	56 Ba	57 *La	72 Hf	73 Ta	74 W	75 Re	76 Os	77 Ir	78 Pt	79 Au	80 Hg	81 Tl	82 Pb	83 Bi	84 Po	85 At	86 Rn	
7 87 Fr	88 Ra	89 +Ac	104 Rf	105 Ha	106	107	108	109	110									

Group labels: IA, IIA, IIIB, IVB, VB, VIB, VIIB, ——— VIII ———, IB, IIB, IIIA, IVA, VA, VIA, VIIA, 0

* Lanthanide Series	58 Ce	59 Pr	60 Nd	61	62 Sm	63 Eu	64 Gd	65 Tb	66 Dy	67 Ho	68 Er	69 Tm	70 Yb	71 Lu
+ Actinide Series	90 Th	91 Pa	92 U	93	94	95	96	97	98	99	100	101	102	103

With a better understanding of atoms, the periodic table was better organized. Scientist now had a greater understanding of the chemical behavior of the 100+ discovered elements. As of the writing of this book there are about 117 elements that have been discovered thus far. The limited number of elements and their atoms combine in a multitude of ways to produce compounds that make up all of the living and nonliving things that exist.

Common elements found in living and nonliving things include carbon, nitrogen, oxygen, iron, magnesium, selenium and hydrogen. You do not have to memorize the entire periodic table. Just understand its meaning and the pattern of its organization. Keep the following in mind:

1. There are 18 vertical columns called **_groups_** or **_families_**. Each element of a group share similar chemical properties. Each of the 7 rows going across horizontally is called a **_period_**. Below period 7 are two rows of elements. These are the **Lanthanides** and **Actinides** series. They are placed below to conserve space and make the periodic table more narrow.

2. The elements can be a solid, liquid or gas and are characterized as being either **_metal_** (elements that like to give off electrons), **_nonmetals_** (elements that like to gain electrons), or **_metalloids_** (elements with chemical properties of both metals

- 64 -

and nonmetals). Most elements of the periodic table are metals. Metals tend to be chemically reactive (like to form bonds with other elements), shiny, **_malleable_** (can be flattened) and **_ductile_** (can be bent into shape), are good conductors of heat and electric current and are solids at room temperature (except mercury which is a liquid at room temperature). With the exception of hydrogen, metals are found to the left of the zigzag line of the periodic table.   Examples include lithium, magnesium and nickel.

3. Nonmetals tend to have the opposite characteristics of metals. They are not shiny, not malleable, not ductile, and are not good conductors of heat and electricity. Many nonmetals are gases at room temperature. They are found to the right of the zigzag line on the periodic table. Examples include fluorine, bromine, and iodine.   The **_noble gases_** are a group of stable gases found in the last column or group of the periodic table. They include helium and neon.

4. Metalloids share properties of both metals and nonmetals. Some are shiny but not malleable. They are brittle and good conductors of electric current. Metalloids are located bordering the zigzag line. They include boron, silicon, germanium, arsenic, antimony, and tellurium.   Metalloids are also known as semimetals.

5. Reading the periodic table is very easy. Each box represents a different element. Inside the box you will find the name of each element, its symbol, atomic number, and atomic mass (see the example below):

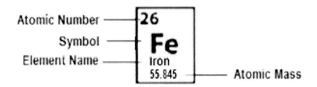

Calculations Using the Periodic Table

You can use the periodic table to solve atomic problems involving the following:

1. **_Atomic Number_** (the number of protons in the nucleus of an atom). Different elements have different atomic numbers (protons).

2. ***Isotopes*** (elements that have the ***same number of protons*** but ***different numbers of neutrons***). Isotopes are always the same element because they have the same atomic number (# of protons).

3. **Mass Number** (the ***sum of the protons and neutrons*** in an atom). This is a helpful number for identifying isotopes because isotopes differ in number of neutrons only. When you write the name of an isotope you always include its mass number. For example, carbon-14 is an isotope of carbon-12 with 2 additional neutrons.

4. ***Atomic Mass*** (the weighted average of all the naturally occurring isotopes for an element). Most elements contain a mixture of two or more isotopes.

Calculations:

1. **Finding the number of protons in a neutral atom:** In a neutral atom (atoms that have neither gained nor lost electrons) the number of protons is equal to the number of electrons (p^+ = e^-). The number of protons is also equal to the atomic number. So, for iron, the number of protons equals 26, which is the atomic number of iron.

---

2. ***Finding the number of neutrons:*** If you know the mass number and the number of protons (atomic #) you can calculate the number of neutrons by doing the following calculation:

atomic mass – atomic number = # of neutrons

Let's use the element iron as our example for the calculation:

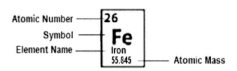

atomic mass		**atomic number**		**# of neutrons**
(56)	-	(26)	=	(30)

[**Note:** The atomic mass # 55.845 was rounded to 56 to simplify calculations.]

This equation can also be re-worked to find atomic mass or atomic number when these entities are the unknowns.

---

3. **Finding atomic mass:** the atomic mass can be calculated by following the steps below. Sample Problem:

Boron-35 (35 is the mass number) makes up 70% of all the boron atoms found in nature, and boron-37 (37 is the mass number) makes up the other 30%. What is the atomic mass of boron?

STEP 1: Multiply each isotope's mass number by the percentage that it is found in nature. You must first convert the percentage into a decimal.

(35 x 0.70) = 24.50
(37 x 0.30) = 11.10

STEP 2: Add the values you calculated in step 1 to determine the atomic mass.

(35 x 0.70) =   24.50
(37 x 0.30) = + 11.10
            _____
            35.60 amu

Exothermic and Endothermic Reactions
Standards: SC.5.P.10.1, SC.6.P.11.1, SC.7.P.11.1, SC.7.P.11.2, SC.7.P.11.3

All chemical reactions involve energy. When a chemical reaction gives off energy it is called an **exothermic reaction** (exo = *go out*   thermic= *heat*). When a chemical reaction absorbs energy it is called an **endothermic** (endo = in   thermic= heat). Once again, the **Law of Conservation of Energy** applies here. In any reaction, the total amount of energy of the system does not change whether the reaction gains or losses energy. Energy cannot be created or destroyed, just changed from one form into another. The energy that is taken in during an endothermic reaction will ultimately be stored in the products.

Factors That Determine the Rate of a Chemical Reaction

Standards: SC.7.P.11.1, SC.7.P.11.2, SC.8.P.9.3

The likelihood of a chemical reaction occurring depends on several factors. These factors determine the **_rate_** or how fast the reaction occurs. They include;

1. The correct amount of **_activation energy_** (the boost of energy needed to start a reaction).

2. Whether a **_catalyst_** or **_inhibitor_** is present or not. These speed up or slow down, respectively, the rate of the reaction.

3. **_Temperature_**. Many reactions proceed faster in warmer temperatures because the molecules have more energy and they bump and collide more.

4. The **_concentration_** of the reactants. As concentration increases the rate also increases because there are more atoms available to collide and react.

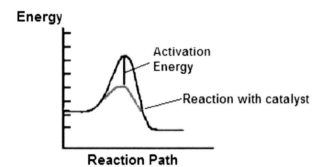

PART III FORMS OF ENERGY

Standards: SC.5.P.10.1, SC.5.P.10.2, SC.5.P.10.3, SC.5.P.10.4, SC.6.P.11.1

This section of **Science Prep Cat** reviews different forms of **_energy_** and how they flow through systems. These various forms of energy include wave, electrical, thermal, chemical, sound, kinetic (motion), gravitational and magnetic energy.

As you will see energy is a very important topic on the science FCAT. Energy is in everything. It is involved in all physical processes. It is the ability to do work or the ability to make things move. It causes change. Without energy nothing could be done. You could not live without energy.

Energy changes create weather, allow organisms to move, and even transmit nervous impulses in the human body. Forms of energy include the following;

1. **_Chemical energy_**- What holds atoms in molecules together. It can be released by chemical reactions, such as burning wood.

2. **_Electrical energy_**- The movement of electrons through matter. Electricity is a form of electrical energy.

3. **_Thermal (heat) energy_**- The random motion or vibration, of atoms in matter. The faster the atoms vibrate the more heat energy they have.

4. **_Light energy_**- The energy carried by light (i.e., sunlight).

5. **_Mechanical energy_**- The energy of moving things. When you ride a bike you use mechanical energy to pedal the bike.

6. **_Nuclear energy_**- Holds protons and neutrons together in an atom's nucleus. It powers the Sun and nuclear power plants.

7. **_Sound energy_**- Vibrates air molecules. You hear sound because air molecules move tiny bones in your ear. These vibrations move to your brain and are interpreted as sound. Sound energy can also vibrate other objects, for example, the vibrations of a speaker when loud music is being played.

When we talk about different forms of energy we have to also mention **_potential energy_** (stored energy) and **_kinetic energy_** (energy of motion). For example, your body stores energy in food (chemical energy) so that you can use it to do work (blink, run, digest food, smile, etc). Thermal energy has kinetic energy because the atoms are in motion.

One type of energy can be transformed into another. If you hold a ball up in the air it will have potential energy (the energy of position or height). When you release the ball it will fall to the ground. The moment it touches the ground the potential energy will be converted to kinetic energy that will make the ball bounce. As the ball bounces in the air some of the kinetic energy will be converted back into potential energy while the ball is in flight. The energy converts back and forth from potential to kinetic as the ball bounces and hits the floor.

A traditional roller coaster demonstrates both potential and kinetic energy. A chain lift uses the mechanical energy of moving chains on a track to lift the car to the top of the hill. At the very top of the roller coaster the car exhibits the greatest amount of potential energy because it is at the greatest height. All the energy of the car is stored energy. This potential energy then converts to kinetic energy as the chain lift releases the car and it begins moving down the roller coaster (by gravity). The faster the car moves the faster potential energy converts to kinetic energy. At the bottom of the roller coaster the car comes to a rest. The kinetic energy of motion converts to stored potential energy once again and the car stops moving.

Law of Conservation of Energy

Standards: SC.6.P.11.1, SC.7.P.11.2, SC.7.P.11.3

Energy changes in form and transfers from one object to another. This is the **_Law of Conservation of Energy_**. The Law of Conservation of Energy is similar to the Law of Conservation of Mass. It says that energy cannot be created nor destroyed but can be changed from one form to another. When we use energy it does not disappear. It can be changed from one form of energy to another. Energy is conserved as it transfers from one object to another and from one form to another.

A generator converts mechanical (moving) energy into electrical energy. The engine of a car converts the chemical energy of gasoline into heat energy and then to mechanical energy to move the car. Electricity produces light and heat in a lamp.

Solar cells convert solar radiation into electrical energy to power homes. Batteries, another type of cell, convert the chemical energy of **_electrolytes_** (mixture of chemicals that conducts electric currents) into electrical energy. Thermal energy in steam can be used to run a turbine (mechanical energy) which in turn produces electrical energy. Potential energy of a ball being converted to kinetic energy as it falls to the ground and bounces demonstrates that energy is not destroyed or created. It is just transformed from one form to another.

Energy conversion is never 100% efficient. This means that when energy is transferred from one form to another there is often energy produced that is not useful. For example, the next time you are in class and your teacher is showing a movie with an LCD projector connected to a computer, go up and feel the projector. What you will see is that an energy conversion is taking place that is not 100% efficient. The projector converts electrical energy into light and sound energy so you can see and hear the video. However, a byproduct of this energy conversion is the production of heat (thermal energy). If you feel the projector it will feel warm to the touch. This heat that is produced is not useful energy for your purposes (unless you are sitting directly near it and it is warming you up in a cold classroom!). You can say it is wasted energy. However, the heat is not destroyed. It is simply returned to the system. Ultimately it will transform to another type of energy. The total amount of energy in the universe will remain the same because energy is not being created or destroyed.

Energy can be classified as **_renewable_** or **_nonrenewable_**. Renewable energy is energy that can be used over and over again. It can be easily replenished. Solar, wind, water (hydro), and geothermal energy (heat inside the Earth) are all renewable.

Nonrenewable energy can't be replenished easily. This is energy the world is running out of. It includes coal, oil, and natural gas. These energy sources are called **_fossil fuels_**. Fossil fuels were formed from the remains of prehistoric plants and animals millions of years ago. The supply of fossil fuels is limited. Renewable and nonrenewable energy sources can be transformed into electrical energy to power our homes, offices, and our entire city.

The Energy of Waves
Standards: SC.5.P.10.1, SC.5.P.10.2, SC.7.P.10.1, SC.7.P.10.2, SC.7.P.10.3

We all experience the energy of waves each and every day of our lives. When we go outside and feel the warmth of the Sun we are experiencing electromagnetic waves. Microwaves from a microwave oven warm our food. X-ray machines from the doctor's office help diagnose our ailments. We hear sound waves with a cell phone and see light waves when we look out into our environment. We have even read about or witnessed firsthand the destruction of earthquake waves on buildings or the flooding of coastal cities by tsunami waves. In this next section you will review the properties of waves that affect our daily lives.

A **_wave_** is a disturbance that travels through space and matter and transfers energy. Waves transfer energy without transferring matter. A toy boat bobbing up and down in a pool experiences the transfer of energy through waves without itself being propelled forward. The toy boat does not travel in the direction of the wave. It simply bobs up and down virtually staying in the same place as the wave travels outward. Waves have the following properties:

1. **crest** - the highest part of the wave
2. **trough** - the lowest part of a wave
3. **wavelength** - the horizontal distance between one crest and the next crest (or one trough and the next trough). The shorter the wavelength the greater the energy of the wave.
4. **amplitude** (wave height) - the height of a wave. The distance between the crest and the trough. The larger the amplitude the greater the energy of the wave.
5. **frequency** - how many waves pass in a certain amount of time.
6. **speed** - measured in meters per second. It is the speed of a point on a wave as it travels.
7. **period** - measured in seconds. It is the time it takes one complete wave to pass a given point.

Some waves, like **mechanical waves**, need a **medium** to travel and some waves can travel in a **vacuum** (an area where matter is absent). A medium is a material through which a wave travels. These include solids, liquids, or gasses. Air is an example of a medium.

Sound waves are mechanical waves. They require a medium in order to travel. Water and sound waves transfer energy through a medium whether it is air or water. Light waves on the other hand can travel through a vacuum and through matter. They are not mechanical waves.

Mechanical waves depend on **vibrations**. Vibrations are the repetitive back-and-forth motion of particles. As individual particles vibrate they transfer energy from particle to particle allowing the wave to travel. This is the reason sound does not travel in a vacuum. There are no particles in a vacuum to transfer sound energy. Ocean waves are also mechanical waves.

Electromagnetic waves (waves from the Sun) can travel without a medium. Energy waves from the Sun travel through space and reach us on Earth without needing a medium. These waves include ultraviolet light, gamma rays, X-rays, visible light, microwaves and infrared rays.

One of the FCAT science benchmarks require that you know that radiation, light, and heat are forms of energy used to cook food, treat diseases, and provide energy. You should be familiar with uses for these waves and how their energy is transferred. For example, microwave ovens are used to heat food rapidly. They work by heating the water molecules inside the food. Microwave ovens transfer microwave energy into thermal energy of water in order to heat the food particles. Other types of radiation which serve a useful purpose are X-rays, which can be used to diagnose broken bones and gamma rays which can be used to treat cancer patients or diagnostically in MRIs.

Two types of waves include **_transverse waves_** and **_longitudinal waves_**. (See the diagram below). These two waves differ in their properties. Transverse waves are made up of crests and troughs. Electromagnetic waves are transverse waves. Longitudinal waves are made up of **_compressions_** (areas where the wave squeezes together) and **_rarefactions_** (areas where the waves spread out). When you think about longitudinal waves think of the waves of a spring. Sound waves are longitudinal waves.

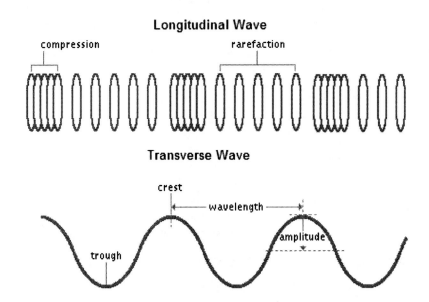

One of the coolest things about waves is how they interact. These interactions include **_reflection_**, **_refraction_** , **_diffraction_**, and **_interference_**. When waves bounce back after hitting a surface this is called re**_FLEC_**tion. An echo is an example of the reflection of a sound wave.

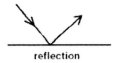

When waves bend or curve this is called diffraction or re**FRAC**tion. They are not exactly the same. Diffraction is the bending of waves around an obstacle and the spreading out of waves past openings. All waves can be diffracted. The diffraction of sound waves is the reason you can hear sound around a corner. The diffraction of light is responsible for the rainbow of colors given off by a CD or DVD.

diffraction

Refraction is when waves bend as they are passing from one medium into another, such as from air into water. Think about the old broken pencil in the water trick. When you insert a pencil into water the pencil appears to be broken. No, this is not magic. Its refraction! The speed of light waves (sound waves and other waves as well) is affected by the different media (plural of medium) they travel through. They also move at different speeds in different materials. The speed and wavelength of light waves change when they travel from air to water. Light travels faster in air than water. So, light slows down when it hits water and the wavelength changes. This gives the pencil the broken appearance.

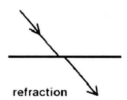

refraction

You can use a **_prism_** to see light refraction. When white light is passed through a prism a rainbow can be seen. This is because white light is made up of a spectrum of many different colors. Each wavelength of light traveling at different speeds are refracted by the prism and are separated into the various colors of the rainbow (red, orange, yellow, green, blue, indigo, and violet). An acronym to remember the colors of the rainbow is "ROY G. BIV" (which kind of sounds like a man's name). The initial letters of each color is contained in the name.

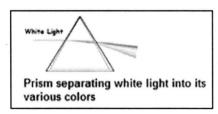

Prism separating white light into its various colors

Interference can be **_constructive_** or **_destructive_**. It is constructive when waves combine and become larger (bigger amplitude). This happens when the crests and troughs of two waves arrive at the same point at the same time.   For example, you are playing the radio while traveling in your parent's car. You arrive at a traffic light next to a car playing the same song. All of a sudden the music gets louder without either party turning up their radios.   The sound waves from both radios combine, the amplitude increases, and the sound is increased.

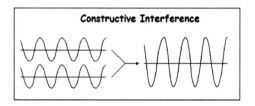

Destructive interference is just the opposite. It is the combining of waves that cause the waves to cancel each other out. It happens when the crest of one wave arrives at the same time as the trough of another wave and they cancel out (perhaps producing a softer sound in the above radio example). Sun glasses cause destructive interference of light to block out certain amounts of light.

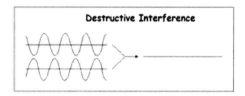

Electrical Energy

Standards: SC.5.P.10.3, SC.5.P.10.4, SC.5.P.11.1, SC.5.P.11.2, SC.6.P.13.1, SC.7.P.11.2, SC.7.P.11.3

Electrical energy and magnetic energy are not the same but they are related. This is why their names are sometimes combined as **_electromagnetism_**. Electromagnetic forces hold electrons and protons together inside atoms, causes friction, and cause iron to become attracted to a magnet, among other things.   They are experienced in both electric fields and magnetic fields.   Electrical and magnetic energy are intrinsically related. A changing electric field generates a magnetic field. Likewise, a changing magnetic field generates an electric field.   We will look at both separately.

Electricity is simply the science of moving charges, specifically electrons (negative charges). It is this movement which gives you light with the flip of a switch. It allows you to listen to your iPod, talk on your cell phone, play your video games, and use your AC on a hot day. The force those moving charges create makes energy available to power all of your modern technologies. Electricity is so amazing in that it can produce light, heat and sound. Often, all at the same time! Your flat screen television is a great example of this. When you plug it in and press the power button electrons begin to move. The force exerted by the moving charges energizes the TV to produce light energy that allows you to see the programming. Sound energy is also produced that allows you to hear the programming. As a byproduct of electrical energy being converted to light and sound energy, heat energy is also produced. After the television has been on for awhile it will feel warm to the touch. Heat is lost to the environment (but remember it is never destroyed). What a great example of the transforming power of electrical energy to make light, sound and heat energy!

Remember that protons and electrons carry charges. Protons carry positive charges while electrons carry negative ones. These charges are in motion. Similar or **_like_** charges **_repel_** (push away from each other) and **_opposite_** charges **_attract_** (pull towards each other). This is called the "**_Law of Electric Charges_**". This law explains the effect of the electric force one charged particle exerts on another. A positive and a positive charge will repel or push away from each other, as will a negative and a negative charge. However, a positive and a negative charge will attract or pull towards each other. This is why protons (+ charge) and electrons (- charge) attract.

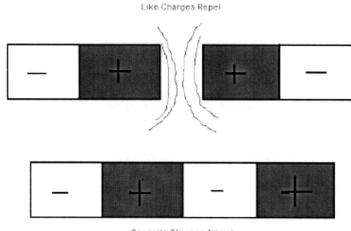

LAW OF ELECTRIC CHARGES

Recall that objects become charged when they gain or lose electrons. Losing electrons give objects a positive charge. Gaining electrons give objects a negative charge. Keep in mind that electrons are moving particles. Electrons can leave one object and travel to another. When it leaves the object that object becomes more positive. The object that it travels to will become more negative (because it is gaining electrons). Let's illustrate this fact. If you rub a glass rod with a cloth it loses electrons and will become positively charged. The electrons will be transferred into the cloth. This process of charging an object by rubbing it is "***charging by friction***".

Not every material can be charged. Wood, for example, conducts no electricity. Other ways of charging an object is by **conduction** and **induction**. Conduction is charging an object by contact. A negatively charged object can transfer a negative charge to a piece of metal by touching it. Induction is the opposite of conduction. In conduction contact is made that causes an object to become charged. In induction a charge is produced in an uncharged metal object without the two touching. If a negatively charged balloon is brought near a piece of metal the balloon would cause the free moving electrons to rearrange themselves away from the negative charges on the balloon ("like" charges repel) and draws or induces the positive charges toward it (opposite charges attract).

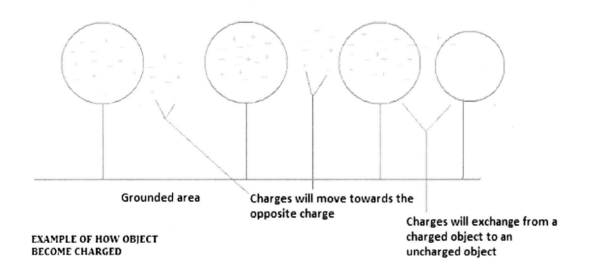

Grounded area

Charges will move towards the opposite charge

Charges will exchange from a charged object to an uncharged object

EXAMPLE OF HOW OBJECT
BECOME CHARGED

Some materials conduct electricity well. They are called **_conductors_** because they allow electrons to travel easily in a material. Electrical wires are made of metal because metal is a good conductor of electricity. The opposite of conductors are **_insulators_**. Insulators do not allow charges to travel well. Rubber is a good insulator. This is why metal wires are typically covered by rubber material to prevent electricity from making contact with your body.

When electrons are not moving we call that **_static electricity_**. Static electricity is the buildup of charges on an object. You see evidence of static electricity or "static cling" when your socks stick to your shirt in the dryer, when you touch a door knob after walking on a carpet or when you take off a wool hat to see your hair stand on end. All of these phenomena happen because electrons are transferred to materials that are good insulators, therefore allowing charges to build up. Built up charges will eventually seek to be released. This is called discharge. More about this in a minute.

Going back to static, if you were to walk across a carpet with rubber soled shoes, electrons from the carpet would be transferred to your shoe via conduction. Because your rubber shoes are good insulators the charges remain built-up in the shoe. When you touch a metal surface such as a door knob, the electrons are free to travel to a good conductor, the metal doorknob. You see a small spark of light and hear a crackling sound. This is the sound of **_discharge_**.

Discharge is the eventual moving of built-up static charges out of an object. Lightening is a major type of static discharge. Charges can rearrange themselves in clouds to form a positive layer above and a negative area below. This is because electrically charged objects can attract or repel a charged or uncharged object without any contact between the objects. Built-up electric charges will attract positive charges on the ground. Lightening is the dramatic discharge of electrons as they make contact with positive electrons on the ground. Remember opposites attract and in the case of lightening this can have dangerous results, not excluding the loss of life and property.

Several terms are used to describe the flow of electrical energy. **_Current_** is one such term. Electric current is the rate of flow of electric charges past a given point in a **_circuit_** (a closed path). A circuit is a complete, closed loop (think "circle"). Electrical systems must be turned on (closed) in order to work. The flow of charges may be carried by moving electrons in a wire as they respond to an electric field or ions in an electrolyte (which is a solution that conducts electricity due to free flowing ions). Each electron transfers energy to the next one as the current flows. The metric unit of measurement for current is the *Amperes* (A) or *amps*.

Two types of current that provide electrical energy include **_direct current_** (DC) and **_alternating current_** (AC). Direct current is what you will find in a battery. Here charges flow in one direction only. Alternating current is what you find in the outlets of your home. These charges flow in both directions (alternating between forward and reverse).

In addition to current, **_voltage_** is also a term used to describe the flow of electrical energy. Voltage is the electrical force that drives (causes them to move) the electric current (of charges) between two points. It is measured with a voltmeter. The metric unit of measurement for voltage is volts (V). The higher the voltage the greater the energy available to move charges. A high voltage battery may be used to power a car, whereas a low voltage battery would be used in small electronics, i.e., MP3 players. Without voltage charges will not flow. Think of voltage as a concentration gradient or hill where charges flow from high to low areas. Voltage provides the energy to move charges down the hill.

Resistance is a measure of how materials resist the flow of electrical charge through it. The metric unit of resistance (R) is ohms (Ω). Just as air resistance is the friction of air, resistance is the friction of electricity. Materials that are good conductors of electric current such as copper will have low resistance. This makes sense. The reason it is a good conductor is because charges flow easily. Materials like rubber have high resistance. This is the reason they are insulators. It is not easy for charges to flow through them. In general, the higher the resistance the lower the current (if voltage stays the same). Resistance also depends on temperature. In higher temperatures atoms in a material will have more kinetic energy to move around more. This interferes with the flow of electric current. So, in general, the higher the temperature the higher the resistance. Ideally, the perfect material having the lowest resistance will meet the following criteria;

1. It will be made of conducting material (such as copper)
2. It will have low temperature
3. If it is a wire it will have thickness (wide diameter). It is easier for more charges to pass through a wide wire than to pass through a thin wire.

4. If it is a wire it will have a short length because charges will pass through a short wire at a faster rate than if travelling down a long wire.

In essence, a short, fat, cold, metal wire would have the least resistance. Super-conductors (usually substances cooled to temperatures approaching absolute zero) have no resistance.

Electric Fields
Standards: SC.6.P.13.1

Earlier we spoke of forces that can act at a distance (without contact). Electricity is one of those forces. One of the reasons electricity can act at a distance is due to the presence of **_electric fields_**. An electric field is the area or space around a charged particle. Here, other charged particles can feel the electric force. So, the field is like an extension of the charged particle that other particles can feel at a distance. Think of it as an "invisible force field".

Magnetic Energy
Standards: SC.6.P.13.1

Magnetism is the force of attraction or repulsion of certain substances for each other due to a **_magnetic field_**. A magnetic field is formed by the movement of electrically charged particles. It is a region where a magnetic force can be detected. As electrons move around they **_induce_** (make) a magnetic field. Although it is hard to really explain what a magnetic field is, you can visualize it by doing a little experiment using a **_magnet_**. A magnet is any material that attracts iron-made materials. It is surrounded by a magnetic field and exerts force on other magnets. In the experiment you will take a bar magnet and place a sheet of white paper over it. You will then pour a thin layer of iron filings over the paper. What you will see is magnetic field lines outlining the shape of the magnetic field. See the diagram below:

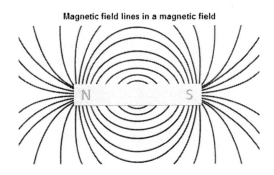
Magnetic field lines in a magnetic field

The closer the magnetic field lines the stronger the magnetic force. From the experiment you will see that the field lines are closer together at either end of the magnet. These ends represent the north and south poles of the magnet. Here the magnetic force is the strongest. The north end of the magnet always points north and the south end always point south.

Magnetic forces have properties that are unique to them. For one, magnets always have both a north and south pole. Even if you cut the magnet, the newly formed pieces will also have a north and south pole.

Another property of magnetic forces is that they **_act at a distance_** (without contact). Like gravitational and electrical force, magnetic forces can act at a distance. You can visualize this by using a strong magnet to pick up a paper clip without it touching it or by using a magnet to hold a piece of paper to a refrigerator. The magnet holds the paper to the refrigerator door even though it is not in direct contact with the refrigerator (it is in direct contact with the paper).

As with electric charges "opposites" attract and "like" repels. **_Like poles repel (pushes away from) and opposite poles attract (pull together)_**. So, if you hold the north poles of two magnets together they will push apart (repel). Likewise, if you hold the south poles of two magnets together they will also repel. However, if you hold the north pole of one magnet near the south pole of another magnet they will attract (pull together). Keep in mind that a force is a push or a pull. You can actually feel this force when you work with magnets.

Another unique property of magnetic forces is that magnets have **_domains_**. These are areas in the substance where atoms line up and arrange themselves like miniature magnets with north poles and south poles aligned. See the diagram below. Materials containing domains, such as iron and nickel will be magnetic while materials, such as plastic and aluminum foil, lacking domains will not be. High temperatures interfere with magnetism because it causes the atoms to move more quickly so that domains lose their alignment. This is called **_demagnetizing_** the magnet.

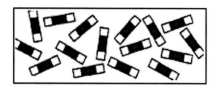
domains before magnetization

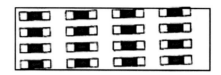
domains after magnetization

There are various types of magnets. These include;

a. **_ferromagnets_**-- strong magnets made out of iron, nickel, or cobalt.

b. **_electromagnets_**-- magnets formed from an electric current. You can make a simple electromagnet by attaching a battery to a nail with a copper wire wrapped around it. The nail will then become magnetic. This shows you can get magnetism from electricity.

c. **_permanent magnets_**-- magnets made from materials that are magnetized and can hold its magnetization for sustained periods of time.

d. **_temporary magnets_**-- magnets made from materials that can be easily magnetized but lose their magnetization easily.

Thermal Energy

Standards: SC.5.P.10.1, SC.5.P.10.2, SC.7.P.11.1, SC.7.P.11.4,

Students tend to get **_thermal energy_** and **_temperature_** confused. Although they are related, thermal energy is not temperature. Temperature is the **_average_** kinetic energy of all the particles in a substance (because not all the particles move at the same speed). It is the energy resulting from the random movement of atoms and molecules inside a substance. The atoms in an object with higher temperature will vibrate more. The higher the temperature the greater the kinetic energy of the molecules in the substance and the faster the molecules move. We may say the object is "hot". The lower the temperature the lower the kinetic energy and slower the rate of movement the molecules have. We may say the object is "cold". Temperature does not depend on quantity. A spoonful of water could have the same temperature reading as a wide area of the Atlantic Ocean!

Effect of temperature on particles
More temperature = more movement

Thermal energy, on the other hand, is the measure of the **_total_** kinetic energy of a substance. Like temperature, it comes from the movement of atoms and molecules in matter. However, thermal energy depends on temperature as well as the quantity or amount of the matter. A barrel of hot water has more thermal energy than a cup of hot water because it has more water. Thermal energy is measured in metric energy units of joules (J) or calories.

Our ultimate source of thermal energy is the Sun. Another source of thermal energy is geothermal energy from inside the earth. This includes volcanoes and geysers. Scientists are discovering ways to tap into these thermal energy sources as an alternative to fossil fuels. Geothermal energy from volcanoes, for example, can be converted into electricity to power homes. Solar panels are used to convert solar energy to electricity to power buildings. Once thermal energy leaves the Sun it is called heat.

Heat
Standards: SC.7.P.11.4

In scientific terms **_heat_** is the transfer of thermal energy between objects that are at different temperatures. We like to think of it as hot or cold but this is not very accurate. A metal spoon feels cold because it has a lower temperature than your hand. When you touch the spoon you are experiencing heat, the transfer of thermal energy from your hand to the spoon. Your hand cools down somewhat which gives the sensation of a cold spoon. In reality, people tend to use the terms heat and thermal energy to mean the same thing. The difference may not be extremely critical for FCAT purposes either. One thing you should keep in mind is that when thermal energy (heat) is added to a substance its temperature increases and when it is removed its temperature decreases.

Thermal energy tends to flow from a system of *higher* energy to a system of *lower* energy. It flows from *warmer* objects to *cooler* objects until equilibrium (they reach the same temperature) is reached. When an ice cube is placed in a cup of hot water thermal energy will flow from the hot water to the ice cube. The heat will cause the molecules in the ice cube to increase in kinetic energy and vibrate more. Moving molecules bump into each other transferring more energy and increasing the temperature. This will occur until the temperature of the ice is equal to the temperature of the hot water. If the atoms achieve enough energy to escape the force of attraction of the particles for each other, they will experience a change in state from a solid to a liquid. In other words, the ice will melt. Thermal energy can be increased or decreased.

Matter transfers thermal energy through **conduction**, **convection**, and **radiation**. Remember, no matter what form of energy transfer is utilized you will never have 100% of the energy being transferred. Some energy is lost as heat to the surroundings.

Conduction is the transfer of thermal energy through contact. When a cold pot is placed on a hot stove the pot will eventually become hot through conduction. Heat is transferred from the stove to the pot via direct contact. Molecules inside the pot will increase in kinetic energy and begin bumping into each other until the temperature of the pot rises to equal the temperature of the stove's burner. **Thermal conductors** are substances that conduct thermal energy very well. Thermal energy travels easily through the substance. This includes metals. **Thermal conductivity** is how well or how fast a material conducts thermal energy. Metals have a high thermal conductivity. This is the reason why they heat up quickly. Cloth has low thermal conductivity. They will stay cooler in comparison to metals as temperature rises. **Thermal insulators** are substances that do not conduct thermal energy very well. Thermal energy does not easily travel through these materials. Examples include wood, cloth and plastics. These types of materials could be at a lower temperature than your hand when touching them but they may not feel cold because thermal energy from your hand does not transfer well to them.

Convection is the transfer of thermal energy through the movement of liquids or gases. It is responsible for ocean currents, the circular path of ocean water. Thermal energy from the sun heats ocean waters creating differences in temperature and density between the cooler and warmer water. The heat increases the temperature of the water as molecules increase in motion and expand.   The warmer water will have a lower density than the cooler water and rise. This causes the cooler water, which now has a higher density, to sink. The rising warmer water will cool and sink and the sinking cool water will warm and rise. The process occurs over and over. This repeating cycle of cold water sinking and warm water rising is called a **_convection current_** which moves in a circular path. Convection currents allow the colder water to heat up and rise and the warmer water to cool down and sink. Convection currents also drive weather in the atmosphere. The similar cycle of less dense warm air rising and denser cold air sinking is responsible for atmospheric conditions and changes in the weather.

The third form of heat transfer is _radiation_; the transfer of thermal energy through space (a vacuum). The Earth receives thermal energy from the Sun through radiation.

Specific Heat is the ability of a substance to absorb heat energy. Different substances absorb heat at different rates. The greater the mass of the object the more heat is absorbed. The higher the specific heat of something, the more energy it takes to increase its temperature.

Thermal expansion is an important property of thermal energy. It is the expansion of a substance due to heat. It is the increase in volume as temperature increases. Thermal expansion is the working concept behind thermometers. Alcohol and mercury in thermometers rise in response to higher temperatures due to thermal expansion. Increasing temperature increases the motion of the molecules and causes them to spread out more. This also tends to decrease the density of the material. The rise in temperature reading on the thermometer corresponds with this decrease in density.

In addition to thermometers, hot air balloons also operate on the principal of thermal expansion. When air inside a hot air balloon is heated the molecules will move faster and spread out. This makes the warmer air less dense than the cooler air around it and the balloon rises. Engineers employ this concept when designing bridges as well. We often see metal grids installed into bridges. These are called expansion joints. These are areas of metal that allow the bridge to expand during higher temperatures and not collapse.

It is important to note that most solids, liquids, and gases expand as they are heated. Water, however, is an exception. Water expands as it cools. Between 4°C and 0°C water experiences expansion as it cools into a solid (ice). In addition, its density also decreases slightly. This is evidenced by the fact that ice will float when placed in a glass of water.

Many physical and chemical changes are affected by temperature. In general, as temperature increases so does the rate of physical and chemical reactions. Since temperature affects the motion of molecules the higher the temperature the more motion produced. Molecules will bump into each other more and have more interactions. In chemical reactions this increases the rate at which old chemical bonds are broken and new ones are formed. Keep in mind that the addition of heat increases temperature and causes reactions to go faster. Removal of heat decreases temperature and tends to slow down the rate of physical and chemical reactions.

In terms of physical changes, adding heat to or removing heat from a system could result in a temperature change and lead to a change in state. A change in state is a physical change that requires energy in the form of heat (addition or removal). When an ice cube is placed in hot tea it is not the ice cube that cools down the tea. It is the hot tea that warms up the ice. In doing so the tea becomes cooler. Because heat transfers from warmer objects to cooler ones thermal energy in the hot tea transfers as heat to the ice cube. The ice molecules will begin to increase their kinetic energy and break out of their solid, crystalline lattice. The temperature will rise and the ice changes state to a liquid (it melts). A hot object can make a cold object warm when they touch due to the transfer of heat and the increase in the motion of the molecules.

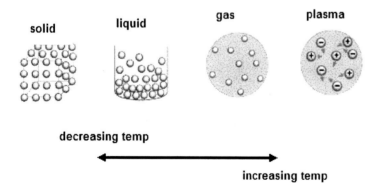

Facts About Temperature Scales

1. Temperature is measured with a ***thermometer*** in metric units of ***Celsius*** (°C), ***Fahrenheit*** (°F) and ***Kelvin*** (K).

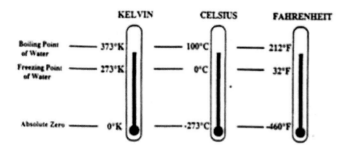

2. Water freezes at 0°C and boils at 100°C

3. To convert Celsius to Kelvin use the formula: K = (273+°C)

4. To convert Celsius to Fahrenheit use the formula: F= C x 9/5 + 32

5. To convert Fahrenheit to Celsius use the formula: C= (F – 32) x 5/9

6. The temperature in which all molecular motion stops = (0 K)

7. Adding heat increases temperature. Removing heat decreases temperature.

8. The metric unit for measuring heat is the Joule (J).

9. A ***calorie*** is the amount of heat needed to raise 1 gram of water one degree Celsius.

How is heat measured? Unlike temperature, heat cannot be measured directly. It must be calculated. Heat is measured in Joules (J). A calorie is also a unit for measuring heat.   A ***calorimeter*** is a device used to measure the heat given off during chemical reactions or physical changes and to measure heat capacity. [**Note**: Please refer to your class textbook for the heat calculation formula and sample questions].

PART IV MOTION OF OBJECTS

Standards: SC.6.P.12.1

Motion is always observed and measured relative to a ***point of reference*** (something that is stationary—like a landmark). When you are giving someone directions to the store you might use the corner barber shop as a point of reference. You would tell them that the store is 5 miles east of the barber shop.

There is a relationship between motion and force. Motion is due to forces. It takes energy to change the motion of objects. When objects have no motion we say they are at rest or motionless. Motion can be described, predicted and calculated by using velocity, speed, acceleration, distance, direction, and time.

1. **_velocity_**-- velocity describes how fast an object is moving in a particular direction. **v= d/t** Directional terms include north, south, east, west, left, right, up, down. Velocity is often measured in **meters/sec**.

2. **_speed_**-- speed describes the distance and time in which an object is moving. It describes how far an object travels in a given amount of time. Speed is measured by distance divided by time or **v=d/t** (notice that the formula for speed is the same for velocity except that velocity involves direction as well).

3. **_acceleration_**-- acceleration describes an object's change in velocity over time. Acceleration can result in a change in direction or speed. It is measured in **m/s²**

$$a = \frac{vf - vi}{t}$$

vf = final velocity,   vi = initial velocity, and t = time

Another way to write this is: $a = \Delta v / t$ (Δv = the change in velocity)

4. **_time_**- time describes how long the motion lasted. It is typically measured in seconds, minutes, and hours. Traveling longer distances takes more time. Walking to your front door takes less time than walking to school.

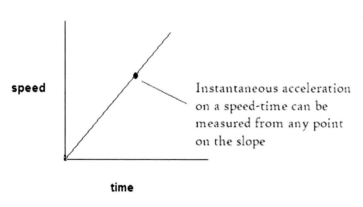

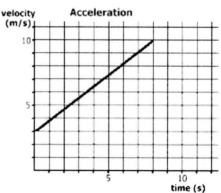

- 88 -

Sir Isaac Newton, the great physicist and astronomer (among other things) came up with three laws of motion that helped explain the relationship between force and motion. They are outlined below:

Newton's Three Laws of Motion

Law #1: ***An object at rest remains at rest and an object in motion remains in motion unless an unbalanced force acts upon it***. In other words, objects prefer to keep doing what they are doing forever. If they are moving they prefer to keep moving. Because of friction we know that objects won't keep on moving forever. If they are not moving they prefer to stay that way. It would take an unbalanced force to change the speed and direction of objects at rest or in motion.

Another way of saying this is ***inertia***. Inertia is the tendency for an object to resist changes in motion. For example, in a car crash where the motorists are not wearing seatbelts they tend to keep traveling in the original direction of motion which is forward. Unfortunately, this forward motion could be right through the windshield! Seatbelts create a resistance against inertia and keep you from going forward in a crash. (Always wear seatbelts when driving!!).

Inertia and mass are related. The greater the mass the greater the inertia experienced. The opposite is also true. Small masses experience less inertia. It's so much easier to stop a small rubber ball from rolling than to stop a huge boulder! It's obvious that heavier objects take more force to move than lighter ones. That is why a heavier object is harder to move than a lighter one. So, we learn another very important fact about matter; not only does it takes up space and has mass but its mass gives it inertia.

Law #2: ***Force is equal to mass times acceleration***. You can write this in equation form as **F=ma**. From the equation it is easy to see that force and acceleration are directly proportional. The greater the force, the greater the acceleration of the object. If you push your friend with a small amount of force it may affect him very little. If you apply a great amount of force to push your friend it may knock him to the ground and cause him to become very angry with you! Mass and acceleration are inversely proportional. Objects with less mass can accelerate faster. Have you ever noticed that racing bikes tend to be made of material that give them less mass than regular bikes? This difference in mass allows racing bikes greater acceleration.

Law #3: ***For every action there is an equal and opposite reaction***. If you push against a wall, the wall will exert an equal and opposite force back on you. If the wall didn't exert a force on you, you would go right through it. Or worse yet, if the wall exerted a greater force back on you it might knock you down. How embarrassing to admit you where knocked down by a wall! The fact that the wall doesn't knock you down shows that an equally opposing force is being applied by the wall so that the forces are balanced.

Related to Newton's laws is the concept of ***momentum***. Momentum is an object's mass multiplied by its velocity. In equation format momentum is written as **p=m•v**. The standard metric unit of momentum is the kg•m/s. Objects in motion have momentum which means they also have direction. The momentum of an object is not fully described until you state the direction of the momentum (which should be the same direction as the velocity of the object).

The greater the mass of the object the greater the momentum it has. It would require a greater effort to stop. Which do you think would be easier to stop, a runaway empty shopping cart or a runaway truck? If you answered the shopping cart you are beginning to understand momentum. In order to stop the shopping cart or runaway truck a greater opposing force has to be applied in the opposite direction of its motion. Also, two objects with the same mass but different speeds would have a different amount of momentum. The faster object would have more momentum.

Momentum, like energy is one of those things that is conserved (you don't lose it). Momentum is transferred from one object to another. When two cars on the highway collide momentum is not lost. Some or all of the momentum from one car is transferred to the other. This could cause both cars to stick together or one car to stop and the other to become accelerated. [**Note:** The FCAT requires you to become familiar with simple machines that can be used to change the direction or magnitude of a force. Please refer to your school textbook for information on simple machines].

PART V   FORCE AND CHANGES IN MOTION

Standards: SC.5.P.13.1, SC.5.P.13.2, SC.5.P.13.3, SC.5.P.13.4, SC.6.P.12.1, SC.6.P.13.1, SC.6.P.13.2, SC.6.P.13.3, SC.8.P.8.2

A **_force_** is a **_pull_** or a **_push_**. A force can act on an object and make it move. Pushing or pulling on an object makes it move. In fact forces give objects the energy it needs to speed up, slow down, stop, or change direction. Types of forces include **_gravity_**, **_friction_**, **_air resistance_**, **_pressure_**, and **_electromagnetic force_**, just to name a few. Forces can be in contact with objects or act at a distance (without contact).

Gravity is a very important type of force. It is the attraction or pull between objects having mass. Every object exerts a gravitational force on every other object. That's why it's called a universal force. Whether this gravitational force is felt or not depends on the mass of the objects and how far apart they are. Objects with small masses seem to have very little gravitational pull. However, massive objects such as the Sun or the planets have a very large gravitational pull. It is the strong gravitational pull of the Sun and the relatively close distance of planets of our solar system that cause them to orbit around it.

Gravity on Earth pulls objects down towards its center. It causes an object to move. An object falling from a shelf is responding to the pull of gravity. When you throw a ball up into the air it eventually falls down to the ground under the pull of gravity. Gravity is always pulling objects downward. Objects fall unless supported by something.

Gravitational force acts at a distance (without contact). The Sun's gravitational force keeps the Earth in orbit as it revolves around it. It does this without making contact with it.

Knowledge of gravity allows us to make the distinction between mass and **_weight_**. Mass is the amount of matter (or "stuff") in an object. Weight, on the other hand, is the measure of force of attraction or gravitational pull between an object and Earth. Weight is however, proportional to mass. The greater the mass of something the heavier its weight.

The Difference Between Mass and Weight

Since we are talking about gravity it is important for the science FCAT that you know the difference between mass and weight. We often use both words interchangeably but they are not the same. Mass is a physical property of something. It is the amount of substance contained within the object. Mass is measured in kilograms. You would use a triple beam balance or electronic scale to measure mass. Weight, on the other hand, is a measure of the pull of gravity on an object. It is measured in Newtons. You would us a spring scale to measure weight. Your weight depends on gravity but your mass does not. If you were to travel outerspace your weight would change depending on how much gravity you experienced. If you traveled to a planet with more gravity than Earth's, then your weight would increase on this planet. The same would be true if you visited a planet with less gravity than Earth's. Your weight would decrease. In either scenario your mass would not change regardless of which planet you visited because mass is how much "stuff" is inside something.

Friction is a force that acts opposite to the direction of motion. Friction resists motion. It is based on the characteristics or roughness of a surface or the molecular attraction of materials that come in contact with each other. Friction is a contact force. It causes sliding objects to slow down and come to a stop. In order to slow down your bicycle there has to be a lot of friction between the brakes and the tires. Try stopping your bike on a sheet of ice. Not easy to do!! There are two types of friction, static and kinetic.

Static friction - the friction between non-moving objects in touch with each other. It is static friciton that, for example, makes a block of wood sitting on a ramp stay in place. Before the block can move static friciton has to be overcome. If a great enough force is applied to the wooden block it will "break free" of static friction and begin to move.

Kinetic friction - the friction between moving objects in contact with each other. In the wooden block example above, kinetic friction must be overcome in order for the block to keep moving.

Air resistance is the "friction of air". It pushes against moving objects in the air and opposes their motion. Air resistance slows down a parachute in the air to provide a safe landing. It also makes a car burn more fuel as it is traveling on the highway. Air resistance works to slow down the car. Paper that has been crumpled up into a ball will fall to the ground quicker than a flat sheet of paper which has not overcome air resistance.

Electromagnetic force- is the force that holds an atom's molecules together, among other things. This force was addressed earlier in the chapter.

Balanced and Unbalanced Forces
Standards: SC.6.P.13.1, SC.6.P.13.3

Balanced forces produce no motion. When an object's **position** or **location** changes in respect to time this is called **motion**. Balanced forces have an overall or net force of zero. If two people standing on either side of a box attempt to push the box in opposite directions toward the other person and they are pushing with the same force the box will not move. The forces will cancel themselves out and result in a net zero force. Remember when forces are in opposite directions you must subtract them to calculate the net force.

Unbalanced forces produce motion. If in the above example person #1 exerts a greater force on the box than person #2 the box will experience motion in the same direction as the greater force. Unbalanced motion produces motion in the direction of the force. They have a net force greater than zero. Remember that when more than one force acts on an object the forces combine if they are in the same direction and are subtracted if they are in opposite directions. An unbalanced force acting on an object changes its direction of motion and/or speed

SECTION REVIEW

CHAPTER 2 SAMPLE QUESTIONS

1. Mixtures are two or more substances that are NOT chemically combined. Which of the following statements about mixtures is true?
    a. Human blood is a heterogeneous mixture.
    b. Iced Tea is a heterogeneous mixture.
    c. Whole cow's milk (unprocessed) is a homogeneous mixture.
    d. Red vinegar is a homogeneous mixture.

2. The periodic table displays the properties of each known element.   What should you do when you discover what you think is a new element?
    a. You should compare its chemical properties to existing ones to place it in the table.
    b. You should compare its physical properties to existing ones to place it in the table.
    c. You should just assign it a number and place it in the table.
    d. You should look at both its chemical and physical properties in comparison to existing elements to place it in the table.

3. Which of the following examples show correctly pared compounds?
    a. Covalent compound – NaCl (sodium chloride)
    b. Ionic Compound – H_20 (Dihydrogen Oxide)
    c. Covalent Compound – H_2O_2 (Dihydrogen Dioxide)
    d. Ionic Compound – Mg_2 (Di Metallic Magnesium)

4. Solubility refers to the relative ability of a solute (solid, liquid or gaseous substance) to be dissolved in a solvent (solid, liquid or gaseous substance) under normal conditions.   Solubility depends on many factors. Which of the following situations would result in an increase in the solubility of a solid dissolved in water?
    a. Decreasing the temperature of the water
    b.   Stirring the mixture
    c. Increasing the amount of the solid
    d.   Decreasing the amount of water

5. Amanda is excited about her upcoming laboratory activity.   In her experiment she is asked to provide a visual demo to explain both physical and chemical properties using a single sheet of paper. How could she accomplish this?
    a. She could burn the paper to demonstrate a physical change and crumble the paper to demonstrate a chemical change.
    b.   She could rip the paper to demonstrate a physical change and pour acid on the paper to demonstrate a chemical change.
    c.   She could wet the paper to demonstrate a physical change and crumble the paper to demonstrate a chemical change.
    d. She could rip the paper to demonstrate a physical change and throw away the paper to demonstrate a chemical change.

6. When two immiscible liquids are poured into a graduated cylinder a two-layered solution forms. Liquid A has a volume of 16 mL and a mass of 87 g. Liquid B has a volume of 234 mL and a mass of 100 g. Based on this information which liquid will form the top layer and why? (**Density = mass/volume**)
    a. Liquid A because its density is less than liquid B so it floats.
    b. Liquid B because its density is less than liquid A so it floats.
    c. Liquid B because its density is greater than liquid A so it floats.
    d. Not enough information was provided to solve the problem.

7. Based on the Law of Conservation of Mass, which of the following chemical equations are correctly balanced?
    a. $CO \rightarrow C_2 + O_2$
    b. $C_6H_{12}O_6 + 6 O_2 \rightarrow 6 CO_2 + 6 H_2O + Energy$
    c. $6 CO_2 + 6 H_2O \rightarrow C_6H_{12}O_6 + 5 O_2$
    d. $Na(s) + Cl (g) \rightarrow 2NaCl_4$

8. If you were trying to balance the chemical equation below, keeping in mind that you need to abide by the Law of Conservation of Mass, what would be the correct order of coefficients?

$$\_\_\_Al + \_\_ O_2 \rightarrow \_\_ Al_2O_3$$

    a. 4,2,3
    b. 2,3,4
    c. 1,2,3
    d. 4,3,2

9. In the gas state of matter, which of the following assumptions could be made regarding the levels of kinetic and potential energy of the atoms that compose that matter?
    a. The amount of kinetic energy of the molecules is quite less than that of the amount of potential energy being stored in the molecules.
    b. The amount of kinetic energy of the molecules is far more than that of the amount of potential energy being stored in the molecules.
    c. Gas molecules have a lot of kinetic energy and no potential energy.
    d. The amount of kinetic energy of the molecules is the same as the amount of potential energy being stored in the molecules.

10. Aurora borealis and aurora austrailis are examples of how gases can become super charged and emit colors in the sky. How has this understanding met societal demands for better entertainment technology?
    a. Scientists are able to utilize the concept of the excitement of liquid matter to develop newer types of lava lamps.
    b. Scientists are able to devise newer ways to control free radicals and project them onto 3-D movie screens.
    c. Scientists are able to understand how electricity can be used to generate colors and redefined television sets that use plasma screen technology.
    d. None of the above

11. Based on your understanding of the evolution of atomic theory which of the following best explains what is currently known to be the atomic structure of an atom?
   a. The atom consists of a region of probability where protons can be found and a negatively charged center where electrons and neutrons can be found.
   b. The atom consists of a region of probability where protons can be found and a positively charged center where electrons and neutrons can be found.
   c. The atom consists of a region of probability where electrons can be found and a negatively charged center where protons and neutrons can be found.
   d. The atom consists of a region of probability where electrons can be found and a positively charged center where protons and neutrons can be found.

12. A decrease in the rate of a chemical reaction would result from
   a. Increasing the temperature
   b. Adding an inhibitor to a chemical reaction
   c. Increasing the concentration of the chemical reactants
   d. None of the above

13. If in nature carbon is found 90% of the time as carbon-12, 9% of the time as carbon-13 and 1% of the time as carbon-14 what is the atomic mass of carbon?
   a. 11 amu
   b. 12 amu
   c. 13 amu
   d. 14 amu

14. All chemical reactions involve energy. When a chemical reaction gives off energy it is called an exothermic reaction (exo = go out   thermic= heat). When a chemical reaction absorbs energy it is called an endothermic (endo = in   thermic= heat). Which of the following statements best identifies the type of thermic reaction with the example given?
   a. Cellular respiration is an endothermic reaction.
   b. Photosynthesis is an exothermic reaction.
   c. Baking a loaf of bread requires an endothermic reaction.
   d. All of the above

15. Based on the Law of Conservation of Energy which of the following scenarios is correct as written?
   a. James' body converts the chemical energy in the food he eats into potential and kinetic energy, thus no energy is destroyed.
   b. James' body converts the chemical energy in the food he eats into potential and kinetic energy, thus energy is destroyed.
   c. James' body converts the chemical energy in the food he eats into nonrenewable energy and kinetic energy, thus no energy is lost.
   d. James' body converts the chemical energy in the food he eats into light and kinetic energy, thus no energy is created.

16. Omar wanted to explain to his friend why during a rain storm lightening can be seen before thunder is heard. Which statement below would provide the best explanation?
    a. The wavelengths of light waves are longer than that of sound waves but because they leave their point of origin in clouds first before sound waves so you see lightning before you hear thunder.
    b. Light waves require a medium to travel.
    c. Light waves are transverse waves that travel at a faster speed than sound waves which are longitudinal waves.
    d. Light waves are longitudinal waves that travel at a faster speed than sound waves which are transverse waves.

17. A force is a pull or a push. It can act on an object and make it move. Which of the following is the correct force that is acting on the listed object?
    a. The force of gravity preventing a parachute from opening up.
    b. The force of friction that is pushing a car to go faster.
    c. The force of gravity changing your weight as you travel to other planets.
    d. The force of air resistance that makes falling objects in air fall faster.

18. Ravi is traveling to his aunt's house for dinner. He takes approximately 55 minutes to travel 11 miles.   He travels northwest to reach his aunt's house. What is Ravi's velocity?
    a. 0.20 miles/ minute northwest
    b. 5 miles/ minutes north
    c. 12.2 miles/ minute northwest
    d. Cannot be determine from the information given

19. The calculations below relate to the concepts of speed and acceleration. Which problem below shows the correct calculation?
    a. Acceleration — 40m/s to 60 m/s in 5 seconds = $4m/s^2$
    b. Speed — 40 miles in 2 hours = 12.5 mph
    c. Acceleration — 20m/s to 10m/s in 5 seconds = $4m/s^2$
    d. Speed — 20 miles in 2 hours = -12.5 mph

20. Electromagnetic forces are composed of both electric fields as well as magnetic fields. Which of the following best describes the relationship between electricity and magnetism as it relates to the Earth's atmosphere?
    a. Electricity and magnetism work hand in hand to repair the hole in the ozone layer that protects the Earth from solar radiation.
    b. Electricity and magnetism are two forces that interact with Earth's atmosphere to produce precipitation.
    c. Electricity and magnetism are involved when solar winds interact with Earth's magnetic field to produce electric charges responsible for auroras.
    d. Electricity and magnetism are two forces that interact with the atmosphere to produce global warming.

21. The difference between thermal energy and temperature is
    a. Thermal energy is the total kinetic energy of all of the particles in a substance and temperature is the average potential energy of all the particles in a substance.
    b. Thermal energy is the total kinetic energy of all of the particles in a substance and temperature is the total potential energy of all the particles in a substance.
    c. Thermal energy is the total kinetic energy of all of the particles in a substance and temperature is the average kinetic energy of the particles in a substance.
    d. Thermal energy is the total kinetic energy of all of the particles in a substance and temperature is the chemical energy of all the particles in a substance.

22. Which statement about heat is incorrect?
    a. When you touch a cold spoon you experience thermal energy transferring from the spoon to your hand which makes it feel cold.
    b. A calorie is the amount of heat needed to raise 1 gram of water one degree Celsius.
    c. Cloth has low thermal conductivity so it will stay cooler in comparison to metals as temperature rises.
    d. Adding heat to or removing heat from a system could result in a temperature change and lead to a change in state.

23. Mass is the amount of matter (or "stuff") in an object. Weight, on the other hand, is the measure of force of attraction or gravitational pull between an object and Earth. Weight is proportional to mass. Which of the following situations would result in an increase in weight but not an increase in mass?
    a. Travel to a planet with more gravity
    b. Increase in the normal consumption of food over a two hour period
    c. Travel to a planet with less gravity
    d. None of the above

24. The foods we eat enable us to run, jump and to carry out all our life functions. The type of energy transformation *Not* involved in these activities are
    a. Chemical energy to thermal energy
    b. Chemical energy to geothermal energy
    c. Chemical energy to kinetic energy
    d. Chemical energy to mechanical energy

25. Which material listed below is predicted to experience the most electrical resistance?
    a. Copper wire
    b. Steel cables
    c. Superconductors
    d. Molten Lava

(A) says that thermal energy would flow from the spoon to your hand which is not likely because it would be flowing from a cooler object to a warmer one and this is incorrect.

23. Feedback: Correct Answer (A)
Reasoning: Choice (B) is incorrect because increasing your consumption of food would increase your mass and also increase your weight. Choice (C) is incorrect because to travel to a planet with less gravity would decrease your weight but have no effect on your mass. Choice (D) is wrong for the reasons already stated. The only true answer and correct statement is choice (A).

24. Feedback: Correct Answer (B)
Reasoning: Choices (A), (C), and (D) are true statements. Chemical energy contained in food can be converted to thermal energy (as waste energy) or kinetic and mechanical energy for movement. These choices are thus eliminated.   Choice (B) is the correct answer because it is a false statement which suits the condition of the question.   Geothermal energy is the energy found in the Earth.

25. Correct Answer (D)
Reasoning: Things that are good conductors of heat and electricity do not have high resistance therefore we can eliminate choices (A) and (B). Choice (C) is also incorrect. Superconductors have practically zero resistance. Thus, choice (D) is the only possible answer since molten lava is at a high temperature and the higher the temperature the higher the resistance of the material.

CHAPTER 3   LIFE SCIENCE

All through science the presence of "patterns" often appears. Learning to recognize patterns in nature will make the study of science more interconnected and easier to understand. Connections are everywhere.   In this chapter you will study the patterns that help maintain the life of every organism in the biosphere. We'll begin by introducing ecosystems and then move on to a review of the human body. If you look closely you will see that ecosystems and the human body function in very similar ways. You will also see that you can better understand the natural world through careful observation.

PART I: INTERDEPENDENCE (INTERACTIONS BETWEEN LIVING THINGS AND THEIR ENVIRONMENT)

Standards: SC.5.L.15.1, SC.5.L.17.1, SC.6.L.14.1, SC.6.L.14.2, SC.7.L.17.1, SC.7.L.17.2, SC.7.L.17.3

Ecosystems

An ecosystem describes the interaction between **_biotic_** (living)and **_abiotic_** (nonliving) things in an environment. Don't let the terms biotic and abiotic confuse you. Remember, **"bio"** means life. The prefix **"a-"** means not. So **a-biotic** means "not-life" or nonliving.

Examples of _biotic_ factors

1. animals

2. plants

3. humans

4. bacteria

5. fungi

Examples of _abiotic_ factors

1. air

2. water

3. light

4. temperature

5. soil

Important terms

1. **_population_**-- group of organisms of the same species (able to reproduce together) living in a given location. For example, all the brown bears in a forest make up a population of brown bears.

2. **_community_**-- all the different interacting populations living in the same area. For example, the different populations of animals in a park make up a community.

3. **_biosphere_**-- the location on Earth where all life exists. It is made up of many complex ecosystems. It includes water, air, and soil.

4. **_competition_**--when two or more organisms seek the same resources for survival at the same time. These organisms share a habitat and will struggle for these resources. Plants in a forest compete for sunlight. Without sunlight they could not survive. Taller growing plants will out-compete their shorter growing plants for sunlight. Organisms compete for mates, food, shelter, etc.

5. **_niche_**-- the role an organism plays in the environment. This includes the type of nutrients it requires, how it lives, how it reproduces and its relationships with other individuals in its environment.

6. **_habitat_**--an organism's home.

Organization of Life (from greater to lesser)

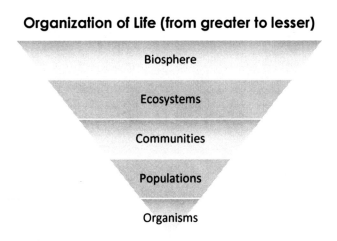

Factors That Determine the Characteristics of Populations

Standards: SC.7.L.17.3

A **_limiting factor_** (or limiting resource) is anything that determines the size or distribution of a population in an ecosystem. They include the things that make it possible or impossible for a population to survive in an area. For example, climate is a limiting factor. Polar bears can survive in cold climates because of their **_adaptations_** (i.e., fur and fat storage beneath their skin). On the other hand, cows could not survive in the same cold climate. The climate limits the types of organisms that can survive in the area. It is therefore a limiting factor.

Other limiting factors include type of food (vegetation and organisms), presence and amount of water, shelter, disease, predator-prey relationships, parasitism, etc. Any changes in a limited resource could affect the size of a population and could lead to the elimination of those populations from Earth. For example, when humans cut down trees (**_deforestation_**) it limits the amount of shelter available for animals that make their homes in trees. Without shelter these animals may be more vulnerable to predators. The long-term effect of this could lead to **_extinction_** (the dying out) of that species.

Living things compete with each other to get the things they need to live in their local environment. However, there are limited amounts of resources in an ecosystem. Food, water, and minerals for example may not keep up with the demand for these resources. The amount of resources limit the number of organisms an environment can support. The total amount of organisms an environment can support is called its **_carrying capacity_**. If a population increases above its carrying capacity many individuals will die off as the competition for limited resources increases.

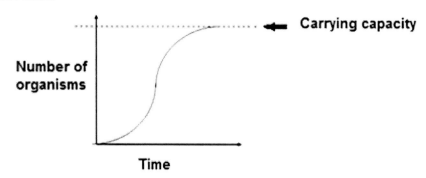

Biomes

Biomes are large ecosystems. They are complex communities characterized by a particular climate, plant life, and animal life. These broad habitats can be divided into six major land (terrestrial) biomes and two aquatic (water) biomes. Refer to the chart below.

Table 3-1 Major Land Biomes on Earth

BIOME	CHARACTERISTICS	ANIMAL LIFE	PLANT LIFE
tundra	extremely cold temperatures; permafrost (permanently frozen subsoil)	musk oxen, lemmings, reindeer, and caribou	treeless; short shrubs and grasses
taiga	long, severe winters; plenty of snowfall; summers with thawing subsoil	beavers, grizzly bears, and wolverines	forests of dense evergreen trees
temperate deciduous forest	moderate precipitation; cold winters; warm summers	wolves, birds, squirrels, and foxes	deciduous trees (maple, oak, beech), plants and shrubs
tropical rainforest	dense vegetation; heavy rainfall; seasonally warm temperatures;	monkeys, bats, frogs, and insects	many broad-leaved plant species
grassland (savannas)	little rainfall; dry climate; strong winds; large open grassy areas	lions, elephants, zebras, and antelope	grasses, very few trees
desert	dry areas; extremely small rainfall; extreme daily temperature fluctuations (can be either cold or hot)	lizards, snakes, birds, and rodents	shrubs and cactus plants

☐ Tundra
■ Taiga
▨ Temperature deciduous forest
▩ Tropical rain forest
▤ Grassland
▦ Desert

Aquatic biomes make up the largest ecosystems on Earth. These biomes are the most stable because of less variation in water temperature. However, they are affected more so by abiotic factors such as light intensity, amounts of dissolved oxygen and carbon dioxide and the mineral content of the water. The two aquatic biomes are marine and freshwater biomes.

1. **_marine biomes_** -- salt water biomes include all the oceans of the world. They serve as large habitats for a wide variety of organisms since the majority of all living things on Earth live there. Marine biomes absorb a lot of solar energy and help determine Earth's climate. They contain a constant supply of nutrients and are the source of much of the oxygen produced by photosynthesis.

2. **_freshwater biomes_**—fresh water biomes include all the rivers, streams, ponds, lakes and wetlands on Earth. Fresh water biomes have a very low concentration of salt. As such they have plant and animal life that are adapted for living in low salt conditions. Some fresh water biomes are still bodies, such as ponds and lakes and others are rapidly moving bodies such as streams and rivers. Wetlands, such as swamps, marshes, and bogs are areas of standing water that support aquatic plants specially adapted for moist, humid conditions. The Florida Everglades is an example of a wetland.

Organisms Have Adaptations That Enable Them to Survive in Their Environment
Standards: SC.5.L.17.1

A lack of food, water, shelter, and other needed resources affect plants and animals in their habitats. **_Adaptations_** increase an organism's rate of survival in an ecosystem. They are characteristics that help organisms compete in their habitats. For example, colors that camouflage (blend) animals with their environment help them to hide from their predators. Skin or fur color is therefore an adaptation. Adaptations become even more important when an ecosystem changes. When this happens, organisms that are better adapted to compete for limited resources (i.e., food and water) will have a better chance for survival.

Two types of adaptations are **_behavioral_** and **_structural_** . Behavioral adaptations are things organisms do to survive. Some behaviors are inherited (i.e., instincts) and some are learned. Bird migration is an example of a behavioral adaptation, as is animals moving in large groups. Structural adaptations are physical characteristics that help an organism to survive (i.e., coloration, speed, sharp teeth, beak shape and size, etc). **Table 3-2** compares the adaptations of plants and animals living in a desert habitat. Desert habitats are characterized by harsh conditions such as extreme temperature variations (extremely hot in the daytime and extremely cold at night), water scarcity, and nutrient-poor soil.

Table 3-2 Adaptations of Desert Plants and Animals

Desert Plants (i.e., cactus, bitterroot, night-blooming cereus)	Desert Animals (i.e., bats, elk, rodents, coyote)
Behavioral Adaptations	Behavioral Adaptations
Night Blooming Many desert plants are night bloomers. They have flowers that open at night when it is cooler as opposed to the day when it is hotter. Because many animals and pollinating insects are nocturnal (they sleep or are inactive during the day and are active at night) night bloomers expose their pollen when it has the best chance of being spread.	Burrowing Many desert animals strive to stay out of the Sun during the hottest times of the day. Some animals burrow underground during the day where it is much cooler. Many desert animals are also nocturnal. They sleep during the day when it is hot and actively hunt for food at night.
Tumbling Some desert plants adapt to dry conditions by tumbling. This allows the plant to remove itself form environments that grow too dry to support it. During tumbling the plant breaks away from their roots, dry out and roll with the wind. As the tumbleweed rolls it spreads its seeds to the new places that the wind takes it. Some tumbling plants reverse the process when water is available. They unroll, put down roots and germinate. This turns them from a dry bundle of twigs to a flowering green bush.	Desert animals are adapted for water scarcity by obtaining water from the foods they eat. Herbivores obtain water from the plants they eat and carnivores from the blood and fluid inside the organisms they eat. Migration Many desert animals such as the pronghorn migrate to cooler, higher elevations during the summer and back to warmer, lower elevations in the winter.
Structural Adaptations	Structural Adaptations
Roots Desert plants have developed a very effective	Many desert animals have evolved structural adaptations that help them minimize water loss and

transport system to deal with dry desert conditions. They grow long and wide root systems to gather water from deep under the surface.

hot desert temperatures. Many have no sweat glands to prevent loss of water through sweating. Some can further conserve water by passing very concentrated urine or no urine at all. The long ears of jack rabbits are adapted to release body heat so as to cool the body.

<u>Xylem and Stomates</u>
Desert plants also have a water absorption system that is effective in absorbing, storing, and utilizing water. This system involves **_xylem_** located in the roots, stem, and leaves that transport water from the roots to the leaves. They also have **_stomates_** which are little pores in the leaves and stems of a plant that permits water evaporation via transpiration. Desert plants are adapted for less transpiration (and thus less water loss) by having smaller and fewer stomates than non-desert plants. Also, many desert plants open their stomates only at night when temperatures are cooler and there is less water loss.

Other types of structural adaptations include thick coats that insulate against cold temperatures and pale skin that absorbs less heat and provides protection from predators.

Trophic (Feeding) Levels

Organisms are classified by how they obtain nutrients (**trophic levels**).

1. **_autotroph_** -- organisms (plants and certain types of bacteria) that can synthesize their own food from substances in the environment, such as sunlight and water. (**Auto** = *self* **troph**= *feeder* **auto+troph** = *self feeder*).

2. **_heterotroph_** -- organisms, like humans or tigers for example, that cannot synthesize their own food and must eat other organisms for nutrients. (**Hetero**= different **troph** = feeder **hetero+troph**= different feeder).

3. **_producer_**-- autotrophic organisms. Examples: plants, grass, and algae.

4. **_consumer_**-- organisms that eat other organisms. Examples: bears, humans and skunks. Types of consumers are shown on the next page.

a. **carnivore**- eats animals (meat). (Secondary consumers)

b. **herbivore**- eats plants only. (Primary consumers)

c. **omnivore**- eats plants and animals.

d. **prey**- the animal that is hunted and eaten.

e. **predator**- animals that kill and eat their prey.

f. **scavenger**- feeds on the remains of animals they have not killed.

5. ***decomposer (saprophytes)***--obtain nutrients from the remains of dead organisms. They help to recycle nutrients back into the soil. Examples: bacteria and fungi (i.e., mushrooms).

Whether predator or prey, autotroph or heterotroph, all organisms contribute to the cycle of life on Earth. Organisms are born, grow, die, and decay as new ones are being produced daily. Another pattern!

Food Chains and Food Webs

Standards: SC.7.L.17.1, SC.8.L.18.4

Trophic relationships are all connected by a pattern of energy flow. This shows how energy (nutrients) moves through an ecosystem. The easiest way to demonstrate this flow of energy is with a ***food chain***. In a simple food chain energy transfers from the Sun to plants (producers), to animals (consumers), and finally to decomposers (fungi and bacteria) which decays organisms and recycle nutrients back into the soil for plants to utilize. A food chain is a pattern of eating and being eaten.

The majority of all food chains begin with the Sun. We say the *majority* due to the existence of organisms that are capable of using inorganic and organic compounds found in their environment as their primary energy source. These organisms are chemotrophic as opposed to photosynthetic. Some are found in the depths of the ocean where sunlight does not penetrate.

Autotrophic organisms, such as plants (producers) use the energy source of sunlight along with other materials to make food (energy). This energy is transferred to animals that eat the plants.

These herbivores (1st level consumers) eat the plants to obtain its energy. Carnivores (2nd level consumers) and omnivores (consumers) eat the animals that eat plants as well as other animals. Scavengers eat the remains of dead organisms. Decomposers (fungi and bacteria) transfer energy back into the ground and recycle nutrients into the soil for plants to use. This continuous pattern or cycle is a food chain. The arrows of the food chain mean "eaten by". So, in the food chain below the grass is "eaten by" the rabbit, who in turn is "eaten by the owl" and so on and so forth. You may not realize how you participate in a food chain but when you eat vegetables and fruits you are eating plants. When you eat meat you are eating animals that may have eaten other animals and plants.

FOOD CHAIN

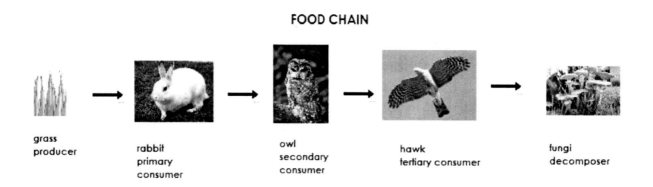

grass
producer

rabbit
primary
consumer

owl
secondary
consumer

hawk
tertiary consumer

fungi
decomposer

The energy in one organism is never transferred 100% to another organism when it is eaten. You learned in chapter 2 that energy transfer is never 100% efficient. Some energy is converted to heat and lost to the environment. In the case of food chains, the animal being eaten uses some of its energy for its own metabolism (digestion, reproduction, etc). The animal doing the eating only gets a fraction of that energy.

Keep in mind, that because science is interconnected that the Laws of Conservation of Mass and Energy applies to ecosystems as well. Remember from chapter 2 that energy is neither created nor destroyed. It is just transformed from one form to another. This is the Law of Conservation of Energy. The energy from the Sun that was transferred to the plant was used to create food for the plant through the process of photosynthesis. Whatever amount of energy that was not lost to heat or the environment was transferred to the organism that ate the plant. Likewise, this energy will be transferred to the organism that eats this one (and so on and so on). The Law of Conservation of Mass also applies here. Matter is simply recycled from one organism to another and the total amount of matter doesn't change.

Because no animal typically eats only one type of organism, **_food webs_** are used to more accurately describe feeding relationships. A food web is a group of connected food chains. It demonstrates the flow of energy from one organism to another as one is eaten by the other. Below is an example of a food web.

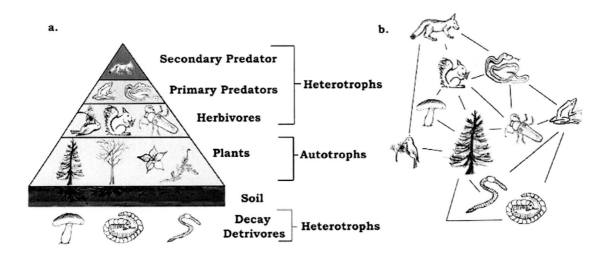

Source: Author, Mark David Thompson

Biodiversity

Plants and animals, including humans, interact with and depend upon each other and their environment to satisfy their basic needs. **_Biodiversity_** refers to the presence of a wide range of different organisms in an ecosystem and how they interact with abiotic factors and with each other. It is variety. Each organism, carrying out its own niche, helps to promote better interactions and overall stability of an ecosystem. Because individuals do not eat only one type of organism, the reduction in one species has less of an effect where variety of other food choices exists than where there is no variety. Biodiversity also insures that some organisms will survive in the event of a devastating environmental event such as disease, drought, famine, or volcanic eruption. Tropical rainforests are the most diverse ecosystems on Earth. Here, there are a wide variety of plants that are used to make medicines and useful products.

Ecological Relationships

Standards: SC.7.L.17.2

Ecological relationships can be described based on who benefits and who is harmed by the relationship. **_Symbiosis_** is the term used to describe when two different organisms live together in close association. Examples of symbiotic relationships include:

1. **_commensalism_**-- when one organism benefits from the relationship and the other one is neither helped nor harmed. For example, the remora are tiny fish that attach themselves to sharks as a quick mode of transportation and for protection. The shark isn't helped by the remora but it isn't hurt either.

2. **_mutualism_**-- when both organisms benefit from the relationship. For example, the bacteria that live in the intestines of cows provide them with an enzyme that allows them to digest the plants they eat. In turn the cows provide the bacteria with a stable supply of nutrients.

3. **_parasitism_**-- when one organism (the **_parasite_**) benefits from the relationship and the other one (the **_host_**) is harmed. For example, eating undercooked meat can cause tapeworms to grow in the digestive tract of humans. The tapeworm get a steady supply of nutrients from the human. In return the human may develop a disease and become very sick from the tapeworm infection.

Photosynthesis, Cellular Respiration and Other Patterns in Nature

Standards: SC.5.E.7.1, SC.5.E.7.2, SC.8.L.18.1, SC.8.L.18.2, SC.8.L.18.3, SC.8.L.18.4

Common examples of patterns in nature are listed on the next page. The exchange of energy and matter by the living and nonliving parts of the environment sets up a pattern of recycling that allows materials to be used over and over again by living things. Energy and matter are continuously exchanged between organisms and their physical environment. In all the examples below, the Law of Conservation of Mass applies in that the total mass of the system never changes. The amount of material present at the beginning of the reaction is accounted for at the end. No material is ever wasted.

1. ***carbon-hydrogen-oxygen cycle***-- the elements carbon, hydrogen, and oxygen are recycled in the environment by the process of ***photosynthesis*** and ***cellular respiration***. In the process of photosynthesis green plants use ***chlorophyll*** (the green pigment found in ***chloroplasts***) to capture sunlight.   Sunlight is used to split water (H_2O) molecules (***photolysis***) to release hydrogen molecules. Hydrogen combines with carbon dioxide (CO_2) from the environment to make the sugar, ***glucose*** ($C_6H_{12}O_6$). Oxygen is released into the environment as a by-product (waste product).

Organisms (including green plants and animals that eat the plants) break down glucose to release the energy (***ATPs***) present inside through the process of cellular respiration (***aerobic respiration***).   Oxygen is used in this reaction. It is the same oxygen the plants released into the environment from photosynthesis. Cellular respiration occurs in the ***mitochondria*** of the cell. The glucose made by plants is combined with the oxygen to make energy. A waste product of cellular respiration is carbon dioxide. Plants use the carbon dioxide that animals breathe out. This carbon dioxide is used by plants for photosynthesis as the process begins over again. Notice that no form of matter (carbon, oxygen and hydrogen) is wasted in these two processes. They are recycled over and over again. The diagram below demonstrates that in the chemical reaction of photosynthesis and respiration the same quantities of reactants are present in the same amounts as products. No matter is wasted; it is all conserved. The Law of Conservation of Mass applies here. We should mention that carbon dioxide is also released into the air by other processes, such as the ***combustion*** (burning) of ***fossil fuels*** (natural gas, oil, and coal). The ***decomposition*** (rotting) of dead organisms also returns carbon, oxygen and hydrogen (and other matter)to the soil for plants to use for growth and photosynthesis.

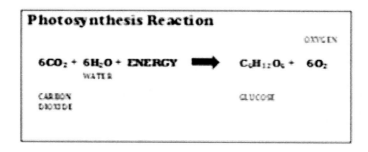

Photosynthesis Reaction

$$6CO_2 + 6H_2O + ENERGY \longrightarrow C_6H_{12}O_6 + 6O_2$$

OXYGEN

WATER

CARBON DIOXIDE

GLUCOSE

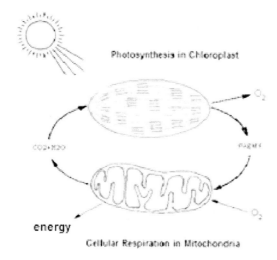

Photosynthesis in Chloroplast

O_2

CO_2+H_2O

sugars

energy

O_2

Cellular Respiration in Mitochondria

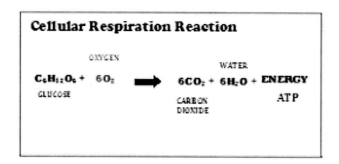

Cellular Respiration Reaction

OXYGEN

$$C_6H_{12}O_6 + 6O_2 \longrightarrow 6CO_2 + 6H_2O + ENERGY$$

GLUCOSE

WATER

CARBON DIOXIDE

ATP

2. _**water cycle**_- (See the diagram on the next page). The water cycle demonstrates the movement of water through the Earth as it changes from the liquid form in oceans, ponds, etc., to a gas (water vapor) by _**evaporation**_ and _**transpiration**_ (evaporation of water from the leaves of plants).   Water vapor cools and condenses to form clouds (_**condensation**_) which become heavy and release the liquid water as _**precipitation**_ (any form of water that falls from the sky, i.e., snow, rain, hail, etc). That water then returns to the oceans and other bodies of water as _**runoff**_ or seeps into the ground as _**groundwater**_.

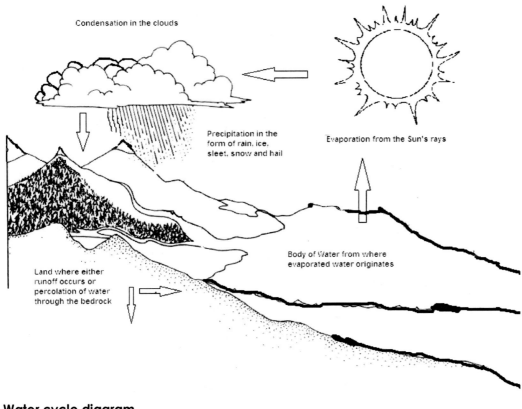

Condensation in the clouds

Precipitation in the form of rain, ice, sleet, snow and hail

Evaporation from the Sun's rays

Body of Water from where evaporated water originates

Land where either runoff occurs or percolation of water through the bedrock

Water cycle diagram

Human Impact on the Environment

Standards: SC.7.E.6.6

Like natural events, human activities can have a major impact on the environment. Humans are a part of ecosystems and have the greatest capacity to change them--in both positive and negative ways. Sometimes their activities can be destructive and alter the balance in an ecosystem. This affects other organisms.

Deforestation is the cutting down of forest. This destroys animal habitats and can lead to their extinction as well as the extinction of medicinal plant species. Deforestation leads to **erosion** of topsoil since trees that anchor the soil and keep it moist and firm, are removed. Poor agricultural practices and over-grazing (feeding on too much grass, for example) depletes (reduces) nutrients in soil and erodes topsoil.

Desertification is the process by which an area becomes a desert. This may occur in areas bordering desert areas when excessive plant life and soil depletion occurs.

Urbanization is the physical growth of urban or city areas. Urbanization also has a negative effect on ecosystems. Land is cleared, which removes necessary vegetation and soil. Without trees and ground cover, which absorbs solar radiation, local temperatures will increase. Urban areas tend to have higher temperatures than rural areas. They also tend to have higher concentrations of carbon dioxide emissions since there is less vegetation to absorb this greenhouse gas.

As human populations continue to grow the increase in urbanization occurs. More than half of the world's population now lives in urban areas. We can attribute advances in medicine and technology as major reasons for people living longer and increases in human population growth. Around the world human populations are growing at such an alarming rate and exceeding the carrying capacity of the environment. In these countries populations are growing faster than the ability to produce food, leading to hunger and starvation.

Over-hunting, fishing, and trapping leads to extinction of some species and the endangerment of others. Importing of **invasive** and **exotic** species (species that are not natural inhabitants of an area and have no natural enemies or competitors) disrupt ecosystems. Because they have no natural enemies, these species out-compete native plant and animal species for resources, resulting in a loss of biodiversity.

The quality of the air, water, and land is compromised by harmful chemicals, sewage, solid wastes, thermal pollution, and by other human means. These forms of pollution not only harm wildlife but they harm humans as well. We are not immune from the harmful effects of our own destructive practices. The burning of fossil fuels contributes to air pollution and increases the **greenhouse effect** (the natural heating of the planet by the absorption of solar radiation by the atmosphere). This leads to **global warming** (the increase in temperature of Earth's climates).

Climate change caused by global warming will begin to affect the weather. As the Earth's climates heat up it will cause the melting of polar ice caps. Water that was trapped in the ice of glaciers will be released more and more into the water cycle. This inundation of water is expected to affect the frequency of extreme weather events such as drought, extreme temperatures, flooding, high winds and severe storms.

The depletion of the **ozone layer** (the natural shield in the Earth's atmosphere that blocks the

Sun's harmful UV rays from reaching the surface) allows more UV rays to penetrate the atmosphere and increase the rate of skin cancers in humans and harm to plants as well.

Solutions to Environmental Problems

A mutual relationship exists between humans and other living things. We rely on plants, animals and other organisms for food, shelter, medicines, clothing, etc. We therefore have a responsibility to correct and learn from our mistakes by taking positive steps in preserving the environment. There are many ways humans have sought solutions for environmental problems. For one, humans have adopted legislation to protect the Earth from harmful activities. For example, there are laws in place that regulate hunting and fishing.   Endangered species are being protected by the creation of national parks and wildlife refuges. Other environmental solutions are outlined below.

Recycling paper, glass, metals and plastics allows products to be reused over and over. It reduces the loss of trees and other natural resources used to make these products. It also reduces the amounts of these materials in landfills.

Conservation (saving) of energy by turning off lights and plugging out appliances and electronics is being practiced. Humans also practice energy conservation by finding more energy saving ways of getting around. They are commuting more and more by walking, riding bikes and carpooling. This reduces the burning of fossil fuels and conserves the limited amounts we have left on Earth. Remember, fossil fuels are ***nonrenewable*** resources (they cannot easily be replaced). It took millions of years for them to be formed and would take millions of years more to recreate them. ***Renewable*** resources are more readily available. These include water, wind, and solar power.

Reforestation prevents further loss of trees by replanting. This helps to prevent erosion of topsoil and reduction in carbon dioxide emissions. Reforestation also creates habitats for organisms that rely on trees for shelter and food.

In countries such as China, population control laws have been created to limit population growth by reducing the number of children per family. Individuals in other countries have also made personal choices to limit family size by the use of biological birth control methods. Controlling population size takes a strain off of limited resources and frees some up for reserves.

Biological control is a method that replaces chemical pesticides as a way of controlling insects and pests. It is the use of living organisms to control the population of these pests. Natural parasites are used to kill harmful insects. Sex hormones are also used to attract and trap environmental pests. Biological control is a better option over toxic pesticides because it doesn't contaminate the land and water or disrupt food webs.

PART II: ORGANIZATION AND DEVELOPMENT OF LIVING ORGANISM

Cells

Standards: SC.6.L.14.1, SC.6.L.14.2, SC.6.L.14.3, SC.6.L.14.4

All living things share certain characteristics. A major similarity among all organisms is that they are all made of **_cells_**. Cells are the smaller parts in all living things, too small to be seen without magnification. The cell is the smallest basic unit of structure and function in living things. It carries out all the processes necessary for life. Some organisms are made up of only one cell. We call them **_unicellular_** (uni = one) or single-celled. These are the simplest cells. Other organisms are more complex and are made up of many cells. We call them **_multi-cellular_** (multi = many). Most organisms are multi-cellular. Living things are also classified as either **_prokaryotic_** or **_eukaryotic_**. **Table 3-3** on the following page shows a comparison between prokaryotic and eukaryotic cells.

Table 3-3 Comparison of Prokaryotic and Eukaryotic Cells

PROKARYOTIC CELLS	EUKARYOTIC CELLS
Bacteria	Cells of plant, animal, protist and fungi (Eurkaryotes include some single-celled and all multi-cellular organisms)
cell membrane, cell wall, cytoplasm, ribosomes, but no membrane bound organelles present	cell membrane, cytoplasm, ribosomes, organelles, and membrane bound organelles
one circular DNA. no nucleus present	DNA found within the nucleus of the cell

Inside the cell are small structures called **_organelles_** that perform specific life functions for the cell. These include such functions as getting energy from food (respiration), growth, maintenance, regulation and reproduction. These physiological functions maintain life and are determined by what occurs within the cell. The chart below summarizes the names of the organelles and their functions. Note which structures can be found in plant cells only and which can be found in animal (humans, dogs, rabbits, insects, etc.,) only.

Table 3-4 Cell Organelles and Their Functions

Name of Organelle	Function
nucleus	The "brain" of the cell. The cell's command center. Contains DNA that caries information needed for cells to live, grow, and reproduce. All eukaryotic cells have a nucleus.
cell membrane	The "bodyguard" for the cell. Protection for the cell. Controls what goes into and out of the cell (selective permeability). Allows nutrients to enter the cell and wastes to exit. Separates the cell from its environment. All cells have a cell membrane.
nuclear membrane	Surrounds the nucleus and allows materials to pass into and out of the nucleus.
cytoskeleton	The "skeleton" for the cell. Supports the cell's shape and helps the cell move just as the human skeleton gives us support and helps us to move.
ribosomes	Make proteins.
endoplasmic reticulum (ER)	The "highway" of the cell. A system of channels that transports proteins and other materials made inside the cell.
smooth ER	No ribosomes attached. Makes lipids. Breaks down toxic substances that could damage the cell.
rough ER	Has ribosomes attached. Packages the proteins made by ribosomes.
golgi complex (or golgi bodies)	Modifies and enhances proteins made by ribosomes (e.g., adds a sugar or phosphate group to the protein).
lysosomes	The "garbage disposal" of the cell. It gets rid of wastes. Found in animal cells only.
mitochondria	The "powerhouse of the cell". Breaks down glucose in cell to make energy (ATP) for the cell.
vacuole (small)	The "refrigerator" of the cell. Stores water and nutrients. Found in animal cells only.
central vacuole (large)	Found in plants only. Stores water for plants. Breaks down wastes in plants (just like the lysosomes in animal cells). When water levels here are low, plants wilt (become shriveled up).
cell wall	Found in plants and some prokaryotic cells only. Rigid and tough for support of plant to help it stand upright. Surrounds the plant cell outside of its cell membrane.
chloroplast	Found in plant cells only. Helps the plant to create its own food by the process of photosynthesis. Contains the green pigment chlorophyll that captures the energy from the sun necessary for photosynthesis.
nucleolus	Make ribosomes

The cells of all organisms undergo similar processes to maintain **_homeostasis_**. Homeostasis is maintaining a stable internal environment in spite of internal or external changes. "Homeo" = **same** + "stasis"= **staying** so, homeostasis is the process of staying the same. Organisms become sick or die when they fail to maintain homeostasis. Each cell of the human body has organelles that are adapted/and or specialized to perform its own life functions. All of these processes serve to maintain homeostasis.

Metabolism is the term given to all the chemical activities an organism must carry on in order to remain alive. To be considered living, all organisms must perform the following eight life functions (metabolic activities):

1. **respiration** --making energy for the cell
2. **growth**--increasing in cell size or cell number
3. **synthesis**-- combing small molecules to make larger ones.   example: photosynthesis
4. **regulation**--maintaining a stable internal environment
5. **nutrition**--obtaining and processing nutrients
6. **transport**-- circulation of materials throughout the organism
7. **excretion**-- removing metabolic wastes. example: carbon dioxide, water, and ammonia.
8. **reproduction**--producing new individuals

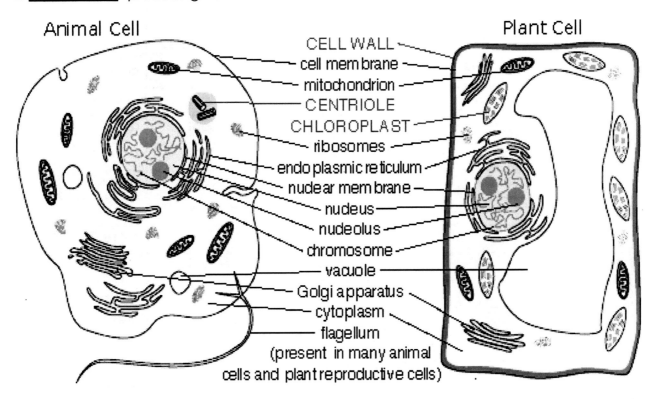

Animal Cell   Plant Cell

CELL WALL
cell membrane
mitochondrion
CENTRIOLE
CHLOROPLAST
ribosomes
endoplasmic reticulum
nuclear membrane
nucleus
nucleolus
chromosome
vacuole
Golgi apparatus
cytoplasm
flagellum
(present in many animal
cells and plant reproductive cells)

Table 3-5 Organelles of Human Cells and Their Life Functions

Life Function	Cell Organelle Responsible for Carrying out Life Function
1. respiration	mitochondria
2. growth	nucleus, cytoskeleton
3. synthesis	chloroplast, ribosomes, nucleolus, golgi bodies
4. regulation	nucleus, cell membrane and all organelles
5. nutrition	vacuoles, lysosomes
6. transport	cell membrane, endoplasmic reticulum (ER)
7. excretion	cell membrane, smooth ER
8. reproduction	nucleus, centrioles, cytoskeleton

Plant and animal cells share many similarities. For one, both plant cells and animal cells are eukaryotic. This means they have a nucleus and other membrane bound organelles. They even have many of the same organelles in common. However, although they do share many similarities, there are some differences between plant cells and animal cells. **Table 3-6** below will help you differentiate between the two. Keep in mind that the term animal cell includes everything from tiny eukaryotic microorganisms to humans. Students tend to forget this.

Table 3-6 Plant Cells vs. Animal Cells

Characteristics	Plant Cells	Animal cells
cell Wall	present	absent
chloroplast	present	absent
chlorophyll	present	absent
large central vacuole	present	absent
small vacuole	absent	present
lysosome	absent	present
cell membrane	present	present
cytoplasm	present	present
centrioles	absent	present
ribosomes, golgi bodies, endoplasmic reticulum, nucleolus, nuclear membrane, mitochondria	present	present
shape	rectangular	round
ability to make own food through photosynthesis	yes	no

The Cell Theory (The Scientific Theory of Cells)

Standards: SC.6.L.14.2

The **_Cell Theory_** is a major theory that governs the classification of living organisms. It is a fundamental organizing principle of life on Earth. The cell theory has three parts:

1. All living things are made of cells (single-celled or multi-cellular)
2. The cell is the basic unit of structure and function (basic unit of life)

3. All cells come from preexisting cells (i.e., new cells form when parent cells divide).

As with any other theory, there are a few exceptions to the Cell Theory:

1. Viruses are not living cells. They are made up of a core of DNA or RNA surrounded by a protein coat. They do not have organelles, yet viruses can reproduce themselves inside a living host cell. A virus is like a parasite. It lives off of living organisms. Outside the organism it shows no sign of life.

2. Mitochondria and chloroplasts, which are organelles found inside of cells, have their own DNA and can reproduce themselves.

3. The very first living cells on Earth could not have come from a preexisting cell. They must have been formed from non-cellular materials in their environment.

Similarities Between the Organization of Complex Organisms and Ecosystems

Standards: SC.6.L.14.1

We have mentioned the concept of patterns many times in this book. When it comes to living things more patterns can be seen when close observations occur. There is a pattern in the hierarchical organization of organisms that is very similar to that of ecosystems. Remember in an ecosystem, the smallest level of organization is a **_species_**. A group of species inhabiting an area is called a **_population_**. A group of populations inhabiting an area is called a **community**. A group of various communities inhabiting an area (along with the abiotic factors) is called an **ecosystem**. The largest ecosystem on Earth is called the **_biosphere_**.

Complex organisms are organized in a similar fashion. The smallest functional unit of life is the **cell**. A group of similar cells that perform a specific function is called a **_tissue_**. A group of tissues that work together to carry out a specific function is called an **_organ_**. A group of organs that work together to perform a bodily function is called an **_organ system_** and all the organ systems make up the total **_organism_**.

Example: cells— form tissues—which forms the organs of breathing (lungs, trachea, bronchi, bronchioles, alveoli)—which are collectively known as the respiratory system (an <u>organ system</u>) and can all be found in an <u>organism</u> (i.e. , a human)

Our pattern of hierarchical organization can even be expanded to include atoms, molecules and organelles. ***Atoms*** (the smallest units of matter) make up ***molecules***. Molecules form organelles, which are the structural and functional parts of cells. The rest of this you already know: cells form tissues, which form organs, which form organ systems, which form the organism. [**Note**: Cells with similar functions have similar structures. Those with different structures have different functions].

Reproduction   (Cell Division and Growth)
Standards: SC.7.L.16.3

Body cells grow and divide to make more cells. This process is called ***cell division*** or ***mitosis*** and is a part of reproduction. Reproduction is characteristic of all living things and is essential for the survival of the species. Cell division allows organisms to reproduce, grow and repair damaged tissues. This is the reason why broken bones and cuts heal.

For cells to grow and divide successfully, they must pass on their DNA, which contains the genetic information (more on DNA later). In mitosis, the new cell formed, the ***daughter cell,*** is genetically identical to the original cell (the ***parent cell***) therefore, they are clones. All cells divide at least once in their life time. The cycle that describes the repetitive process of cell reproduction is called the ***cell cycle***. The steps of the cell cycle, which includes mitosis, are outlined in **Table 3-7** on the following page.

Table 3-7 Mitosis and the Cell Cycle

Cell Cycle Stage	Description
Interphase	Cell appears to be at rest. Most of its time is spent here. Nucleus is visible but the DNA is not. It appears as chromatin which looks like a plate of spaghetti. DNA is duplicated during interphase. Cell makes more organelles and materials needed to ensure each new cell will have all of the necessary structures to function properly.
Mitosis	This stage occurs after interphase. It is the actual cell division. Mitosis is divided into four stages: prophase, metaphase, anaphase and telophase.
Prophase	Nuclear membrane disappears. Chromatin coils into chromosomes and become visible. Spindle fibers form that help to split chromosomes apart. Sister chromatids form.
Metaphase	Chromosomes attached to spindles line up in the middle of the cell
Anaphase	Sister chromatids separate.
Telophase	Final stage of mitosis. New cell is formed. The nuclear membrane and nucleolus re-form. Chromosomes unwind to form chromatin again. Cytokinesis usually occurs after telophase which causes the actual separation of the cells in animal cells.

Mitosis

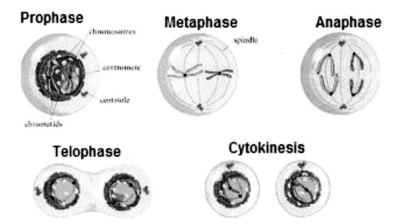

Having knowledge of mitosis is helpful in understanding disorders like cancer. Cancer cells no longer respond to natural signals of mitosis that tell a cell when to start and stop dividing, so they keep dividing. This leads to an overproduction of cells. Eventually a lump of cells form called a **_tumor_**. Tumors cause problems in the body because they take up space within the body and prevent normal metabolic functioning. Sometimes they also press against nerves or blood vessels, restricting their functioning. Exposure to sunlight over a period of time increases the likelihood of developing skin cancer.

Mitosis is a form of **_asexual reproduction_**. Asexual reproduction does not involve **_sex cells_** (**_sperm_** and **_egg cells_**) and it makes genetically identical cells (clones). Only one parent cell is needed. Most of the cells in your body divide by mitosis. Some multi-cellular organisms asexually reproduce by a process called **_budding_**. In budding, a part of the parent organism pinches off and forms a new organism which is genetically identical to the parent cell. The bud stays attached to the parent cell while it grows. When it is fully grown it detaches.

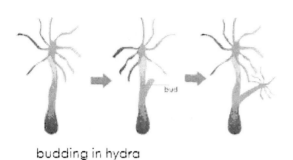

budding in hydra

Advantages of Asexual Reproduction
1. Asexually reproducing animals do not have to use energy to find a mate, resulting in a more efficient usage of their energy.
2. Organisms can produce many offspring in a short period of time. This improves their survival rate.
3. Organisms do not have to depend on other organisms in order to reproduce.

Another form of cell division that occurs in multi-cellular organisms is called **_meiosis_**. Meiosis is a form of **_sexual reproduction._** It forms sex cells (**_gametes_**) that are **NOT** genetically identical to the parent cell although they will share some similarities.   These cells have half the number of chromosomes or DNA of their parent cell. Offspring receive half their genes from each parent in sexual reproduction. Animals, including humans, inherit some characteristics from one parent and some from the other. Examples of a characteristics or traits that are passed from parent to child are hair color and eye color.

Gametes are **_haploid_**.   On the other hand, cells produced by mitosis are **_diploid_**. They have the full chromosome number. In humans, the diploid number of chromosomes is 46 and the haploid number is 23. When a haploid egg joins a haploid sperm, the combining of their genetic information (**_fertilization_**) makes a cell with a full set of chromosomes (diploid). Meiosis only occurs in sex cells. Plants use asexual reproduction or **_vegetative propagation_** to grow, as well as sexual reproduction to form fruit and increase the species.

Sexual reproduction creates **_variations_** (variety) in organisms because each cell is not genetically identical to the parent cell. A process called **_crossing over_** occurs during prophase of meiosis which results in an exchange of genetic information between similar chromosomes (**_homologous chromosomes_**). This creates new genetic combinations. The steps of meiosis are outlined below. Notice they are very similar to the steps of mitosis with the exception of meiosis having two cellular divisions (meiosis I and II).   Both involve PMAT (prophase, metaphase, anaphase, telophase) and cytokinesis. The second division in meiosis is identical to mitosis.

Table 3-8 Stages of Meiosis

Stages of Meiosis	
Interphase 1	DNA is copied (replicated). Cell prepares to enter meiosis.
Meiosis I	The first division
Prophase I	Chromosomes condense. Nuclear membrane disappears. Spindles form. Homologous chromosomes pair up (**_synapsis_**). Crossing over occurs.
Metaphase I	Homologous chromosomes move to center of cell.
Anaphase I	Homologues separate.
Telophase I	Nuclear membrane usually does not re-form.
Cytokinesis	May or may not occur. Two cells form that are diploid.
Interphase II	No DNA replication occurs. Cell may immediately enter into meiosis II.
Meiosis II	Proceeds just like mitosis
Prophase II	Spindle fibers form. Nuclear membrane disappears. **_Chromatin_** coils up to form chromosomes.
Metaphase II	Sister chromatids line up in the middle of the cell.
Anaphase II	Sister chromatids separate.
Telophase II	Spindle fibers disappear. Nuclear membrane and nucleolus re-form. New cell forms.
Cytokinesis II	Cell divides into two cells each having half the number of chromosomes (**_haploid_**). A total of four cells form after meiosis II.

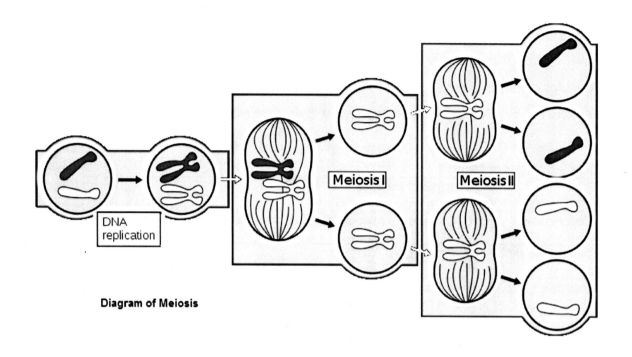

Diagram of Meiosis

Advantages of Sexual Reproduction

1. The genetic recombination that occurs during crossing over of prophase I of meiosis creates cells which are not genetically identical to their parent cell. This results in variations (differences) in populations.

2. Differences in organism's genes allows populations to adapt to changes in their environment which increases their survival rate.

Comparison of Cell Division in Eukaryotic and Prokaryotic Cells

When prokaryotes reproduce they simply divide in half. This is called ***binary fission***. Each half becomes a separate organism. The new daughter cell is genetically identical to the parent cell. Before the cell splits in half the DNA is copied and each cell gets a copy. They are clones. This whole process can take as little as 30 minutes, which is the reason bacteria can reproduce quickly. This is also the reason you become very ill when you have a bacterial infection because the bacteria can multiply so quickly.

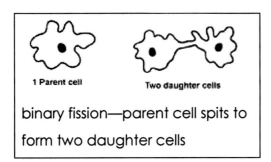

binary fission—parent cell spits to form two daughter cells

Comparison of Cell Division in Plant and Animal Cells

Standards: SC.7.L.16.3

Table 3-9 Comparison of Animal and Plant Cell Division

Animal Cell Division	Plant Cell Division
1. Have <u>centrioles (structures</u> involved in cell division).	1. No centrioles present.
2. Spindle fibers help chromosomes to separate and move.	2. Spindle fibers help chromosomes to separate and move.
3. Cytokinesis splits the cell to form two completely separate cells.	3. Cytokinesis does not form two completely separate cells. Plant cells remain attached after cell division. A ***cell plate*** is formed after cytokinesis. This cell plate eventually becomes the cell wall.

Sexual Reproduction in Plants

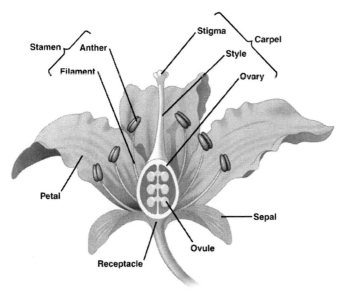

The Flower is the reproductive structure of flowering plants (angiosperms). It consists of various parts. The male reproductive structure is the **stamen**, which consists of the **anther** and the **filament**. The female reproductive structure is the **carpel** (**pistal**) which consists of the **stigma**, **style** and **ovary**.

Pollination begins the reproductive process. It is the transfer of pollen grains from the anther to the stigma of the same flower (self-pollination) or of a different flower (cross-pollination). Pollen is produced by the anther. It contains the male reproductive cell, the sperm cell. Pollen must fertilize an ovule to produce a viable seed. Pollinators include bees, other insects and animals that unknowingly transport pollen grains in their fur.

Once the pollen grain makes contact with the stigma a pollen tube begins to grow down the style on its way to the ovary. The sperm cell travels in the pollen tube and fertilizes the female reproductive cell, the egg cells, located and produced by the ovules in the ovary. After fertilization the ovule becomes the seed. The ovary becomes the fruit.

Organ and Organ Systems
Standards: SC.5.L.14.1, SC.6.L.14.5

Your cells depend on other cells in your body. They all work together to carry out their specialized functions. On a higher level, the human body contains many organs and organ systems to perform different functions. The major organ systems are listed in **Table 3-10** on the following page. A breakdown of each body system follows **Table 3-10**.

Table 3-10 Organ Systems and Their Functions

Organ System	Function
1. respiratory system	removes carbon dioxide from blood and exchanges it for oxygen
2. immune system	made up of the white blood cells and lymph nodes and fights disease and infections in the body
3. reproductive system	produces eggs and sperm cells and provides mechanisms to increase the species number
4. excretory system	removes wastes from the bloodstream
5. nervous system	detects stimuli, secretes chemical and electric signals, and controls all other organ systems
6. endocrine system	releases hormones into the blood to communicate with target cells
7. digestive system	uses enzymes to break down food and release nutrients into the blood stream. removes solid wastes from the body (feces).
8. muscular and skeletal system	works together to move the body
9. circulatory system	delivers nutrients and oxygen to cells and carries metabolic waste and carbon dioxide away from cells

Human Body Systems

NERVOUS SYSTEM (REGULATION)

ORGANS OF THE NERVOUS SYSTEM AND THEIR FUNCTIONS	
ORGAN	FUNCTION
nerve cells (neurons)	Cells that process and transmit information
nerves	Carries signals or nerve impulses that transmit information
brain	Controls the different functions of the body. Functions in learning, memory, movement, etc.
spinal cord	Coordinates activities between the brain and other body structures

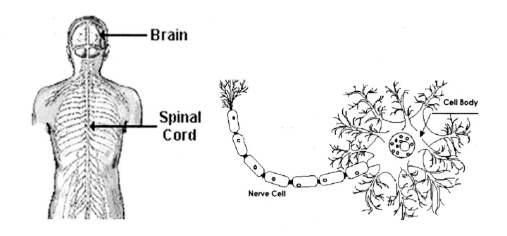

Brain

Spinal Cord

Cell Body

Nerve Cell

HOW THIS SYSTEM MAINTAINS HOMEOSTASIS

Since the nervous system does not store nutrients it must receive a continuous supply of blood from the circulatory system.   Any interruption to the flow of blood may bring about brain damage or death. The nervous system maintains homeostasis by controlling and regulating the other parts of the body.

DISORDERS OF THE NERVOUS SYSTEM		
NAME OF DISORDER	**HOW CAUSED**	**EFFECT ON THE SYSTEM**
CEREBRAL PALSY	Damage or abnormal development in the parts of the brain that control muscle tone and movement	Affects body movement, balance, and posture
MENINGITIS	Viral or bacterial infection	Can lead to seizures, unconsciousness, headaches, etc.
STROKE	Damage to brain by cerebral hemorrhage or blood clot	Loss of bodily functions (i.e., talking, walking, etc.)
POLIO	Virus	May cause paralysis
ALZHEIMER'S DISEASE	Genetic or environmental causes. Degenerative disease in which neurons in brain gradually become destroyed	Fatal. Causes loss of memory, mood swings, unusual behavior, and overall loss of functioning

DIGESTIVE SYSTEM (NUTRITION)

ORGANS OF THE DIGESTIVE SYSTEM AND THEIR FUNCTIONS	
ORGAN	**FUNCTION**
stomach	Stores food. Mechanical and chemical digestion. Protein digestion begins here
mouth	Mechanical and chemical digestion. Carbohydrate digestion begins here. Ingestion occurs here (food enters the body).
esophagus	Moves food to stomach by peristalsis
gallbladder	"Stores" bile which is used to digest fats
small intestine	Chemical digestion and nutrient absorption
liver (accessory organ)	"Makes" bile for fat digestion
large intestine	Absorbs water and minerals from undigested food and forms feces
anus	Feces leaves the body through the anus
rectum	Temporarily stores feces
pancreas (accessory organ)	Produces enzymes that are used by the small intestine to digest foods

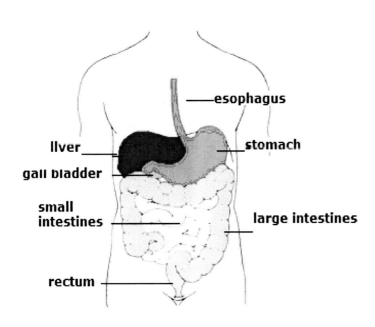

HOW THIS SYSTEM MAINTAINS HOMEOSTASIS

The digestive system breaks down carbohydrates, fats, and proteins before they are absorbed by the body as nutrients and used by the cells. Once the digestive system breaks down the nutrients, the circulatory system works with it to distribute the nutrients to each cell. The digestive system also helps to eliminate wastes (feces) to prevent a toxic buildup in the body. The liver, which monitors the blood, is a very important organ of homeostasis. The liver breaks down toxic substances like alcohol and other drugs and destroys old blood cells.

DISORDERS OF THE DIGESTIVE SYSTEM		
NAME OF DISORDER	HOW CAUSED	EFFECT ON THE SYSTEM
ULCER	Bacterial infection	Causes bleeding (loss of blood) and pain
DIARRHEA	Decreased water absorption in large intestine	Dehydration (loss of vital water)
CONSTIPATION	Increased water absorption in large intestine	Difficulty in eliminating feces
GALLSTONES	Caused by a combination of factors, including inherited body chemistry, body weight, gallbladder motility (movement), and perhaps diet. Gallstones develop when bile contains too much cholesterol and not enough bile salts.	Severe pain, blockage of bile ducts (vessels), and prevention of flow of bile.

CIRCULATORY SYSTEM (TRANSPORT)

ORGANS OF THE CIRCULATORY SYSTEM AND THEIR FUNCTIONS	
ORGAN	**FUNCTION**
arteries	Carry blood away from the heart
veins	Carry blood to the heart
capillaries	Where nutrients and gases are exchanged
red blood cells	Carry oxygen and carbon dioxide and give blood its red color because they contain hemoglobin (an iron-containing protein that binds oxygen in the lungs and transports it to tissues in the body).
white blood cells	Fights diseases (pathogens)
plasma	The liquid portion of blood
blood	Supply oxygen and nutrients to tissue. Removes wastes such as carbon dioxide, urea and lactic acid. Circulates white blood cells and detect foreign material by antibodies. Transports hormones. Regulates body pH levels and core body temperature.
platelets	Cell fragments which play an important part in the clotting of the blood
heart	Pumps blood through the body

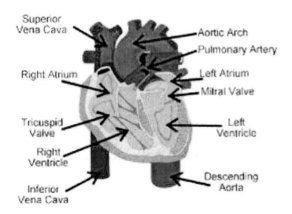
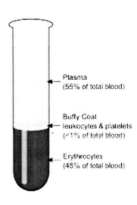

HOW THIS SYSTEM MAINTAINS HOMEOSTASIS

Stabilizes body temperature and pH. Nutrient molecules leave the capillaries to be taken up by the cells and waste molecules given off by the cells are received by the capillaries to be transported away. Blood contributes to homeostasis by transporting oxygen (red blood cells), fighting infection (white blood cells) and clotting blood when necessary (platelets). The circulatory system works with the respiratory system to maintain homeostasis by distributing the oxygen molecules needed for respiration and also by circulating the carbon dioxide waste of respiration as well. The excretory system works with these systems to remove the waste products of respiration (carbon dioxide and water) from the body. Oxygen is utilized during cellular respiration. Fighting infection keeps the body intact and prevents it from succumbing to disease caused by viruses and bacteria. Clotting of blood when a vessel has been cut prevents the loss of this vital fluid. Plasma, too, contributes to homeostasis. The nutrients needed and wastes given off by cells are carried in plasma. Plasma also helps to maintain blood pressure.

DISORDERS OF THE CIRCULATORY SYSTEM (CARDIOVASCULAR DISEASES)		
NAME OF DISORDER	**HOW CAUSED**	**EFFECT ON THE SYSTEM**
HYPERTENSION (HIGH BLOOD PRESSURE)	Dietary, genetic, or unknown medical cause. Can be caused by diseases of other body systems i.e., kidney disease.	Can result in heart attack, stroke or death
HEART ATTACK	Clot inside a blood vessel that blocks the flow of blood. Usually caused by an injury to the vessel's wall, both by trauma or infection and by the slowing of blood flow past the point of injury.	Blockage deprives portions of the heart of needed nutrients and oxygen resulting in destruction of heart tissue
ANEMIA	Genetic or dietary causes. Low red cell count or some abnormality of the red blood cells or the hemoglobin. Dietary (Iron Deficiency Anemia) or genetic (Sickle Cell Anemia).	Low oxygen transport capacity of the blood
LEUKEMIA	Cancer of the blood or bone marrow due to genetic or environmental causes	Damage to the bone marrow. This means people with leukemia may become bruised, bleed excessively, or develop pinprick bleeds and anemia

RESPIRATORY SYSTEM (RESPIRATION)

| ORGANS OF THE RESPIRATORY SYSTEM AND THEIR FUNCTIONS ||
ORGAN	FUNCTION
pharynx	Part of the digestive and respiratory system of many organisms. Because both food and air pass through the pharynx, special adaptations are necessary to prevent choking when food or liquid is swallowed.
trachea	Lets air move from the throat to the lungs
bronchi	Carries air to the lungs
bronchioles	Smaller part of bronchi which lets air move from the bronchi to the alveoli
alveoli	Where gas exchange takes place (carbon dioxide is exchanged for oxygen)
lungs	Its principal function is to transport oxygen from the atmosphere into the bloodstream, and to excrete carbon dioxide from the bloodstream into the atmosphere

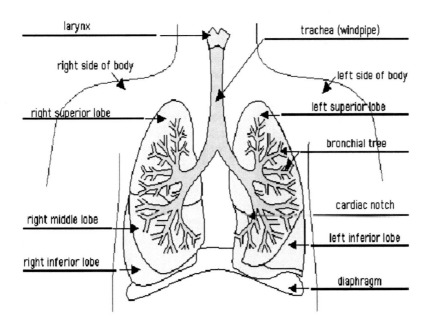

HOW THIS SYSTEM MAINTAINS HOMEOSTASIS

The respiratory system helps to maintain homeostasis by maintaining the carbon dioxide and oxygen balance in the body. When the carbon dioxide concentration rises or when the pH lowers, the respiratory center of the brain is stimulated and the breathing rate increases. The excretory system removes the wastes of respiration.

DISORDERS OF THE RESPIRATORY SYSTEM		
NAME OF DISORDER	HOW CAUSED	EFFECT ON THE SYSTEM
BRONCHITIS	Usually by bacterial or viral infection in the bronchi.	Persistent cough or sputum production. Obstructed airways. Inflamed airways. Shortness of breath and wheezing.
ASTHMA	These episodes may be triggered by such things as exposure to an environmental stimulant (or allergen), cold air, exercise or exertion, or emotional stress. In children, the most common triggers are viruses such as those that cause the common cold.	The airway sometimes tightens and becomes inflamed and is lined with excessive amounts of mucus. This airway narrowing causes symptoms such as wheezing, shortness of breath, chest tightness, and coughing.
EMPHYSEMA	Exposure to toxic chemicals or long-term exposure to tobacco smoke.	Emphysema is characterized by loss of elasticity of the lung tissue, destruction of structures supporting the alveoli, and destruction of capillaries feeding the alveoli. Symptoms include shortness of breath, hypoventilation, and an expanded chest. As emphysema progresses, clubbing of the fingers may be observed, a feature of tissue being deprived of oxygen.

EXCRETORY SYSTEM (EXCRETION)

ORGANS OF THE EXCRETORY SYSTEM AND THEIR FUNCTIONS	
ORGAN	**FUNCTION**
lungs	Excrete carbon dioxide and water vapor
liver	Detoxify drugs
skin	Excrete sweat (water and salts) through sweat glands.
kidneys	Filter wastes (such as urea) from the blood and excrete them, along with water, as urine
ureters	Carry urine from the kidneys to the urinary bladder
urinary bladder	Store urine until it can be excreted from the body
urethra	Carry urine from the bladder to outside of the body

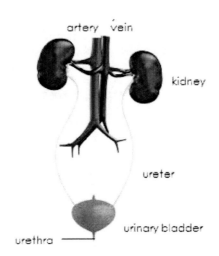

HOW THIS SYSTEM MAINTAINS HOMEOSTASIS

The excretory system helps to maintain homeostasis by removing the wastes of metabolism (ammonia, urea, salts, water, etc) from the body. The skin removes wastes from the body by way of sweating. This also helps to maintain body temperature. The kidneys and the urinary system also help to remove wastes. As blood passes through the kidneys, urine is made and excreted. Urine is composed of substances not needed by cells, end-products of metabolism (i.e., urea) and excess salts and water.

DISORDERS OF THE EXCRETORY SYSTEM		
NAME OF DISORDER	HOW CAUSED	EFFECT ON THE SYSTEM
KIDNEY DISEASE	Long term use of pain killers (i.e., aspirin) and other drugs. Can be caused by other diseases, such as lupus and diabetes. Genetic component.	Increased blood pressure, buildup of waste products in the blood, damage to blood vessels, change in the composition of blood, swelling (edema), heart disease, etc.
GOUT	Caused by a buildup of uric acid in the blood that gets deposited into the joints. Diet and genetics is usually the cause.	Excruciating and sudden pain, swelling, redness, warmness and stiffness in the joint. Low-grade fever may also be present. The inflammation of the tissues around the joint causes the skin to be swollen, tender and sore if it is even slightly touched. For example, a blanket draping over the affected area could cause extreme pain.

ENDOCRINE SYSTEM (REGULATION)

ORGANS OF THE ENDOCRINE SYSTEM AND THEIR FUNCTIONS	
ENDOCRINE GLANDS AND THE HORMONES THEY SECRETE	**FUNCTION**
hypothalamus	The "master gland". Controls metabolism and such things as body temperature, hunger, thirst, and sleep.
pituitary gland	Secretes hormones that control homeostasis and other endocrine glands
thyroid gland	Produces hormones (i.e., thyroxin), that regulate the rate of metabolism and affect the growth and rate of function of many other body systems
parathyroid glands	The sole function of the parathyroid glands is to regulate the calcium level in our bodies within a very narrow range so that the nervous and muscular systems can function properly
adrenal glands	Chiefly responsible for regulating stress.
pancrease	Produce the hormones insulin and glucagon which regulate blood sugar
gonads **1. testes** **2. ovaries**	Produce male sex hormones such as testosterone which function in puberty, and secondary male sex characteristics (penis growth, facial hair, course skin, muscle mass, etc). Produce female sex hormones such as estrogen and progesterone which function in puberty, secondary sex characteristics, the menstrual cycle, and in pregnancy.

Major Endocrine Glands
Male   Female

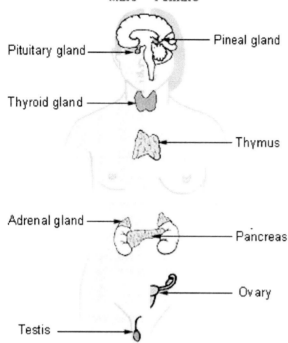

Pituitary gland

Pineal gland

Thyroid gland

Thymus

Adrenal gland

Pancreas

Ovary

Testis

HOW THIS SYSTEM MAINTAINS HOMEOSTASIS

The hormones produced by the endocrine glands are chemical messengers that are transported throughout the body via the circulatory system by the blood. The endocrine and nervous system both coordinate the activities of body parts and help to maintain homeostasis. The nervous system reacts quickly to external and internal stimuli, whereas the endocrine system is slower to act but its effects are longer lasting. A number of different hormones are active in keeping the blood glucose level at a normal level (0.1%). The most important of these is insulin. Immediately after eating, increased glucose concentration stimulates the pancreas to release insulin. Insulin also promotes the uptake of glucose by cells including the liver. Insulin stimulates the conversion of glucose to glycogen in the liver. Between eating, when insulin is not being produced, the liver convert glycogen to glucose and therefore the blood glucose level remains constant. This conversion of glycogen is stimulated by both glucagon and, in times of emergency, also adrenalin. If the supply of glycogen should run out and the blood glucose level remains low, hormones will direct the liver to make more glucose.

DISORDERS OF THE ENDOCRINE SYSTEM		
Name of Disorder	How Caused	Effect on the system
GOITER	Usually due to iodine deficiency. Can be caused by autoimmune disease	At times it does not negatively affect the system (except in appearance) but it could cause breathing and swallowing problems. Swelling of the neck due to an enlarged thyroid gland.
DIABETES	Physical damage to the pancreas or a deficiency in the hormone insulin (produced by the pancreas). Genetic and dietary causes.	Metabolic disorder characterized by high blood sugar. Inability to regulate blood sugar. Diabetic coma, foot amputations, blindness, stroke, death
PITUITARY GLAND DISORDERS	Damage to the pituitary gland resulting in overproduction or underproduction of growth hormone and other hormones produced by this gland. Damage can include those caused by severe head trauma, surgery, brain tumors, etc.	Growth problems in children. In adults can cause loss of strength and muscle tone, poor memory, social withdrawal, and even depression.

LOCOMOTION (MOVEMENT)

ORGANS OF LOCOMOTION AND THEIR FUNCTIONS	
ORGAN	**FUNCTION**
bones	Function to move, support, and protect the body, produce red and white blood cells and store minerals
cartilage	Helps in the formation of bones. Supplies a smooth surface for the movement of bones. Cartilage is found in many places in the body including the joints, rib cage, ear, nose, bronchial tubes and the spine.
joints	Location at which two or more bones make contact. They are constructed to allow movement and provide mechanical support.
muscles	Produce force and cause motion, either locomotion or movement within internal organs
skeletal muscles	"Voluntary" (under conscious control) muscle causes locomotion and affects posture
smooth muscle	"Involuntary" (not under conscious control) muscle found in the walls of organs such as the stomach, esophagus, bladder and small intestine
cardiac muscle	"Involuntary" muscle found in the heart only
tendons	Connects muscle to bone
ligaments	Connects bone to bone

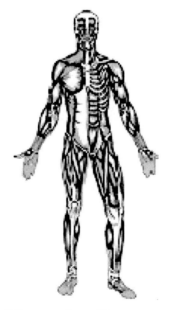
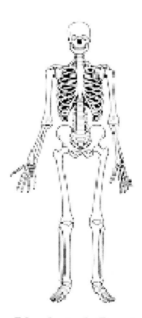

Muscular System   **Skeletal System**

HOW THIS SYSTEM MAINTAINS HOMEOSTASIS

When the body is at rest, body heat is generated primarily by the liver, heart, brain, and endocrine glands, but when the muscles are active they generate many times the heat produced by these organs. Therefore, increased muscle activity by rubbing the hands or stamping the feet is used as a short-term measure to raise body temperature and maintain homeostasis.

DISORDERS OF LOCOMOTION		
Name of Disorder	How Caused	Effect on the system
ARTHRITIS	Inflammation of joints caused by joint infection, autoimmune disease, or other metabolic causes	Damage to joints, pain, loss of use of affected body parts, disability
TENDONITIS	Inflammation of tendons caused by overuse of the tendon as in athletic activity or via other diseases, such as arthritis	Symptoms can vary from an ache or pain and stiffness to the local area of the tendon, or a burning that surrounds the whole joint around the inflamed tendon. With this condition, the pain is usually worse during and after activity, and the tendon and joint area can become stiffer the following day as swelling impinges on the movement of the tendon.

REPRODUCTIVE SYSTEM (REPRODUCTION)

ORGANS OF THE REPRODUCTIVE SYSTEM AND THEIR FUNCTIONS	
ORGAN	**FUNCTION**
ovary	Produces egg cells in females
oviduct (fallopian tube)	Passageway for eggs released from the ovaries or for fertilized eggs to travel to the uterus
uterus	Place where the fertilized egg (zygote) develops into an embryo, fetus, then ultimately a baby
cervix	During childbirth, contractions of the uterus will dilate the cervix up to 10 cm in diameter to allow the child to pass through
vagina	Providing a path for menstrual fluids to leave the body. Sexual activity. Giving birth.
penis	Male reproductive organ adapted for reproduction for the delivery of sperm. It also serves as the external male organ of urination.
testes	Produces sperm in males
scrotum	Keeps the testes at a temperature slightly lower than that of the rest of the body for the protection of the sperm
urethra	The urethra has an excretory function in both genders to pass urine to the outside, and also a reproductive function in the male, as a passage for sperm
vas deferens	Functions in male ejaculation to propel sperm forward in order to eject it from the penis
seminal vesicles	They secrete a significant proportion of the fluid that ultimately becomes semen. Semen is composed of sperm cells and seminal fluid.
prostate gland	The main function of the prostate is to store and secrete a clear, slightly alkaline fluid that constitutes up to one-third of the volume of semen

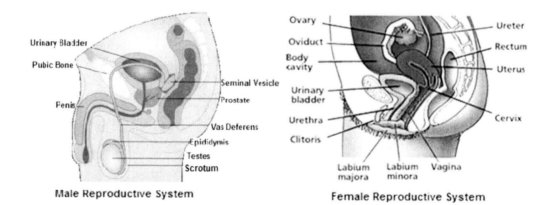

Male Reproductive System

Female Reproductive System

- 148 -

DISORDERS OF THE REPRODUCTIVE SYSTEM		
NAME OF DISORDER	HOW CAUSED	EFFECT ON THE SYSTEM
CERVICAL CANCER	Genetic or environmental. Most scientific studies have found that human papillomavirus (HPV) infection is responsible for virtually all cases of cervical cancer. HPV is contracted during sexual intercourse.	Symptoms of advanced cervical cancer may include: loss of appetite, weight loss, fatigue, pelvic pain, back pain, leg pain, single swollen leg, heavy bleeding from the vagina, leaking of urine or feces from the vagina, and bone fractures.
PROSTATE CANCER	Genetic or environmental	Pain, difficulty in urinating, erectile dysfunction and other symptoms
MALE INFERTILITY	Inability to produce children naturally due to problems such as low sperm count, testicular cancer, physical damage to testicles, etc.	Impairs the ability to reproduce
FEMALE INFERTILITY	Inability to conceive children or to carry a pregnancy to term due to issues such as genetics, uterine fibroids, blockage to fallopian tube due to excessive scarring from venereal disease, etc.	Impairs the ability to reproduce

Comparison of Human Organ Systems and Plant Structures

Standards: SC.5.L.14.2

All plants and animals, including humans, are alike in some ways and different in others. They all have internal parts and external structures that function to keep them alive and help them grow and reproduce. The physical structures of plants may differ from humans but the functions they carry out serve a similar purpose. Certain differences between plants and animals are quite obvious. Animals are motile. They have legs and other structures to help them achieve movement. Plants on the other hand lack locomotion. While they lack many of the structures of animals, plants manage to accomplish the same life functions.

Xylem and **phloem** are tissues in plants that function as a circulatory system. Xylem transports water from the root to the leaves and phloem distributes food from the leaves downward. Plant stems provide structure to a plant in the same manner as a skeleton or exoskeleton provides structure to an animal.

Plants, like animals, have hormones that control such life functions as growth and development. One such hormone is **auxin**. Auxin regulates the amount, type, and direction of plant growth. Hormones are part of the endocrine system of animals.

Plants perform sexual reproduction as do animals. They have ovaries that make egg cells. They have pollen grains that transport sperm cells inside to the ovaries for fertilization. The stamen and the pistil are the reproductive organs of the plant. Animals have a much more highly developed sensory and nervous system than plants. Plants have almost no ability to sense.

Table 3-11 Comparison of Human and Plant Organ Systems

Functions	Human Organ System	Plant Organ System
support	skeletal system (exoskeleton in some animals)	stem system (adds height and seeks light as well
transport water and nutrients	circulatory system(i.e., heart pumps blood)	stem system (vascular—xylem and phloem tissue)
reproduce	reproductive system	flower system (sexual). **stamen** = male reproductive organ. **pistal** = female reproductive organ
waste removal	excretory system	root and leaf system (**stomates** = structures in leaves that allow gases such as carbon dioxide, water vapor and oxygen exit and enter the leaf)
energy usage or production	all systems respiratory system	all systems
provide a barrier to the outside environment	integumentary system (skin)	epidermal system
takes in water and nutrients	digestive system	root and leaf systems

STRUCTURE OF A PLANT

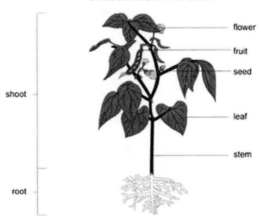

Infectious Agents

Standards: SC.6.L.14.6

An **_infectious agent_** is one that causes a disease or infection that can be spread from one individual to another. These include viruses, parasites, bacteria and fungi. They are also referred to as **_pathogens_**. One way to prevent infection from bacteria and viruses is by washing your hands often. Parasitic infections can be avoided by not drinking contaminated water or eating undercooked food.

Table 3-12   Infectious Agents

Type of Pathogen	Examples of Diseases Caused	Typical Mode of Transmission	Treatment	Size of Pathogen
Virus	Small pox, influenza (flu), mumps, measles, chickenpox, Ebola, rubella, HIV	Blood- borne	Anti-viral drugs	20-300 nanometers in length
Parasites	Malaria	Through contaminated food and water, via vectors (insects), blood - borne, air-borne	Clinical medicines	From microscopic-well over 30 feet
Bacteria	Tuberculosis, pneumonia, tetanus, syphilis, typhoid fever, and diphtheria	Airborne, water-borne, Blood-borne	Antibiotics	1-5 micrometers in length
Fungi	Most common cause of disease in plants. Apart from athletes foot fungus most life threatening fungal infections occur in humans with weak immune systems. Skin, nail or yeast infections.	Through soil	Fungi are eukaryotic organisms which create a treatment challenge when other eukaryotic cells are infected. Fungicides or anti-fungal agents disrupt the fungi's homeostasis in order to kill it.	A typical fungal cell is 1-40 micrometers in length.

PART 3: HEREDITY

Standards: SC.7.L.16.1, SC.7.L.16.2, SC.7.L.16.3, SC.7.L.16.4

How does a heart cell know that it's supposed to be a heart cell or bone tissue know that it's supposed to make red blood cells? Why do you look similar to your parents? The answer is all in your **deoxyribonucleic acid**, or as it is more commonly known as, **DNA**. Every organism requires a set of instructions that specifies its traits. DNA is the set of instructions that determines if an animal will have a particular fur color; whether a flower will grow to be a rose or an orchid; or whether you will be tall or short. DNA controls the traits of an organism.

DNA is the genetic material that is passed from generation to generation. Genes are sections of DNA arranged linearly. Genes are located on chromosomes. These chromosomes are located in the nucleus of the cell. **Genetics** is the study of DNA and how characteristics (**traits**) are passed down from parent to **offspring** through **gametes** (sex cells). The process of parents passing on genetic information to their offspring is called **heredity**. Heredity is the passage of these instructions from one generation to the next.

DNA Molecule

From the picture above you can see that DNA's shape resembles a twisted ladder. We call this a **double helix**. **James Watson & Francis Crick** are the scientists who created the first accurate model of DNA. This is what we know about the structure of DNA:

1. DNA molecules are very long
2. DNA is made of thousands of repeating units called **nucleotides**. A nucleotide is made up of three parts; a sugar (**deoxyribose**), a phosphate, and a nitrogenous base.
3. DNA contains four nitrogenous bases:
    - adenine (A)
    - cytosine (C)

- guanine (G)
- thymine (T)

4. The four bases in DNA bond together in only one way: guanine (G) pairs with cytosine (C) and adenine (A) pairs with thymine (T). We call this **_complementary base pairing_**. This principle was first observed in the 1950's by a scientist named **_Erwin Chargaff_**. We call base pairing rules in DNA, **_Chargaff's Rules_** . He observed that the amount of thymine in DNA always equals the amount of adenine. And the amount of cytosine always equals the amount of guanine.

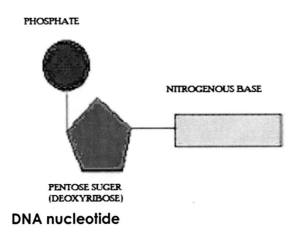

PHOSPHATE

NITROGENOUS BASE

PENTOSE SUGER
(DEOXYRIBOSE)

DNA nucleotide

The study of heredity began in the 1800's with an Austrian monk named **_Gregor Mendel_**. Using regular garden pea plants he performed important experiments to explore heredity. Without having the knowledge we have today of DNA and genes his discoveries helped scientists better understand how traits are passed from one generation to the next. Mendel observed traits such as seed shape, plant height, and flower color. He observed the results of pollination and fertilization of gametes from plants having same characteristics (i.e., both tall) and plants having different characteristics (i.e., one tall and one short). He observed the characteristics of the offspring (the F1 generation). Mendel then **_crossed_** (mated) these offspring (F2 generation) and observed the outcome.

Based on the characteristics observed in the offspring, Mendel developed principles of inheritance and concluded that these characteristics must have been due to certain "factors" originating from the parents. We now know these factors to be genes. It is genes that determine traits. In sexually reproducing organisms, half of inherited traits in the offspring come from the mother and the other half comes from the father. Therefore, no offspring is identical to its parents. Organisms inherit some characteristics from one parent and some form the other. This combination creates variety.   In fact, no two organisms are identical (apart from identical twins) because no two organisms have the same DNA.

The principle of **dominance**, which helps to explain the pattern of heredity, was one that Mendel developed.

Rules of Dominance
1. The trait that is observed in the offspring is the **dominant trait** (represented in genetics problems with an uppercase letter). Dominance occurs when certain **alleles** (different genes that control a trait) mask the expression of other alleles. 2. The trait that disappears in the offspring is the **recessive trait** (represented in genetic problems with a lowercase letter). A recessive trait or allele is expressed only when two recessive alleles for the same characteristic are inherited.

We will tie in dominance when we introduce **Punnett squares** in the next section.

Important Genetics Terms
1. **phenotype** -- the way an organism looks (i.e., red hair or brown eyes)
2. **genotype** -- the gene combination of an organism (i.e., in genetics problems letters are used to represent traits. So, the gene combination could look like this: AA or Aa or aa).
3. **heterozygous** -- when the two alleles for a trait are different (i.e., Aa)
4. **homozygous** - when the two alleles for a trait are the same (i.e., AA or aa).

Punnett Squares
Standards: SC.7.L.16.2

It is possible to predict whether a person is likely to inherit a particular trait from parents. This prediction can be made using diagrams called **Punnett squares**. Punnett squares are diagrams that show the possible offspring (children) of a genetic cross. The following example shows how they are used in genetics. Let's use one of Mendel's pea plants in our example:

Problem: *In pea plants tallness is a dominant trait. What are the possible offspring of a cross between a homozygous tall pea plant and a short pea plant?*

> **Step 1—** List the given information from the problem and determine which letter combinations to use to represent the parent's traits

Given:

T= tall trait

t = short trait [You have to use the same letter to represent the trait of "height"]

TT = gene combination of the tall parent. [Remember every trait has 2 alleles—one from the mother and the other from the father. That's why this parent has 2 T's. Both T's are capital because tallness is a dominant trait. Dominant traits are given a capital letter. Both letters are the same capital letter because this parent is homozygous, meaning both alleles are the same.]

tt = gene combination of the short parent. [Remember this parent has the recessive trait of shortness. This parent is homozygous for shortness so, they have two lower case t's]

> **Step 2— Draw a square and divide it into 4 sections**

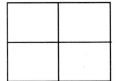

> **Step 3—** Write the letters that represent alleles from each parent along the top and side of the square. It does not matter which parent is placed at the top or along the side. Write one letter per box.

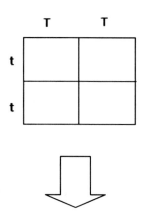

Step 4— Fill in the squares. Each square represents one offspring of the cross. Each offspring must receive one gene from each parent since we get half our genes from our mother and the other half from our father. For each empty square distribute one letter from the top and one letter from the side. Capital letters are always written first. The letters written inside the boxes represent the gene combinations of the offspring.

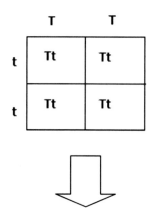

Step 5— Go back and answer the original question

The possible offspring of a cross between a homozygous tall pea plant and a short pea plant are:

    Tt (100%)   This represents the genotype of the offspring

    The phenotype of the offspring is they all are tall.

Remember, whenever a dominant trait is present it will be shown (expressed). Dominant traits are stronger than recessive ones (the lowercase letter).

Pedigrees

Another way of representing the inheritance of traits is with the use of a chart called a **_pedigree_**. A pedigree traces a gene through the family line.

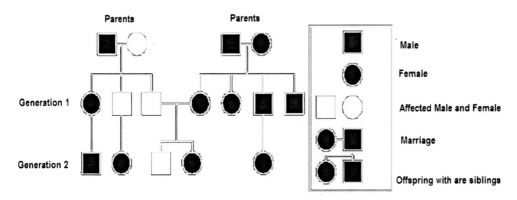

Pedigree diagram

DNA Replication

We mentioned earlier that in order for cells to reproduce during mitosis and meiosis DNA must make an exact copy of itself. This is called **_DNA replication_** and it occurs during interphase. Each new cell formed gets a complete copy of the DNA. When DNA replicates the following events happen:

1. The double stranded DNA unwinds, the two strands separate and unzip by breaking the hydrogen bonds between the nitrogenous bases.
2. Free nucleotides in the nucleus bond to their complementary bases on the DNA strand. This is all controlled by enzymes.
3. A DNA molecule is produced that is identical to the original strand.

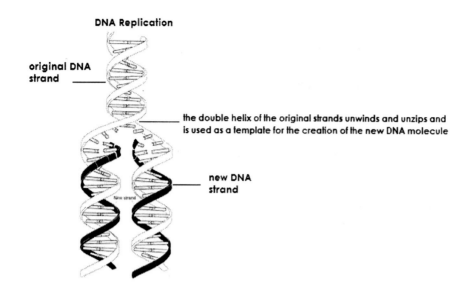

DNA Replication

original DNA strand

the double helix of the original strands unwinds and unzips and is used as a template for the creation of the new DNA molecule

new DNA strand

DNA and its Control of Cell Activities

Standards: SC.7.L.16.1

You already know that an organism's unique qualities are determined by the DNA located on its genes. Genes control proteins that control cell activities. This is how DNA controls cell activities.

Many of the proteins made in the cell are **_enzymes_** (molecules that speed up chemical reactions). For example, genes control the enzymes that determine eye color and height during fetal development. In fact, most of the differences you can see among organisms are due to their different types of proteins. Proteins also help cells to function. DNA's nucleotide sequence determines the sequence of **_amino acids_** (the building blocks of proteins) found in the enzyme and other proteins made. So, each gene is a set of instructions for making a protein.

DNA and Protein Synthesis

Standards: SC.7.L.16.1

1. The first step in making a protein is for DNA to unwind its double helix, open up and make a copy of one of its strands. This copy is called **_mRNA_** (messenger RNA) because it brings the message of DNA from the nucleus into the cytoplasm. This processes is called **_TRANSCRIPTION_** because DNA is being copied. The word

"transcribe" means to make a copy.

2. mRNA leaves the nucleus and attaches itself to a ribosome in the cytoplasm of the cell.

3. The ribosome becomes a protein assembly line. The mRNA is fed through the ribosome three bases (**_codon_**) at a time.

4. Another RNA molecule called **_tRNA_** (transfer RNA) picks up specific amino acids from the cytoplasm and brings them to the ribosome. A long string of amino acids form a protein. The amino acids become linked in a growing chain. This process is called **_TRANSLATION_** because the instructions on the original DNA strand which was copied onto the mRNA strand is interpreted; it is turned from one "language" (DNA) to another (amino acids).

Note: RNA (ribonucleic acid) is a nucleic acid similar to DNA with the exception of being single stranded, having ribose as its sugar and having uracil (U) instead of thymine (T) as one of the four bases.

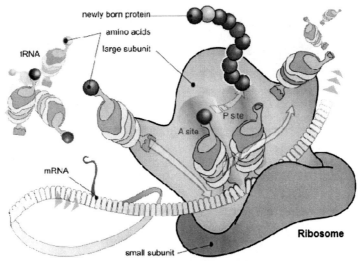

Ribsomome mRNA Translation

DNA Mutations

Changes in DNA are called **_mutations_**. This change can be in the amount and type of bases present or in their sequence on the DNA molecule (A, T, G, C). Mutations often occur due to random errors during DNA replication. They can lead to no damage to the organism, an improvement in the organism's traits, or to a harmful trait. Changes in the DNA of an organism can cause changes in traits. Some mutations are beneficial, such as seedless watermelon or pink grapefruit.

Sometimes in a mutation a nitrogen base is left out. This is called a **_deletion_**. On the other hand, if during a mutation an extra nitrogen base is added this would be called an **_insertion_**. Sometimes the wrong base is used. This is called a **_substitution_**. If a mutation occurs in the DNA of sex cells (egg and sperm), it can be inherited. Cells have proteins that can often detect and fix errors in DNA. When the mutation cannot be fixed it becomes a part of the genetic code. DNA mutations can be caused by chemicals (**_mutagens_**) or even UV rays from the Sun. Examples of mutagens include certain drugs, high doses of vitamin A, asbestos, and X-rays.

Biotechnology and its Impact on Individuals, Society and the Environment

Standards: SC.7.L.16.4

Biotechnology is the use of living organisms or other biological material (i.e., DNA) to develop new products for use in daily life. It has been used to develop new foods and medicines and other products. Other useful applications of biotechnology include environmental cleanup. Cloning, genetic engineering and artificial selection are some examples of biotechnology. Biotechnology can be applied to health care, agriculture and crop production, industrial, and environmental uses.

Biotechnology has an environmental application when bacteria are used to clean up ocean oil spills or when biodegradable plastics, that breakdown over time to lessen pollution, are created. In many third world countries genetic engineering is being used to create bigger and stronger crops and livestock to alleviate hunger and starvation.

Genetic engineering is the transfer of genes from one organism into another. Human genes that control the synthesis of insulin hormone can be inserted into bacteria. The bacteria will then be genetically engineered to produce human insulin that can be given to diabetic patients.

Biotechnology has social benefits by the use of genetic testing to detect genetic diseases in fetuses before they are born or in paternity testing to determine the identity of a child's father.

Gene therapy, which is the use of biotechnology to treat patients with genetic disorders such as cancer improves the quality of life in these patients. Genes are inserted into the cancer patient to correct defective genes and replace them with more functional ones.

PART IV DIVERSITY AND EVOLUTION OF LIVING ORGANISMS

Evolution
Standards: SC.5.L.15.1, SC.6.L.15.1, SC.7.L.15.2, SC.7.L.15.3

When some people think of **evolution** they think about apes changing into humans over time. But that is not the Theory of Evolution. The Theory of Evolution suggests that existing forms of life on Earth may have evolved from earlier forms that may have been very different in looks, structure, and behavior. The Theory of Evolution is the organizing principle of life. It is an attempt to describe the change in populations over time and not individual species.

Differences in the characteristics of organisms sometimes give individuals an advantage in surviving and reproducing. These genetic variations often give organisms favorable traits that help them to better adapt to changes in their environment. Although great diversity of living things exists on Earth, changes in the environment can threaten the survival of populations.

When environmental changes occur organisms that can adapt well to these changes are said to have favorable traits. As such, these individuals will survive and reproduce over time, thus passing down favorable traits from generation to generation. Special characteristics that help an organism survive and reproduce in its environment are called **adaptations**. Adaptations can be physical, such as fur color, or involve behaviors that give the individual an advantage in hunting, mating, or protecting itself from predators. The gills of a fish are adaptations that allow fish to breathe underwater and as such, survive in aquatic environments.

To demonstrate adaptations let's use the example of a population of leaf-eating animals (herbivores) with variations in neck length. Some individuals of the species have long necks and others have short necks. The animals with the long necks eat leaves from trees higher up. The shorter neck animals eat leaves from low-lying bushes and shrubs. If a virus infects all the bushes and shrubs in the environment the food source of the short neck animals will decrease. As a result, they will begin to compete for what little food remains. Eventually over time, with no food, the short neck animals will begin to starve and die out. Eventually, they may become **_extinct_** (when a species has died out and no longer exist on Earth). Extinction is the end of the organism. Examples of organisms that no longer exist on Earth today (are extinct) include the Dodo, the Passenger Pigeon, the Bali Tiger, the Cuban Ruta Tree, the Tasmanian Wolf, the Caspian Tiger, and the Quagga.

The inability of the short neck animals to adapt to their changing environment would result in their extinction. The long neck animals possessed a genetic variation (long necks) that enabled them to survive the virus attack on the food source. Because of this variation they were better adapted for survival in their environment. Because they survived they would be able to reproduce and pass on this favorable trait to their offspring. In time, the long neck species would have proven to be more genetically fit than the short neck animals. Long neck animals will replace the short neck variety. It can then be said that evolution occurred in this population of animals. This is known as **_natural selection_** or survival of the fittest. The environment serves as the selecting agent for survival.

The "fittest" individual is not necessarily the biggest or the strongest. They are the ones that are more adaptable to changes in their environment. Millions of years ago when a meteor hit Earth and caused the climate change which resulted in the extinction of the dinosaurs, small mammals present at that time, survived. They were able to burrow into the ground for food and protection. Although they were much smaller than the mighty dinosaurs they proved to be more fit. They survived the catastrophic event and reproduced to increase the number of species over time.

Natural Selection is a primary mechanism leading to change over time in organisms. It is a theory that was created in the 1800's by **_Charles Darwin_**, a naturalist.   For this, he is given the distinction of "Father of Evolution". His theory was based on three ideas:

1. **_overpopulation_**-- populations produce more species than can possibly survive.
2. **_competition_**-- organisms compete for food, shelter, mates, etc.
3. **survival of the fittest**-- variations among individuals in a population make some better suited for the environment.   As such, they survive to reproduce and pass on their traits.

4. The environment is the agent of natural selection, choosing which variations are advantageous and which are not. Darwin's theory could not explain why variations occurred (the study of genetic mutations had not yet begun).

A modern example of evolution that occurs in bacteria is antibiotic resistance (the ability of bacteria to resist the harmful effects of antibiotics). When exposed to antibiotics many bacteria are killed. A genetic variation in a few would allow them to not be affected by the antibiotics and to survive the treatment. They become adaptable to the drugs. These bacteria are more genetically fit and have greater adaptation abilities for survival. Due to natural selection they would reproduce and pass on the favorable trait to their offspring. In time an entire population of bacteria is produced that carries the adaptation of antibiotic resistance.

Natural selection deals with variations in genes that occur randomly by mutations or spontaneously during crossing over of meiosis. However, humans have found ways to deliberately select which traits in plants and animals are favorable, and therefore more desirable. This practice is called _**artificial selection**_ as opposed to natural selection. Humans have an impact on the genetic traits of organisms when they breed plants and animals for the inheritance of favorable traits. Deciding, for example, that red roses are more profitable than white, a gardener may breed red roses repeatedly until the population increases over white roses. Humans, as opposed to nature, now becomes the selecting agent.

Evidence for Evolution
Standards: SC.7.L.15.1

The scientific theory of evolution is supported by multiple forms of evidence. Documented evidence in support of evolution includes the _**fossil record**_, the _**geologic time scale**_, _**comparative anatomy**_, _**comparative embryology**_, _**comparative cytology**_, and _**comparative biochemistry**_. These pieces of evidence are described below;

The Fossil record

1. _**Fossils**_ are the remains or imprints of organism that no longer exist. They help people learn about living things that once existed on Earth.

2. Fossil evidence is consistent with the theory of evolution that populations change over time. By studying fossils, scientists are able to develop a picture of past organisms in order to determine the changes in plant and animal life that has occurred.

3. Scientists have made a time line known as the **_fossil record_** that organizes fossils by estimated age and physical similarities.

4. Fossils found in younger layers of sedimentary rock tend to be similar to present-day organisms.

5. Relatively intact and fully preserved prehistoric organisms have been found in ice, **_amber_** (sticky plant material) and tar.

Geologic time scale

1. The geologic time scale is a scale that divides Earth's 4.6 billion year history into distinct intervals of time. The age of Earth has been estimated based on radioactive dating of the oldest known rocks from Earth's crust.

2. **_Eon_** is the largest division of geologic time (Hadean eon, Archean eon, Proterozoic eon and Phanerozoic eon).

3. **_Era_** is the second largest division of geologic time. The Phanerozoic eon is divided into three eras.

4. After era, the next largest division of time is the **_period_**. The three eras are further divided into periods.

5. The smallest division of geologic time is the **_epoch_**. Periods are divided into epochs.

6. The appearance and disappearance of species mark the boundaries of geologic time intervals.

7. Mass extinctions cause the number of species to greatly decrease over a

relatively short period of time. This extinction could be due to such changes as ocean currents or global climate changes.

8. The beginning of the Paleozoic era ushered in a flourishing time for marine life. Halfway through this era land plants appeared. By the end of the Paleozoic era, insects, amphibians and reptiles populated the land.

9. The Mesozoic era was the famous age of the dinosaur. This era includes the Triassic, Jurassic and Cretaceous periods where dinosaurs and other reptiles inhabited the land. Small mammals were also present during this time. Birds appeared in the late Mesozoic era.

10. The Cenozoic era is the age of mammals. It is the era we currently live in.

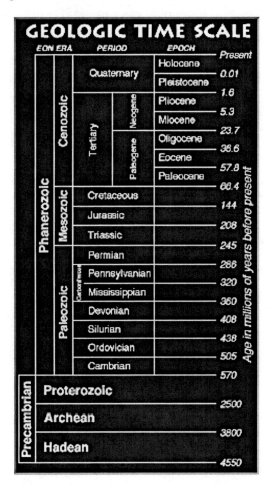

Comparative anatomy

Observations of the anatomy or structure of various body parts of organisms provide evidence of similarities between various organisms. For example, there are many similarities in structure between the flipper of a whale, the wing of a bat, the arm of a human and the forelimb of a dog. This may suggest a common ancestor.

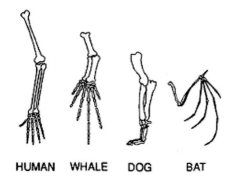

HUMAN   WHALE   DOG   BAT

Comparative embryology

Comparing the embryos of various organisms shows similarities in this early stage of development.   It is suggestive of a common ancestor.

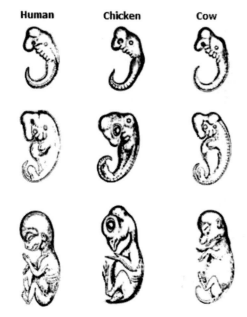

Comparison of embryological structures in human, chicken and cow

Comparative cytology

 Most living organisms have cell organelles that are functionally and structurally similar. These include ribosomes, mitochondria and the cell membrane. Comparing these cell structures in organisms can establish an evolutionary relationship.

Comparative biochemistry

All living things contain DNA and other biochemical compounds such as enzymes. The closer two organisms are the more similar their DNA and biochemistry. The more similar these compounds are the closer the evolutionary relationship between organisms.

Classification

Standards: SC.6.L.15.1

1. **_Classification_** -- the grouping of different types of organisms based upon similarities in structure and evolutionary relationships.

2. **_Taxonomy_** -- the branch of biology concerned with naming and classifying the diverse forms of life.

3. **_Carolus Linneaus_** devised **_binomial nomenclature_** (two names in Latin) consisting of using the genus and species of organisms to form their scientific name.   It is called the LInnaean system of nomenclature.

Example: scientific name of humans = Homo sapiens

Homo is the genus name   **sapiens** is the species name.

Note that scientific names have the genus name starting with a capital letter and are underlined or written in italics.

4. Taxonomic Hierarchy—groups are arranged in order from the largest, broadest group (kingdom) to the smallest, most closely related group (species).

Kingdom
     Phylum
        Class
           Order
              Family
                 Genus
                    Species

** The species is the fundamental unit of classification.

5. Organisms become more closely related and their grouping becomes smaller as you move down the taxonomic hierarchy.

6. The 6 Kingdom System is based on the following criteria:

1. Presence or absence of a nuclear membrane (cell type—simple or complex)

2. Unicellularity versus multicellularity (the # of cells in the organism)

3. Type of nutrition (organism's ability to make food)

Kingdoms of Living Things (in order from simplest to most complex)

1. Archaebacteria

-- Most primitive life form. These bacteria often live in extreme environments (thermal vents under conditions with no oxygen or highly acid environments).
-- Unicellular and no nucleus (prokaryotic)
--Examples: halophiles (live in extremely salty environments), methanogens (produce methane) and thermophiles (thrive in extremely hot environments)

2. Eubacteria

--Bacteria with primitive cell structure (prokaryotic)
--Have no organized nucleus or nuclear membrane
-- Most common type of bacteria but are classified in their own kingdom because their chemical makeup is different from archaebacteria.
--Examples: bacteria (i.e., E. coli and bacillus pneumonia) and blue green algae (cyanobacteria)

3. Protist

--Eukaryotic
--Unicellular. Consist of organisms that are animal-like or plant-like in their mode of nutrition
--Examples: ameba, slime mold, paramecium, euglena, and spirogyra (green alga)

4. Fungi
-- Eukaryotic
--Cells are usually organized into branched, multinucleate filaments which absorb digested food from the external environment (heterotrophic).

--Examples: yeasts, molds, and mushrooms

5. **Plant**

--Eukaryotic, multi-cellular

--Possess chloroplast, cell walls and are photosynthetic

--Examples: flowering plants, mosses, ferns, trees, grasses, shrubs

6. **Animal**

--Eukaryotic

-- Consist of multi-cellular organisms which ingest their food (heterotrophic)

--Examples: humans, insects, fish, reptiles, mammals, and birds

When Linnaeus developed his system of classification there were only two kingdoms, plants and animals. This two-kingdom system became obsolete with the use of microscopes. This lead to the discovery and identification of new organisms possessing distinguishing characteristics and differences.   The six-kingdom system is widely used today.

The three-domain system is a classification system devised in 1990 by Carl Woese, an American microbiologist. It is based on the six-kingdom system but divides living things into three groups; **_archae domain_** (archaebacteria), **_bacteria domain_** (eubacteria), and **_eukarya domain_** (all eukaryotes).   Woese based the placement of organisms into each domain based on cellular information, genetics and evolutionary lineage. The domains are divided into several kingdoms.

SECTION REVIEW

CHAPTER 3 SAMPLE QUESTIONS

1. Which of the following situations below would **Not** be involved in an evolutionary process that could lead to extinction of species?
   a. Tall plants out-competing short plants for sunlight
   b. Large polar bears storing fat and energy for long periods during winter months
   c. Humans hunting elephants with tusks for ivory
   d. Natural disasters and human interference

2. Biomes provide an area for several organisms to exist and to acquire the basic necessities for survival. How does the type of biome affect the type of organism that can exist in that biome?
   a. A biome is specifically designed for whatever organism exists in it.
   b. A biome is designed only for organisms that are aquatic.
   c. Only organisms that are specially adapted to survive in a particular biome can live there.
   d. Any organism can exist in any type of biome.

3. Which statement below best describes the relationship between producers, consumers and decomposers?
   a. Producers make food, decomposers eat producers, and consumers break down decomposers to release their nutrients because consumers are nature's recyclers.
   b. Consumers make food, producers eat consumers, and consumers break down decomposers to release their nutrients because consumers are nature's recyclers.
   c. Consumers make food, decomposers eat producers, and producers break down decomposers to release their nutrients because producers are nature's recyclers.
   d. Producers make food, consumers eat producers, and decomposers break down dead consumers and producers to release their nutrients because decomposers are nature's recyclers.

4. How does the Law of Conservation of Mass relate to photosynthesis and cellular respiration?
   a. The mass of the end products of photosynthesis is equal to the mass of the reactants of cellular respiration.
   b. The oxygen that is given off as a waste product of photosynthesis is utilized as a reactant in the cellular respiration reaction.
   c. The mass of products and reactants of both photosynthesis and cellular respiration in the environment remains constant over time.
   d. All of the above

5. Which of the following types of symbiosis is correctly paired with the example given?
    a. Commensalisms—The relationship between moss growing on the trunk of a tree in which the moss gets the light and nutrients they need and the tree is unaffected.
    b. Commensalisms—The relationship between a child growing up in a 3rd World Nation and the fluke worm inhabiting its stomach resulting in the malnourishment of the child.
    c. Mutualism—The relationship between remora fish and sharks in which the remora attaches itself to sharks for transportation and protection and the shark is unaffected.
    d. Parasitism -- The relationship between cows and the bacteria that lives in their stomachs that enables cows to digest complex chitin found in grass blades and the bacteria to obtain nutrients from food eaten by the cow.

6. Which of the following situations correctly identifies the environmental problem and the solutions created to resolve that environmental problem?
    a. Overuse of natural resources solved by exhaustion of them.
    b. Keeping all water faucets and light fixtures on to solve energy crisis.
    c. Overuse of trees for furniture building solved by reforestation.
    d. Use of exotic insect species to eradicate native nuisance.

7. Which situation below is most likely the result of a gene mutation?
    a. Skin cancer in a young child exposed to too much sunlight.
    b. A blister-like growth from an infection of the upper jaw of a wild pig.
    c. A polar bear shedding as it ages
    d. A human baby losing its baby teeth as it grows up

8. Which of the following examples correctly organizes organisms in an ecosystem by their level of complexity (from the least to the most complex)?
    a. House fly–ameba– human – horned frog
    b. Snap dragon plant– protist — mushroom – chimpanzee
    c. E. coli bacteria – reindeer – grasshopper– ameba
    d. Halococcus bacteria – snap dragon plant – horned Frog – human

9. Which statement below is true of both mitosis and meiosis?
    a. Mitosis results in the production of identical diploid cells, while genetic variation is the result of haploid cell production in meiosis.
    b. Mitosis results in the production of identical haploid cells, while genetic variation is the result of diploid cell production in meiosis.
    c. Meiosis results in the production of identical diploid cells, while genetic variation is the result of haploid cell production in mitosis.
    d. Meiosis results in the production of identical haploid cells, while genetic variation is the result of diploid cell production in mitosis.

10. Which of the following statements below concerning the life functions of an organism is **Not** correct?
- a. Respiration is necessary for the removal of unwanted oxygen and the supply of carbon dioxide to the body's cells.
- b. Excretion is necessary for the removal of urea and other metabolic wastes from cells and the filtration of impurities from the blood stream.
- c. Muscular contraction and relaxation are necessary for motile organisms to move so as to locate food, shelter and protect itself from prey.
- d. Reproduction is necessary for the continuation of the species in its ecosystem.

11. The statement below that demonstrates a correct match between an organ and its organ system is
- a. Motor neurons cause you to flinch as your nervous system reacts in response to your friend pretending to throw a punch at you.
- b. You develop diabetes as your pancreas, a part of your reproductive system, fails to produce enough insulin.
- c. Your cardiovascular system works hard at responding to stimuli in your surroundings through the various nerves it employs throughout your body.
- d. Your liver secretes bile that helps regulate the urinary system.

12. Given the Punnett square results below predict the genotypes of the parent organisms.

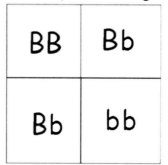

- a. Both parents are genotype **Bb**, thus they are homozygous.
- b. Both parents are genotype **Bb**, thus they are heterozygous.
- c. At least one parent is genotype **BB**, thus the parent is homozygous recessive.
- d. Both parents are genotype **bb**, thus they are heterozygous.

13. What does a pedigree chart reveal about recessive genetic disorders?
- a. Recessive genetic traits are passed on from generation to generation until descendents develop the genetic disorder, having received a recessive allele from only one parent.
- b. Recessive genetic traits are passed on from generation to generation until descendents develop the genetic disorder, having received a recessive allele from both parents.
- c. Recessive genetic traits are passed on from generation to generation until descendents develop the genetic disorder, having received a recessive allele from a spouse.
- d. Recessive genetic traits are passed on from generation to generation until descendents develop the genetic disorder, having received a recessive allele from a sibling.

14. Predict what the complimentary base pair sequence of mRNA would be for the following DNA strand.

ATGGTCTTTGATTCC

    a. TACCAGAAACCAAGG
    b. UACCAGAAACTAAGG
    c. UACCAGAAACUAAGG
    d. TACCAGAAACCAAGC

15. Which of the following statements below best identifies the similarities between various types of infectious agents?
    a. Viruses, parasites, bacteria, and fungi need a host to survive and reproduce.
    b. Viruses, parasites, bacteria, and fungi are capable of surviving outside of the hosts' body.
    c. Viruses and parasites need a host to survive, while bacteria and fungi are capable of surviving without a host.
    d. Bacteria and viruses need a host to survive, while fungi and parasites are capable of surviving without a host.

16. If Tashi were to find the complete bone set of a limb belonging to an unidentified organism how could comparative anatomy help her to determine the origins of the organism?
    a. Comparative anatomy would allow Suzy to classify the organism based on similar structures in the biochemistry of another organism.
    b. Comparative anatomy would allow Suzy to classify the organism based on similar body structures of another organism.
    c. Comparative anatomy would allow Suzy to establish evolutionary relationships between organisms.
    d. Choices (b) and (c) only
    e. Choices (a) (b) and (c)

17. The flower is the reproductive structure of angiosperms (flowering plants). It consists of various male and female parts that allow sexual reproduction to occur in the plant. Which statement correctly explains the relationship between the flower's parts and its function?
    a. The anther sends the carpel to the stigma of another flower for self-pollination.
    b. The stigma of the flower receives pollen from an anther on the same flower during cross-pollination.
    c. The anther produces pollen which is transferred to the stigma on the same flower during self-pollination.
    d. Pollinators must be stationary insects that transport the pollen knowingly.

18. Knowledge of organelles is necessary when trying to understand the overall function of the cells. Which of the following situations would cause a cell to become dysfunctional?
    a. Mitochondria not producing energy
    b. Nucleus compromised by viral infection
    c. Ribosmes not producing proteins
    d. All of the above

19. What benefit does the Linnaean system of taxonomy provide for classifying organisms?
   a. Organisms are classified scientifically, which avoids the problem of regional classification.
   b. Organisms are classified regionally, which allows for flexibility in identifying organisms.
   c. Organisms are specifically identified by their genotypes, which makes them unique.
   d. Organisms cannot be identified by the Linnaean system since it uses uninominal nomenclature.

20. Which organism is correctly matched to the correct kingdom based on the 6 Kingdom System of taxonomy?
   a) Animal Kingdom – Bacteria
   b) Archaebacteria kingdom – Salt tolerant bacteria
   c) Fungi kingdom – reptiles
   d) Plant kingdom – domestic felines (house cats)

21. The Cell Theory is a major theory that governs the classification of living organisms. It is a fundamental organizing principle of life on Earth. Which of the following statements is supported by the Cell Theory?
   a. Only certain living things are composed of cells.
   b. The cell is the basic unit of life.
   c. The Cell Theory is an accepted theory that is absolute—there are no exceptions.
   d. Viruses can be classified as living things because they can reproduce outside the host organism.

22. Biotechnology is the use of living organisms or other biological material (i.e., DNA) to develop new products for use in daily life. It has been used to develop new foods and medicines and other products. Which of the following are current technologies that employ the idea of biotechnology?
   a. Nintendo Wii system for gaming and interactive play via the Wii remote controller.
   b. Cochlear implants designed to interact with the human brain to produce hearing in deaf individuals.
   c. Nose hair trimmer that contours to the inner curves of a person's nostrils.
   d. Push button start for a new vehicle that has just been released for consumer purchase.

CHAPTER 4   EARTH AND SPACE SCIENCE

This section of the FCAT explores very interesting issues about Earth and space. Because humans love to explore new territories our knowledge of Earth and the universe has expanded greatly. We are beginning to understand more how they work, their history, and how to apply this knowledge toward the creation of technologies that benefit mankind.

PART 1   EARTH IN SPACE AND TIME

Human Space Exploration

Standards: SC.5.E.5.1, SC.8.E.5.2

For millions of years humankind has gazed at the stars and the heavens and wondered about their origins. They have pondered the existence of other life forms and mysterious planetary bodies in space.   Man's need to explore has opened up windows of opportunities for the development of knowledge and understanding of our Solar System and the universe.

Scientists believe the universe began with a tremendous explosion of matter, bright lights, and intense energy. They call this theory the ***Big Bang Theory***. As with all scientific theories, the Big Bang Theory must be tested with observations and experiments. The desire for answers brought on the science of astronomy dating back to ancient times. Astronomy allowed scientists to observe objects in space using the naked eye and eventually telescopes. Ultimately, with the development of the first rocket in the early part of the 20th century, man was finally able to physically explore space.

Man's desire to explore space helped to advance scientific research and further the development of knowledge about the ***universe***, ***galaxies***, and the ***Solar System***. If we were to arrange these in size order we would see a hierarchy of increasing size. First we find that the Sun and its orbiting planets form our solar system. The Solar System is found within our galaxy, the **_Milky Way_**. The Milky Way is one of billions of galaxies within the universe. Scientists believe that the universe is expanding (becoming wider) causing galaxies to move further and further apart.

While we may never have the ability to travel to the Sun, our closest star, we have gleaned so much information about it from space travel and scientific investigations. Furthermore, space travel is also used as a tool for understanding properties and processes of Earth. The discovery of the hole in the ozone was detected and visualized via artificial satellite in space. These and many more benefits make exploring space extremely vital in obtaining data that can be further utilized for the betterment of humankind.

Technology and Space Exploration

Standards: SC.8.E.5.10

Technology is essential in science. A fact that is especially true in the arena of space exploration. Technology is responsible for unimaginable access to space once only possible in science fiction movies. Technology permits special satellites and cameras to take pictures of distant objects in space.

One of the earliest forms of technology in space exploration was the telescope. Telescopes extend human vision tremendously. Its invention in the 17th century was responsible for the discovery of many of the planets and their moons which could not be seen from Earth. Included on the list were the planets Uranus, Neptune, and their moons.   These early telescopes were limited in that they could only see visible light. Space dust prevented many planets from being seen.

The 20th century brought great advancements in telescope technology. Large optical, radio, infrared, and X-ray telescopes allowed astronomers to see beyond space dust and far into space. Furthermore, the invention of rockets, space shuttles, space probes, space stations and the like have allowed for communication of information, data collection and storage, measurements, sample collection, and computation involving space.

Technology, such as the Mars Rover allowed scientists to remotely collect data on Mars in unmanned robotic operations. Rovers can record thermal readings, collect soil and water samples with their robotic arms, take color images of landscapes and can use their sensors to gather information to send back to Earth. Various information gathering missions to Mars were accomplished by such spacecrafts as the *Mars 2* (1971), the *Mars Pathfinder (1997)*, and the *Mars Odyssey (2001)*.

The Hubble Telescope was valuable in discovering other universes and in determining what our universe actually looks like. Satellite imagery has been one of the single most technological and scientific advancements in piecing together the puzzle of the universe. Satellite-borne cameras have even helped scientists learn more about Earth's environment (atmosphere, water, living organisms, etc).

The Effects of Space Exploration on the Economy and Culture of Florida

Standards: SC.8.E.5.12

As 2011 brings an end to NASA's space program, Florida has been a state that has particularly benefited from space exploration. The U.S. space program has changed the economy and culture of Florida in positive ways. It has done this by creating jobs in aerospace and non-aerospace industries. The corporate and personal income taxes raised has lead to economic growth in the state.

Tourism in Florida increased as a result of the building of the Kennedy Space Center (the launch site for NASA space flights) in the 1960's. This not only generated great revenues from the millions of visitors worldwide, it also caused many people from European, Asian, and South American countries (just to name a few) to relocate to the state bringing their distinctive cultures with them.

Space technology has led to advancements in computers such as Internet access, virtual reality, and software development. It has also led to improvements in health and medicine such as better digital imaging diagnostic equipment. Examples of other inventions developed from NASA technology includes scratch-resistant glasses, enriched baby food, Global Positioning System (GPS), water purification systems, portable coolers/warmers, athletic shoes, weather forecasting aids, solar cells, voice-operated wheelchairs, and fire resistant materials. Many technology tools specifically created for space exploration was adapted for usage in every day mainstream life. These include the personal computer, telescopes, and satellites.

The Measurement of Distance in Space

Standards: SC.8.E.5.1

On Earth we measure distances directly. We use metric terms such as centimeters, meters or kilometers or English units such as inches, yards, or miles. Measuring distances in space is altogether different. The distances between objects in space are **ENORMOUS**. In fact the distances are generally much larger than the objects themselves. Our knowledge of light and space travel helps us to comprehend this expansive distance. Some of the terms are listed in **Table 4-1** on the following page.

Distances of astronomical objects located near Earth, such as the Moon and the Sun, can be measured using scientific knowledge. Once again, using properties of light and knowledge of space travel we can measure these distances accurately. For example, we know the distance of Earth to the Moon roughly ranges from 357,000 km to 407,000 km. This distance can be measured by using light pulses. Since we know how fast light travels we can send a light pulse to the Moon and measure how long it takes to get there and back. Knowing that light travels 300,000 km/s or 186,000 miles/s we can multiply the time it takes the light pulse to travel to the Moon by the speed of light. This will tell you how far away the Moon is.

Table 4-1 Astronomical Units of Measurements

Unit of Measurement	Description
Astronomical unit	The **astronomical unit (AU)** is a basic unit of distance used by astronomers. It is the average distance from the Earth to the Sun and is about 93-million miles (150-million km).
light-year	A **light-year** is a way of measuring the gigantic, unimaginable distances of celestial objects in space. It is based on the speed light travels, which is 300,000 km/sec. In one second light can travel 300,000 km (186,000 miles). A light-year is 5,865,696,000,000 miles/year (9,460,800,000,000 km/year). Better yet, a galaxy that is a million light-years away would be 1 million times this number. That's a long distance! Measuring these distances in miles would be ridiculous. It would be like trying to measure the distance from Miami to California in inches. It is therefore easier to speak in terms of light-years than in miles or other metric units. For example, it would take a space shuttle traveling 18,000 mph 37,200 years to go one light-year.
light-minute	A **light minute** is the distance light travels in a minute (18,000,000 km). **Sunlight takes 8.3 minutes to reach Earth. Therefore, the distance from the Sun to Earth is 8.3 light minutes (150 million kilometers or 93 million miles).**
angstrom	**In contrast to astronomically large units of distance such as the light-year the angstrom is an extremely small unit of length.** Astronomers use the angstrom (Å) to express electromagnetic radiation wavelengths. 10,000,000 angstroms is about the width of a paperclip. When used to express the wavelength of visible light we get ranges from about 4,000 angstroms (violet light) to about 7,600 angstroms (red light). One angstrom is equal to one hundred-millionth (0.00000001) of a centimeter, which is about four billionths (0.000000004) of an inch. The nanometer, a SI unit equal to 10 angstroms, is often used instead of the Angstrom. Angstroms are also used to express the size of an atom and the length of a chemical bond. For example, the size of an atom is three to 10 angstroms.

Our Galaxy—the Milky Way

Standards: SC.5.E.5.1, SC.8.E.5.2, SC.8.E.5.4

The universe contains billions of galaxies. Likewise, each galaxy contains billions of stars. A **_galaxy_** is a large system of stars, objects orbiting those stars, gas, and dust held together by gravity. Each galaxy is isolated from similar systems by regions of space. Science has much knowledge yet to be gained from the study of the universe. We are still not 100% certain of the origins of neither the universe nor its eventual fate.

Our galaxy is called the **_Milky Way_**. As incomprehensibly vast as our galaxy is it is only a small speck in the universe. In fact, it is only one in billions of galaxies that exist in the universe. The Milky Way is average sized compared to other discovered galaxies. It is a spiral-shaped galaxy with more than 200 billion stars. It is approximately 100,000 light years in diameter. The Sun is located about 28,000 light years from its center.

A Light-year is not only a measure of distance but of age. A star that is 1 million light-years away is visible to us on Earth only because its light was created and traveled a million years to reach Earth. When we look at this star we would be looking at the past-- how the star looked one million years ago and not how the star currently looks. This is also true of distant galaxies. Astronomers look at distant galaxies to get an idea of what early galaxies may have looked like and how they formed.

The Three Types of Galaxies

Standards: SC.5.E.5.1

There are three main types of galaxies: **_spiral_**, **_elliptical_** and **_irregular_**. Although different in shape and function many galaxies appear to have similarities. They are made up of the same chemical elements and are governed by the same physical laws. In addition, they possess the same forces and forms of energy.

Table 4-2 Types of Galaxies

Type of Galaxy	Description	Illustration
spiral galaxy	The most common type. They look like spirals with a bright bulge in the center and spiral arms. The center bulge is made up of old, red stars. The spiral arms are made up of dust and gas and are areas of new star formation. The Milky Way is a spiral galaxy.	Spiral Galaxy

elliptical galaxy	Also named for its elliptical shape. Is made up of very little gas and dust. Little star formation occurs here. They usually have a bright center and are made up mostly of old, red stars.	Elliptical Galaxy
irregular galaxy	Have irregular shapes. They are usually found in groups or clusters and may be the result of galaxy collisions.	Irregular Galaxy

The Law of Universal Gravitation and the Formation of the Solar System

Standards: SC.5.E.5.3,   SC.8.E.5.3,   SC.8.E.5.4

The Solar System is made up of all the **planets**, **moons**, **asteroids**, **meteors**, **comets**, gas and dust that revolves around (orbits) the Sun.   Everything in the Solar System orbits the Sun due to its large pull of gravity.   Isaac Newton's **Law of Universal Gravitation** helps to explain the role gravity plays in the formation of planets, stars, and solar systems.   It states that objects exerts a force of attraction on other objects that is directly influenced by the size of their masses and decreases as their distance from one another increases.   In other words, massive objects that are close together will exert a greater attraction for each other than objects of less mass or objects that are not close to each other.

Newton's law extends gravity beyond Earth.   Gravity is universal.   All masses exert a gravitational attraction to other objects.   Even in space.   When the Law of Universal Gravitation is applied to the solar system it explains why planets and other solar bodies orbit the Sun.   The entire solar system (planets, moons, etc.) was formed from a giant gas cloud that collapsed under the weight of its own gravity.   The Sun is even made of the same dust and gas as the universe. Gravity then pulls the gas and dust into a ball forming the celestial bodies.   Because the Sun has such a large mass it pulls everything towards it with its strong gravitational force.   The planets of our Solar System also have a large mass (less massive than the Sun however) and are located relatively close to the Sun.   Due to these two factors they form a strong attraction to the Sun's force of gravity.   They stay in orbit around the Sun even as they try to pull away.   They are however kept in place by this strong force.

Hierarchical Relationships Between Planets and Other Astronomical Bodies in Space

Standards: SC.8.E.5.3

Astronomers classify anything that orbits the Sun as a planet, dwarf planet, or small solar system body. A hierarchical relationship exists between all solar system bodies in terms of distance, size and composition. This relationship is demonstrated in **Table 4-3**. Solar system bodies are arranged in decreasing size order.

Table 4-3 Solar System Bodies

Solar System Body	Description
planet	A **planet** is a large, celestial body that orbits a star and shines by reflected light. The planets of our Solar System orbit the Sun. Because of its great mass it gets compacted into a round shape by its own gravitational pull. Planets are made up of rock or gas (more on this later in the chapter).
moon	A **moon** is a natural satellite of a planet. Moons are always smaller than the planet that they orbit. It orbits the planet because it has less gravity. Although moons are smaller than the planets they orbit some moons of our Solar System are larger than other planets. For example, Jupiter's moon Ganymede is larger than both Mercury and Pluto. Moons are made of rock, metals, and minerals.
asteroids	**Asteroids** are small, rocky bodies with irregular shapes that mainly orbit the Sun in the asteroid belt (in between the orbits of Mars and Jupiter). Some asteroids are found too far out into space to be studied. Asteroids are made of mineral, rock, and other substances.
comet	**Comets**, also referred to as "dirty snowballs", are made of ice (water, ammonia, methane, and carbon dioxide), dust, a rocky center (some types), and some type of organic material; probably left over since the time the planets formed. Comets orbit the Sun. However, when they orbit too close to the Sun the ice component melts and it develops a tail of gas and dust that always points away from the Sun.
meteoroids	**Meteoroids** are small, rocky bodies that orbit the Sun. It is called a **meteorite** when it falls to Earth and hits the ground. Most meteoroids burn up as they enter Earth's atmosphere. The light energy that is given off when this happens is called a **meteor**. Scientists collect meteorites and use them to study the early solar system. The composition of meteorites appears to be similar to that of many of the terrestrial planets.

Historical Models of the Solar System

Standards: SC.8.E.5.8

The Sun is the center of our solar system. This fact was not always known. Prior to the 1500's the **_geocentric_** model (theory) was used to explain the Solar System. The geocentric model (geo = earth, centric= center of) stated that Earth was the center of the universe and had different properties than the other bodies in space. Scientists had not accepted the idea of a "solar system" when this model was created. They believed the Earth was stationary while the Sun revolved around it. We know today that this model is not correct. This is an example of how scientific knowledge is modified as new information becomes available. The geocentric model wasn't completely discarded simply because it was proven untrue. It was used for further investigations and to seek out other theories.

The **_heliocentric_** model (*helio* = sun,   *centric* = center of) correctly describes the Sun as the center of the Solar System. Earth and the other planets and moons revolve around the Sun. **_Copernicus_**, the astronomer, developed this heliocentric model in 1543 based on mathematical calculations. Now we know that the Earth orbits the Sun and the Moon orbits the Earth as it orbits the Sun.

Properties of the Sun

Standards: SC.8.E.5.6

The Sun is a mass of hot, burning gases that are on fire.   It is made of plasma (extremely hot, high energy ionized gasses) that produces very high temperatures.   The Sun produces energy as a result of nuclear fusion (hydrogen atoms collide to form a helium nucleus and a lot of energy). It has a core temperature of 15,000,000°C and is 150,000,000 kilometers from Earth. The Sun is 333,000 times the mass of the Earth.   It makes up 99% of the mass of the entire Solar System.

Although the Sun can be described as a big ball of hot gas it can be divided into distinct layers. Like the Earth, the Sun has layers that describe its structure.   The external structure includes:

1. **_photosphere_** -- the visible surface of the Sun (the part of the Sun we actually see).
2. **_chromosphere_**-- located above the photosphere. 2500 km in thickness. Visible during a total

eclipse of the Sun.

3. **_corona_**-- region outside of the chromosphere.   Visible during a total eclipse of the Sun.

The internal structure includes:

1. **_core_**-- the innermost layer of the Sun and the source of its energy.

2. **_radiative zone_**--the outer layer of the Sun next to the core. Thermal energy from the Sun is transferred outward from the core to other parts of the Sun through the process of radiation that occurs in this zone.

3. **_convection zone_**-- The Sun's gases are not hot or dense enough to transfer energy from the core to all parts of the Sun via radiation. In the convection zone, thermal energy is carried from the radiation zone to the surface of the Sun (photosphere) by convection currents. Cooler gases sink to the base of the convection zone and are warmed by heat at the top of the radiative zone. These gases rise to the photosphere and the currents continue.

The density and temperature of the Sun changes drastically as you travel from the innermost regions to the outer layers. Density decreases from the core to the surface but temperature changes variably. Temperature is about 15 million degrees Kelvin at the core and then drops to about 6000 degrees at the photosphere. It then increases to more than 2 million degrees in the corona.

Characteristics of the Sun include **_solar winds_**, **_sun spots_**, **_solar flares_**, and **_prominences_**.

1. **_solar winds_**-- charged particles ejected from the Sun.

2. **_sunspots_**-- dark, planet-sized regions on the surface of the Sun caused by magnetic fields. They appear dark because they are cooler (1800 degrees cooler) than the area around it. Magnetic fields give gas particles extra energy that causes them to shoot out away from the Sun's surface. These particles rise and cool in massive gas clouds called sunspots.

3. **_solar flares_**-- a large, sudden explosion in the Sun's atmosphere that releases a great amount of energy. These increases in brightness occur near sunspots and produce electromagnetic radiation at all wavelengths.

4. **_prominences_**-- great surges of hot gas that rise hundreds of thousands of miles from the Sun's surface. Often loop shaped and very bright, prominences last a day to several months. They consist of cooler plasma.

Solar disturbances (i.e., sunspots,) generate enormous electric currents that disrupt communication on Earth and damage equipment. Streams of electrons and protons from the Sun also become trapped in our magnetic field and cause the beautiful auroras at the North and South Poles.

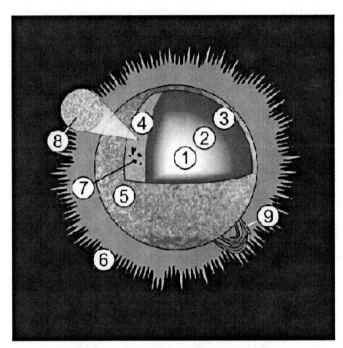

1. Core
2. Radiative zone
3. Convective zone
4. Photosphere
5. Chromosphere
6. Corona
7. Sunspot
8. Granules
9. Prominence

An illustration of the structure of the Sun

Source: Author, Ryan Wilson

Like the planets that revolve around it, the Sun also exhibits motion. The Sun and the other stars in the galaxy revolve once about every 225 million years around the Milky Way. Like other celestial bodies, the Sun also rotates on its axis. Unlike Earth, which is a solid mass, the Sun is entirely made of gasses. Because of this, different parts of the Sun rotate at different rates. The surface regions near the Sun's equator rotate once every 25.6 Earth days. This can be measured by observing the position of sunspots. The rotation decreases with increasing latitude towards the Sun's poles. Here rotation occurs once every 33.5 Earth days. There is variation in the rate that the inner regions of the Sun rotate.

Convection currents in the interior of the Sun also play a role in its motion. Energy from the core spread towards the surface by radiation. At the surface convection occurs. Here, complex swirling motions bring currents of hot, charged plasma originating deep from within the Sun's core to the outer layers of the Sun. These currents strongly influence the Sun's magnetic field. It takes several thousand years to transport heat from the core to the surface of the Sun.

The Electromagnetic Spectrum

Standards: SC.8.E.5.11

Electromagnetic radiation is a form of energy that travels through space in waves. The Sun produces electromagnetic radiation at all wavelengths, from the shortest (gamma rays) to the longest (radio waves) and everything in between (see the diagram on the next page). Electromagnetic waves are transverse waves. They include **_microwaves_**, **_infrared waves_**, **_ultraviolet light_**, **_visible light_**, **_X rays_**, and **_gamma rays_**. All the different waves make up the electromagnetic spectrum.

Different types of radiation originate from different parts of the Sun. The properties of these waves depend on their wavelengths. Study the diagram of the electromagnetic spectrum located on the next page. The diagram illustrates how these waves differ by wavelength. On the chart, wavelength decreases from left (gamma rays) to right (infrared rays). Visible light can be found in the middle of the spectrum. Most visible white light occurs in the photosphere.

In terms of visible light, violet light has the shortest wavelength and red light the longest. Shorter wavelength X rays and UV radiation emitted by solar flares can interfere with radar and other equipment operating under radio wave frequencies. Short wavelength ultraviolet radiation is mostly filtered out by the Earth's ozone layer. Most electromagnetic radiation, except visible light, is blocked by Earth's atmosphere. Measurement of UV radiation can be used to map holes in the ozone layer.

Microwaves are used on Earth to monitor melting of the polar ice caps due to global warming. Longer wavelength infrared (thermal) radiation is invisible to the human eye and is mostly blocked by water vapor in the Earth's atmosphere. Measurement of infrared radiation is used to obtain temperature data of land, ocean surfaces, and clouds. Because electromagnetic waves do not need a medium they can travel through space. Radio waves are used to detect pulsars in space (pulsars emit radio waves).

The electromagnetic spectrum is of particular use in studying hot bodies in space since these objects are the source of short wavelength radiation (UV, X rays, gamma rays, etc). Satellite images use electromagnetic radiation to detect temperature, motion, magnetism and chemical composition of space bodies. Gamma ray telescopes in space give evidence of the creation of the universe. When stars explode into supernovas they emit gamma radiation. Gamma radiation is very lethal (deadly).

Observing wavelength shifts provides information about the direction of travel of objects in space. Whenever an object seems to be traveling away from an observer the light appears to shift to the red portion of the spectrum (red shift). Scientists believe the universe is expanding outward because when observed there appears to be a red shift. When light-emitting objects in space are moving towards an observer there is a shift in the visible light spectrum towards the blue portion (blue shift).

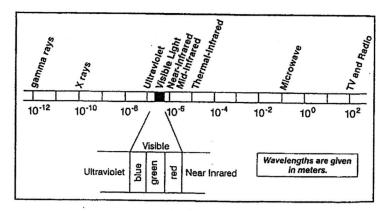

Wavelengths of Electromagnetic Radiation

The Sun and Moon's Impact on Earth

Standards: SC.8.E.5.9

The impact of the Sun on the Earth

The Sun is a massive object which exerts such a strong gravitational force on Earth that it keeps it in orbit around it. Earth greatly benefits from its relationship with the Sun. The Sun provides great amounts of thermal energy to Earth. This energy supports life and creates a stable environment on Earth. The Sun makes photosynthesis possible and drives weather and climate.

Earth's relationship with the Sun influences time, seasons and tides (the Moon is also involved with tides). Time is determined by the rotation or spinning of Earth on its axis (the imaginary line around which the Earth rotates) and the movement of the Earth around the Sun (revolution). Earth makes one complete turn on its axis in 24 hours. This is called a **_day_**. On Earth 1 day = 24 hours. The portion of Earth that is facing the Sun experiences daylight. The portion that is facing away from the Sun experiences night time. Earth takes 365 ¼ days to travel around the Sun. This is called a **year**. So, one Earth year = 365 ¼ days.

The fact of Earth revolving around the Sun creates the four seasons. Seasons are also caused by the 23.5 degree tilt of the Earth on its axis as it revolves around the Sun. You can see this in the diagram below. This tilt causes the northern hemisphere (upper half of Earth) and southern hemisphere (lower half of Earth) to receive different amounts of the Sun's energy at different times. The result is variations in seasons and length of days.

The energy of the Sun hits the southern hemisphere most directly. This produces warmer climates and longer days. In the winter the northern hemisphere is tilted away from the Sun and receives less of the Sun's energy. This produces cooler climates and shorter days.   During the times when the northern hemisphere is tilted toward the Sun, it receives more direct sunlight and experiences warmer climates.

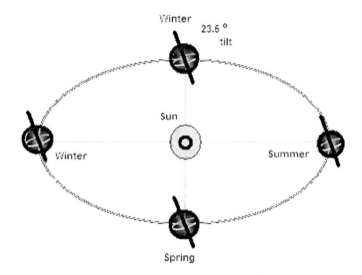

Diagram of Earth's seasons and its tilt on its axis

The Impact of the Moon on the Earth

The Moon's relationship with the Earth influences ocean tides, moon phases, and eclipses. As Earth revolves around the Sun, the Moon likewise revolves around the Earth. The massiveness of Earth creates a strong gravitational pull that keeps the Moon in orbit around it in just the same way as the gravity of the Sun keeps the Earth in orbit around it. The gravity of the Sun keeps both the Earth and Moon in their orbits.

**Tides** are the rise and fall of sea levels, with respect to the land. They are due to gravitational forces (attraction) of the Sun and Moon and the rotation of the Earth. Like a magnet, the Moon is attracted to the Earth and pulls at its water. This gravitational pull causes the oceans to bulge out in the direction of the Moon. On the opposite side the ocean also bulges as the Earth is being pulled towards the moon. Every day there are two high tides and two low tides. The interaction of the Sun, Earth and Moon causes fluctuations (changes) in ocean levels daily. The combined gravitational forces exerted as the Moon travels around the Earth and as they together travel around the Sun causes sea levels to rise and fall daily.   The various types of tides are shown in **Table 4-4**.

Table 4-4 Types of Tides

Type of Tide	Description
spring tides	The gravity of the sun and moon work together to create very high, high tides and low, low tides. These are _**spring tides**_. They occur at or soon after a full or new moon. Spring tides have nothing to do with the season spring. They occur when the Earth, Sun and Moon are aligned (are in line).
neap tides	_**Neap tides**_ occur when the gravity of the sun and moon pull against each other (tide is low). These are weak tides.

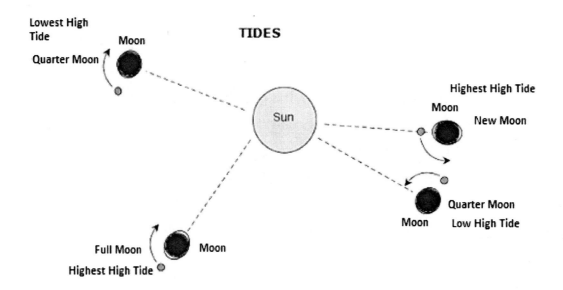

TIDES

**Moon phases** are another effect of the relationship between the Moon and Earth. The revolution of the Moon around the Earth makes the Moon appear to viewers on Earth to be changing shape in the sky. These are called moon phases. They depend on the position of the Moon in relation to the Sun and Earth as it revolves around the Earth. We see the bright parts of the Moon at different angles as it revolves around Earth. The bright part of the Moon appears to shrink from a full disk (full moon) to a thin banana shaped crescent then grow back into a full disk again (sometimes disappearing altogether). Keep in mind that neither the Moon nor any planet emit light. They just reflect light given off by the Sun. So, moon phases are caused by the shadow of the moon as it reflects sunlight. The part of the Moon facing the Sun is lit up while the part facing away from the Sun always looks dark.

Moon phases occur monthly (lunar month = 29.5 Earth days). All eight phases can be easily observed by daily observation of the night sky. It is interesting that we never see the "dark side" of the Moon. On Earth we see only one side due to its rotation on its axis and its revolution around Earth. It takes the Moon the same amount of time to rotate on its axis as it does to revolve around the Earth (29.5 days). Since the moon rotates on its axis at the same rate it takes it to revolve around the Earth we always see the same side of the Moon. If the Moon had a faster rotation we would be able to see the dark side of the Moon as well.

Moon Phases

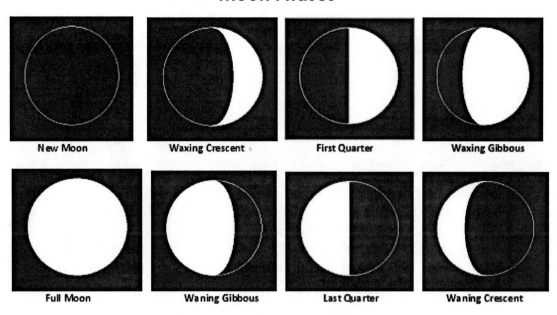

Table 4-5 The Phases of the Moon in Order

Phase	Description
1. new moon	We can't see the moon at all (except during a solar eclipse). The Moon's unilluminated side is facing the Earth.
2. waxing crescent	The Moon appears to be partly but less than one-half illuminated by direct sunlight. The fraction of the Moon's disk that is illuminated is increasing.
3. first quarter	We see first half of the moon. One-half of the Moon appears to be illuminated by direct sunlight. The fraction of the Moon's disk that is illuminated is increasing.
4. waxing gibbous	The Moon appears to be more than one-half but not fully illuminated by direct sunlight. The fraction of the Moon's disk that is illuminated is increasing.
5. full moon	We see a fully round moon. The Moon's illuminated side is facing the Earth. The Moon appears to be completely illuminated by direct sunlight.
6. waning gibbous	The Moon appears to be more than one-half but not fully illuminated by direct sunlight. The fraction of the Moon's disk that is illuminated is decreasing.
7. last quarter	We see the last half of the moon. One-half of the Moon appears to be illuminated by direct sunlight. The fraction of the Moon's disk that is illuminated is decreasing.
8. waning crescent	The Moon appears to be partly but less than one-half illuminated by direct sunlight. The fraction of the Moon's disk that is illuminated is decreasing.

Note: waxing = expanding,   waning = decreasing, crescent = less than half, gibbous = more than half

In addition to moon phases we also experience ___eclipses___ of the Sun and Moon from Earth.

These are due to the relative positioning of each in respect to one another. Eclipses occur when the Earth or Moon blocks light from the Sun and causes a shadow. It is important to note that in terms of distance, the Moon is positioned closer to Earth than is the Sun. However, they are all relatively close to one another. Two types of eclipses are solar eclipses and lunar eclipses.

Table 4-6 Types of Eclipses

Type of Eclipse	Description
solar eclipse	A **_solar eclipse_** happens when the moon passes between the Earth and the Sun. Sunlight is blocked by the moon. A shadow of the moon is cast on the Earth's surface. Solar eclipses are dangerous if you look into one. They can cause blindness.
lunar eclipse	A **_lunar eclipse_** happens when the Earth is between the Sun and Moon. The Earth throws a dark shadow across the moon. Lunar eclipses are safe to look at.

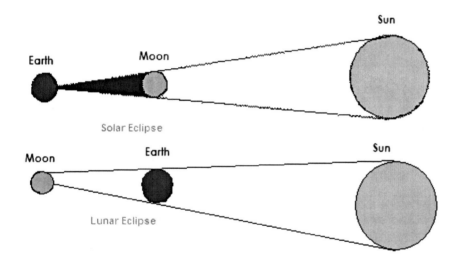

The Planets of Our Solar System

Standards: SC.5.E.5.2, SC.8.E.5.7

Until very recently there were nine planets in our solar system. In the order in which they orbit the sun, the nine planets were _Mercury_, _Venus_, _Earth_ (3rd rock from the Sun), _Mars_, _Jupiter_, _Saturn_, _Uranus_, _Neptune_ and _Pluto_. Pluto however, is no longer considered a planet. This is because Pluto crosses the orbit of Neptune. A main requirement for planetary status is that the planet must have its own orbit. They cannot cross the orbit of another planet. Because Pluto crosses Neptune's orbit it is no longer classified as a planet. Pluto is now only considered a _dwarf planet_. Dwarf planets orbit the Sun as the other planets do. However, they are considered larger than satellites (moons) but smaller than planets. Even so, Pluto is still the focus of several space exploration missions. We now say there are 8 known planets, a few dwarf planet s and their natural satellites (moons).

All planets share the following common characteristics:
1. They all orbit the Sun (the enormous gravitational pull of the Sun keeps all the planets of the Solar System in their orbits).
2. They are all smaller than the Sun.
3. They all rotate on their axis.
4. They all have day and night.
5. They all have seasons.
6. They all have a north and south pole.
7. Most have moons (except Mercury and Venus).

The planets are divided into **_inner_** and **_outer_** planets:

1. The **_inner planets_** are Mercury, Venus, Earth, and Mars. These are all made of rock material. For this, they are known as terrestrial planets. They are the closest planets to the Sun.

2. The **_outer planets_** are Jupiter, Saturn, Uranus, Neptune and Pluto (dwarf planet). These are called gas planets because they all are made mostly of gases. Jupiter, Saturn, Uranus, and Neptune are much larger than the terrestrial planets and are referred to as gas giants. The outer planets are farthest from the Sun. All of the gas giants have rings around them.

Data from various satellite probes show similarities and differences amongst planets and their moons in our solar system. Space shuttles positioned above Earth reports data on the atmosphere, land and life on Earth. This data reveals that conditions on other planets in the Solar System are different than those on Earth. Differences include such aspects as the amount of gravity, temperature, atmosphere, the presence of water, etc.

On the FCAT you may be asked to compare and contrast characteristics of solar system bodies such as period of rotation (length of time it takes to make a complete rotation or spin on its axis), period of revolution (the length of time it takes to completely revolve or orbit the Sun one time), gravitational force, distance from the Sun, speed, movement, temperature, and atmospheric conditions. **Table 4-7** below compares and contrasts these characteristics for you.

Table 4-7 Comparison of Solar System Bodies with Earth

THE SUN AND PLANETS OF OUR SOLAR SYSTEM AS COMPARED TO EARTH					
Name	Classification	Distance from Sun	Surface Temp	Physical Properties	Distinguishing Features
Sun	Main sequence star	-----	5,500 °C	Equatorial radius = 695,500 km Composed of varying layers of gases.	More massive than Earth with greater gravity. Temperature at core exceeds 14 million °C
Mercury	Inner planet Terrestrial (rocky) planet	3.2 light-minutes (nearest planet to Sun)	-173°C to 427 °C	Solid and covered with craters. Almost no atmosphere. Has a greater density than Earth (higher density metals make up Mercury). Diameter = 4,879 km	Smaller and less massive than Earth. Less gravity (38% less). Slower period of rotation (1 day on Mercury = 59 days on Earth). Shorter period of revolution (1year on Mercury= 88 days on Earth). 2nd smallest planet in the Solar System. No moons. Avg. orbital speed = 47.87 km/s
Venus	Inner planet Terrestrial (rocky) planet	6.0 light-minutes	464 °C	Rocky and very hot. Has the densest and hottest atmosphere of all the planets in the Solar System. The atmosphere completely hides the surface and traps the heat. Composed of carbon dioxide and nitrogen. Diameter= 12,104 km	Earth's "twin" because share some similarities. Sixth largest planet. Slightly smaller, massive and less dense than Earth. Slightly less gravity than Earth (91% of Earth's). Slower period of rotation (1 day on Venus = 243 days on Earth). Shorter period of revolution (1 year on Venus = 224 days on Earth). No moons. Avg. orbital speed = 35.02 km/s
Earth	Inner planet Terrestrial (rocky) planet	8.3 light-minutes	-13°C to 37 °C	Liquid covers 71% of the Earth's surface. The atmosphere is composed of oxygen and nitrogen. Diameter=12,756 km	Only planet known to support life. Fifth largest planet and the third from the sun. 1 moon. Period of rotation = 24 hours. Period of revolution = 365 ¼ days. Avg. orbital speed = 29.78 km/s
Mars	Inner planet Terrestrial (rocky) planet	12.7 light-minutes	-123 °C to 37 °C	Thin atmosphere that contains some nitrogen and argon but mostly carbon dioxide. Low air pressure. Martian crust is chemically different	Cold planet. Ice is only form of water found. Have 2 large volcanoes. Smaller and cooler than Earth. Fourth planet from the sun. 2 moons. Less dense and less gravity than Earth (38% of Earth's). Period of rotation is about equal to Earth's. Longer period of revolution (1

				from Earth's crust. Diameter= 6,794 km	year on Mars = 687 days on Earth). Avg. orbital speed = 24.07 km/s
Jupiter	Outer planet Gas planet	43.3 light-minutes	-110 °C	Very large, composed mostly of gases (hydrogen and helium). Deep massive atmospheres made of clouds of water, methane, and ammonia. Very hot interior. Does not have a solid surface. The planet is a ball of liquid surrounded by gas. Radiates more thermal energy back into space than it receives from the Sun. Diameter=142,984km	Largest planet in our solar system. Images from space show The Great Red Spot, a 400 year old storm system of swirling gas with 3 times the diameter of Earth. Thin, faint ring can be seen around Jupiter. Have 63 moons. Much larger than Earth. Less dense. Much greater gravity (236% of Earth's). Faster period of rotation (1 day on Jupiter = 9 hours on Earth). Longer period of revolution (1 year on Jupiter = 12 years on Earth). Avg. orbital speed = 13.07 km/s
Saturn	Outer planet Gas planet	1.3 light-hours	-140°C	Very large, composed mostly of gases (hydrogen and helium). Deep massive atmospheres that contain methane, ammonia, and ethane. Very hot interiors. Radiates more thermal energy back into space than it receives from the Sun. Diameter= 120,536 km	2nd largest planet in the Solar System. Sixth from the Sun. Have the largest rings of all the gas giants. Rings are thin (less than one kilometer thick) and made of small, icy particles. The rings are 250,000 km or more in diameter. Have 62 moons. More massive and less dense than Earth. Almost equal amount of gravity as Earth (92% of Earth's). Faster period of rotation (1 day on Saturn = 11 hours on Earth). Longer period of rotation (1 year on Saturn = 29 years on Earth). Avg. orbital speed = 9.69 km/s
Uranus	Outer planet Gas planet	2.7 light-hours	-195°C	Composed mostly of gases. Deep massive atmosphere composed mostly of hydrogen, helium, and methane. Blue-green in color because of the methane in its atmosphere. Diameter= 51,118 km	Very large. 3rd largest planet and the seventh from the Sun. Has 27 moons. Less dense than Earth. Slightly less gravity than Earth (89% of Earth's). Faster period of rotation (1 day on Uranus = 17 hours on Earth). Longer period of revolution (1 year on Uranus = 84 years on Earth). Tilted 90° on its axis (it's tipped over on its side as compared to Earth). Avg. orbital speed = 6.81 km/s
Neptune	Outer planet Gas planet	4.2 light-hours	-200°C	Composed mostly of gases. Deep massive atmospheres composed mostly of hydrogen, helium and methane. Atmosphere contains belts of clouds. Methane gas gives Neptune its blue color. Interiors release a lot of thermal energy to outer layers. Convection currents allow warm air in atmosphere to rise and cool air to sink setting up wind patterns that create the belts of	Very large. 4th largest planet and the eighth from the Sun. Have 13 moons. Less dense than Earth. Slightly greater gravity than Earth (112% of Earth's). Faster period of rotation (1 day on Neptune = 16 hours on Earth). Longer period of revolution (1 year on Neptune = 164 days on Earth). Set of very narrow rings. Avg. orbital speed = 5.43 km/s

				clouds. Diameter= 49, 528 km	
Pluto	Dwarf planet but located in outer solar system. Terrestrial (rocky) planet	5.4 light-hours Farthest from Sun	-225°C	Small, dense, and rocky. Ice planet. Made of rock and ice and is covered by frozen nitrogen. May have a thin atmosphere of methane. Receives very little light and thermal energy from the Sun. Diameter= 2,390 km	Farthest from the Sun. The only planet that has not been visited by a spacecraft. Have 3 moons. Less dense than Earth. Less gravity than Earth (6% of Earth's). Planet is smaller than the moons of other planets in the Solar System. Slower period of rotation (1 day on Pluto = 6 days on Earth). Longer period of revolution (1 year on Pluto = 248 years on Earth). Avg. orbital speed = 4.66 km/s

The Study of Moons

Standards: SC.5.E.5.3, SC.8.E.5.3

Remember that a natural satellite that orbits a planet or smaller body is called a **moon** (named after Earth's moon, the Moon or Luna). Scientists study moons because they provide information that can help piece together the history of the Solar System. By comparing such things as composition of rocks and atmosphere, scientists can hypothesize about the age and origins of the Solar System. Carbon dating of rocks found on Earth's moon reveals the age of the Solar System to be about 4.6 billion years old.

Moons orbit their planets in a predictable manner. Some even move in a **retrograde** (backward) fashion. It is believed that some moons are captured asteroids caught in the planet's gravitational pull. Gravity keeps moons in orbit around their planets. Moons vary greatly in size and composition. All planets of our solar system have moons, except Mercury and Venus.

Earth's moon is spherical and made of rock (of material similar to the Earth's crust). It has no atmosphere, no water, and no living things. Drastic temperature changes occur. Its surface is covered with craters. The size is about one-fourth of Earth's diameter. The Moon revolves around the Earth every 29.5 days.

Properties of Stars

Standards: SC.8.E.5.5

A star is a massive ball of hot gas that emits light and is held together by gravity. The nearest star to Earth is the Sun which is about 150 million km away. Stars are basically like furnaces releasing large amounts of energy from its core. This energy comes from nuclear fusion reactions that convert hydrogen to helium. The hotter the star the brighter it shines. Gravity pulls the star inward while the pressure from the fusion reactions pulls the star out. This balancing act gives stars their spherical shape.

All stars are pretty much made of the same chemical elements. In the highest amounts these include the gasses hydrogen and helium. Other elements found in stars include the elements carbon, oxygen, sulfur, nitrogen, and silicon, just to name a few. Although stars are made from the same chemical elements, they differ in size, age, brightness, distance, color and temperature.

Scientists study the **_absorption spectrum_** of starlight to determine which elements can be found inside stars. This spectrum is formed when electromagnetic radiation is passed through a medium in which radiation of certain frequencies is absorbed. By studying its absorption spectrum scientist know which wavelength of light each element absorbs, thus, they can tell which chemical elements make up that star.

The color of a star provides information on its temperature and age. In general, you can easily remember this by saying that a **_blue_** star is a **_new_** star and is **_hot_** and a **_red_** star is a **_dead_** (dying) star and it is **_cooler_**. A white star is in between a blue and a red. It is fairly new and hot as well. This classification does not include white dwarfs which are dying stars.

Temperature is used to classify stars. The **_Hertzsprung - Russell diagram_** (H-R diagram) compares stars at various stages of their lives (see the diagram on the next page). It is a graph of a star's **_color_** (surface temperature)vs. its **_luminosity_** (brightness). On it, astronomers not only plot a star's temperature, color and luminosity but its spectral type and evolutionary stage as well. The hot, luminous stars are in the upper left of the graph and the cool, dim stars are in the lower right. Some stars are off of the main sequence. Cool, bright stars are in the upper right and hot, dim stars in the lower left.

The H-R diagram reveals 3 types of stars:

1. **_Main sequence_** (longest stage in life cycle)
2. **_Super giants_**
3. **_White dwarfs_**

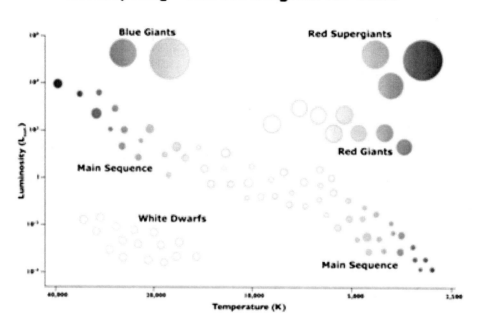

Most stars are main sequence stars. They lie along the smooth diagonal curve in the center of the diagram. Main sequence stars are in the most stable stage of their lives. Our Sun is a main sequence star.

When stars begin to die fusion reactions decrease and less hydrogen converts to helium. For these stars, their hydrogen supply eventually becomes depleted. They are very old. They become **_giants_** and **_super giants_** (above the main sequence curve). The force that once pulled the star outward begins to decrease. Without this outward force, the force of gravity pulling the star together causes the star to consume and ignite matter in its environment. These stars will eventually explode (becoming a **_supernova_** or **_nebula_** (depending on their mass) and then become white dwarfs (hot, white, dim stars), **_neutron stars_**, or **_black holes_**. Super giant stars may be 12 times more massive than the Sun. Because of their size and the fast rate of nuclear fusion happening inside of them these stars are unstable. They burn out quickly, lasting only a few million years. Ultimately, they disintegrate completely into a supernova returning the star's material back to the universe. This material will eventually be used to make another star. What a wonderful example of the Law of Conservation of Mass!

When smaller stars run out of fuel completely they become **white dwarfs**. The star collapses inward under its own gravity. It continues to shine because it is still hot and takes billions of years to cool down. More massive stars than the Sun will explode into supernovas and not white dwarfs when they die. The remaining core of the star becomes a **neutron star** or **black hole**. **Red dwarf** stars are cooler stars than the Sun and have smaller masses. These stars can burn for up to 10 trillion years.

Scientists also classify stars according to their brightness (**apparent magnitude**). The closer the star (to Earth), the brighter it appears to us. The Sun, for example is not the brightest star in the Solar System but because of its close distance to Earth it appears to be. The actual brightness or **luminosity** (**absolute magnitude**) of a star is how much energy or starlight is actually emitted (put out) from the star in a given time. Luminosity and distance (how far it is from us) determines the brightness of the star. A floodlight puts out more light than a penlight. So, it is more luminous. If that floodlight is a mile away from you, however, it will not be as bright because light intensity decreases with distance. Stars that are far away from Earth appear dim.

Luminosity also depends on size. The larger a star is the more energy it puts out and the more luminous it is. Even though two stars may have the same temperature, the larger one will be more luminous. To calculate luminosity scientists use the star's apparent magnitude and its distance. Astronomers measure a star's distance in **light-years** (distance light travels in one year). This term is used for simplicity. It would seem crazy to record the distance of a star as 503,000,000,000,000,000 km. It's so much easier to say the star is 200 light-years (or whatever number) away. To determine the distance of a star astronomers use the star's **parallax**. Parallax is the apparent shifting in position compared to other nearby stars (see the diagram on the following page). If a star's position is measured at two different times there will be a shift in its position. This shift creates an angle that can be used to mathematically calculate distance.

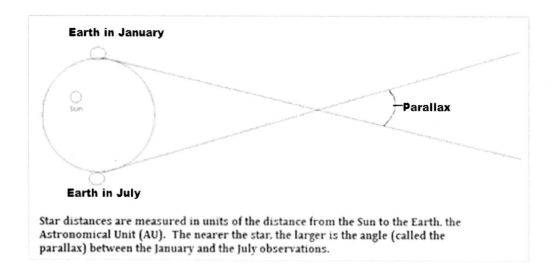

Earth in January

Sun

Earth in July

Parallax

Star distances are measured in units of the distance from the Sun to the Earth, the Astronomical Unit (AU). The nearer the star, the larger is the angle (called the parallax) between the January and the July observations.

In the previous section we talked about red and blue shifts. We can tell which direction a star is moving in the Solar System by observing the wavelength of light it emits. A star is moving towards us if the spectrum of the star is shifted to the blue end of the spectrum. It will appear blue. If a star is moving away from us, its spectrum will be shifted to the red end. It will appear red. A star's rate of rotation can also be determined by observing the red and blue shift.

Comparison of Stars in the Milky Way

Standards: SC.8.E.5.2, SC.8.E.5.5

For the FCAT you will need to be able to compare and contrast our Sun with other stars in the Milky Way Galaxy. **Table 4-8** on the next page will help you. For example, from the table you can see that Sirius is a brighter star than our Sun. Each value (such as size, temperature, etc) is based on relative comparison to that of the Sun.

Mass of Sun = 1.989×10^{30} kg

Luminosity of Sun = 390 billion megawatts or **3.939×10^{26} Watts (W)**

Apparent magnitude of Sun (as seen from Earth) = -26.73 [Note: very bright objects have negative magnitudes]

Approximate Age of Universe= 13.7 billion years

Table 4-8   The Sun as Compared to Other Stars

Name of Star	Size (radius)	Surface Temperature (color)	Luminosity (absolute magnitude)	Evolutionary Age	Brightness (apparent magnitude)
Rigel	5.4×10^7 km	25,200 K (blue)	85,000 times brighter than the Sun	~10 million years old	0.12 - 0.18
Sirius	5843 km	7,500 – 11,000 K (blue)	25 times brighter than the Sun	200 -300 million years old	-1.46
Sun	695,500 km	5,000 – 5,000 K	--	4.6 billion years old	-26.74
White dwarfs	5,564 – 13,911 km	**From over 150,000 K to under 4,000 K**	**100 times the Sun's to under 1/10,000th that of the Sun's**	Final evolutionary state of 97% of stars in the Milky Way	Less than 1.0
Red giants	7.0×10^6 to 7.0×10^7 km	Less than 5000 K	0.4 times that of the Sun	Late phase of stellar evolution	Close to 0
PSR J0108-1431 (neutron star)	6-12 km	8000 K	Very faint 0.04 times the brightness of the Sun	166 million years old	Less than 27.8
Betelgeuse	8.2×10^8 km	3600 K	130,000 -180,000 times brighter than the Sun	~10 million years	0.42 – 0.52
Polaris (the North Star)	2.1×10^7 km	7200 K	2200 times brighter than the Sun	? years	1.97

PART II EARTH STRUCTURES

The History of the Earth

Standards: SC.7.E.6.3,   SC.7.E.6.4

   Physical evidence supports scientific theories that Earth has evolved over geologic time due to natural processes. The Earth is believed to be 4.6 billion years old. How is it possible for scientists to determine the age of the Earth if they were not present at its creation? The answer is they gather evidence about the past based on events currently happening in the present time.   The **_Theory of Uniformitarianism_** helps to explain events that shaped the Earth so many years ago. The theory states that processes we observe today--such as plate tectonics, volcanic and earthquake activity, erosion, weathering, and deposition—occurred in the past as well and created the planet as we know it today. In addition, events in space such as meteorite strikes and collisions from other space objects impacted Earth and played a role in its creation.

Scientists use __*radioactive dating*__ (absolute dating) to date rocks and fossils found on Earth. Elements that are radioactive tend to be unstable and break down over time. When they break down they change into more stable elements. By comparing the ratio of stable to unstable elements in a sample of rock or fossil scientists can determine the age of the sample. The time it takes for half the unstable atoms in the element to decay (breakdown) is called the __*half-life*__ of the sample. Elements with very long half-lives, such as uranium-238 (4.5 billion years) can be used to date objects that are millions of years old.

__*Fossils*__ (the remains or imprints of living things that lived long ago) found in sedimentary rock provide physical evidence to show how Earth has changed over a very long period of time. Fossils can be dated using radioactive dating to reveal their age. The oldest documented fossil organisms date to over 3 billion years ago. Many of these organisms are very different from those that exist today.

__*Relative dating*__ is a way scientists can determine the age of the Earth and its parts by comparing the position or sequence of rock layers. Fossils are often found in layers of sedimentary rock. If the rock layer has not been overturned or disrupted by earthquakes or other geologic processes it would be safe to say that fossils found in the bottom layers would be older than those found in the top layers. This is because the oldest layer tends to be the bottom layer (sediments are deposited in water layer by layer from the lowest layer to the highest). This is the __*Law of Superposition.*__ It states that sedimentary rock layers can be dated based on their relative position. Undisturbed layers that are on the bottom tend to be older than layers on top.

The Earth (and the rest of the universe) is theorized to have been formed from a large rotating cloud of interstellar gas and dust (solar nebular) remaining from the Big Bang. As Earth became more massive in size gravity caused the weight of the gas and dust to collapse on itself and takes on a rounded shape. The newly formed Earth was extremely hot and lacked the atmosphere and oxygen necessary to support life.

Millions of years after the creation of Earth, the Moon was formed. A chemical analysis of moon rocks show they consist of the same components contained in the crust and mantle of Earth. It is believed that the Moon was formed from portions of the Earth. It was created from captured material originating from a solar body collision which blew off a portion of Earth's crust and mantle. Under the influence of gravity these pieces combined to form the Moon.

Earth's first atmosphere lacked oxygen but contained water vapor, nitrogen and carbon dioxide. Because it lacked oxygen it could not support life. Life is hypothesized to have begun in the oceans with primitive marine organisms. The first land organisms may have been ones who could survive in an oxygen-poor atmosphere and perform photosynthesis. Photosynthesis created oxygen in the atmosphere that later made it possible for more complex forms of life to exist on Earth.

The Structure of Earth

Standards: SC.7.E.6.1, SC.6.E.7.4, SC.6.E.7.9

Over geologic time the internal and external features of Earth have changed by means of both constructive and destructive forces. These are forces that either build the Earth up or break it down. The forces responsible for these actions originate in and on the Earth. The scientific theory of Earth's evolution states that changes in our planet are driven by the flow of energy and the cycling of matter through dynamic interactions among the atmosphere, hydrosphere, cryosphere, geosphere, and biosphere. All life on Earth is dependent of this energy and material resources. These resources are used to sustain human civilization on Earth.

Earth should be thought of as a living, global system. It is made up of the various systems that interact to allow life to exist. A few examples of these interactions include the one between Earth, the Sun and the Moon; between the living and nonliving parts of the environment; between the crust and landforms; and between the atmosphere and weather systems. At the core of these interactions is energy. More specifically, changes in energy and the flow of energy through the system. It's all interconnected.

Earth's systems can be divided into 5 major subsystems or spheres: land (**geosphere**), water (**hydrosphere**), ice (**cryosphere**), air (**atmosphere**), and living things (**biosphere**). While these layers may overlap and share some of the same physical space, they have different compositions and serve different purposes.

1. Geosphere

Includes the solid, rocky parts of Earth. It can be divided into 3 layers-- **_crust_**, **_mantle_**, and **_core_**.

a. **_crust_** — Earth's hard outer shell—the surface layer we live on. It is a thin layer that represents only about 1% of the Earth's mass. When we walk on the ground we are walking on a part of Earth's crust.   There are 2 types of crust; **_oceanic crust_** (the crust under the oceans) and **_continental crust_** (the crust that make up the continents).   Oceanic crust is thinner than continental crust (6-11 km thick) and is made up of heavy rocks, like basalt (a volcanic rock). The continental crust is thicker (30 km thick) and is made of lighter igneous rock such as granite.

b. **_mantle_**-- the layer below the crust, measuring about 2900 km thick.   It is denser than the crust and represents about 64% the mass of the Earth. The mantle can be divided into 2 layers, the **_outer mantle_** and the **_inner mantle_**.   The outer mantle is located 300 km below the surface. It is made up of the **_lithosphere_** (the uppermost part of the mantle and crust) and the **_athenosphere_** (layer of hot, tough liquid rock). The plates of the lithosphere float on top of the athenosphere like marshmallows floating in a cup of hot chocolate. Temperatures   here can reach up to 3000°C.

The inner mantle is located about 2,890 km below the Earth's surface. The heat flow from the core creates a convection current that cools as it reaches the Earth's surface.   The convection current in the mantle creates a force that pulls tectonic plates apart and causes them to collide as well. When plates collide earthquakes occur. When they pull apart, magma from within the Earth exit at weak areas in the crust, such as volcanoes. The movement of this hot convecting current is also responsible for the spreading of the sea floor and the building of mountains. Note that the moving of tectonic plates is a slow process, occurring at a rate of about 0-100 mm annually.

c. **_core_** — the innermost part of the Earth. It is the hottest layer. The core is located about 2900 km from the surface and   is made up of an **_outer core_** and an **_inner core_** -- the center of the Earth. The outer core is so hot (4000-5000°C) that the iron and nickel that make it up remain molten (melted).   The inner core has an average temperature of about 5000 -

6000°C but is under such tremendous pressure that it is a solid (iron and nickel). When the Earth rotates the liquid outer core spins around the solid inner core (which doesn't spin because it is a solid) creating the Earth's magnetism. Because of this magnetism the Earth operates as if it has a huge bar magnet located inside it.

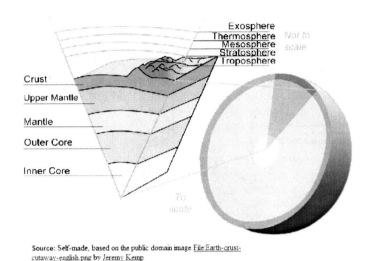

Source: Self-made, based on the public domain image File:Earth-crust-cutaway-english.png by Jeremy Kemp

2. Hydrosphere

Includes all the water found on, above, or under the Earth. It includes oceans, rivers, streams, ponds, water vapor and ground water. Approximately 71% of the Earth's surface is covered by ocean.

The _**water cycle,**_ which is the movement of water through the Earth, is an example of an important process that occurs in the hydrosphere and involves the interaction of other spheres (atmosphere and geosphere). Energy from the Sun drives the water cycle. The Sun's heat causes _**evaporation**_ of water in oceans, or leaves on trees (transpiration) for example. As water evaporates, it becomes less dense and rises into the atmosphere. Water then cools and collects into clouds (_**condensation**_). Clouds release _**precipitation**_ (snow, rain, etc) that return the water to the land. Water that seeps into the Earth is known as _**ground water**_. **Runoff is** water that drains or flows off the land back into streams, rivers and oceans.

In terms of the water cycle it is clear to see how polluting the air and water can harm

Earth. Polluted water circulates repeatedly through the water cycle bringing harm to the air, land, and surface waters all organisms depend on to sustain life. As the polluted water collects on Earth, cycles into the air, and returns back to Earth it would negatively impact such things as our drinking water, the air we breathe, and water plants use for growth.

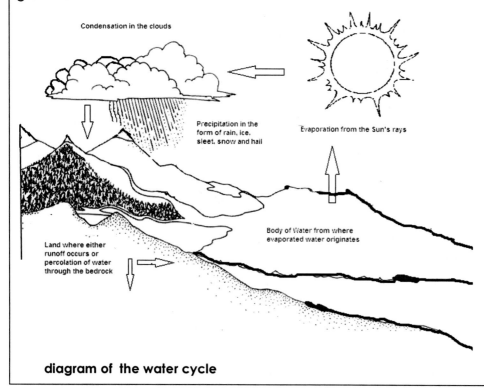

diagram of the water cycle

3. Cryosphere

The cryosphere (*cryo* = cold) is sometimes considered as part of the hydrosphere. It includes all the frozen water on Earth such as snow, permafrost (frozen ground), polar ice caps and glaciers. The warming of the planet due to global warming is contributing to the melting of glaciers and the expansion of the hydrosphere. This creates such problems as rise in sea levels and coastal flooding.

4. Atmosphere

The blanket of air that surrounds Earth is its atmosphere. It is a layer of gases and water vapor and is held in place by Earth's gravity. The composition and structure of the atmosphere protects life and insulates the planet. Firstly, it protects Earth from the intense heat of the Sun. Secondly, the atmosphere absorbs UV radiation from the Sun to reduce its harmful effects on living things. The ozone layer is responsible for this protection. The ozone layer has been compromised by human activity leading to the formation of holes in this layer and the unfortunate increase in the incidence of skin cancer.

The atmosphere maintains the temperature of the Earth's surface so that it is not too hot or too cold to support life. Clouds and air in the atmosphere reflect 25% of incoming solar radiation. Another 25% of incoming solar radiation is absorbed by the atmosphere.

The atmosphere is composed of 78% nitrogen, 21% oxygen, and about 1% other gases (carbon dioxide, argon, methane, hydrogen, helium, etc). It is divided into 5 layers (see the diagram below). In order from lowest to highest layer is the **_troposphere_** (where weather occurs) which is warmed by convection currents; the **_stratosphere_** (contains the ozone layer); the **_mesosphere_** (contains some of the coldest temperatures on Earth) which shows a decrease in temperature with height; the **_thermosphere_** (contains high temperatures) which shows an increase in temperature with height; and the **_exosphere_** (outer space). Air pressure (the weight of the atmosphere pressing down on Earth) decrease as you travel through the five layers. Temperature also fluctuates (increases and decreases depending on the layer).

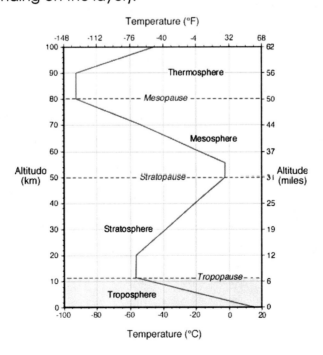

5. Biosphere

Also called the zone of life. It is the area where all life exists on Earth. It can be thought of as the ultimate ecosystem integrating all living things and their relationships. It is also an area where elements of the hydrosphere, atmosphere, geosphere, and cryosphere all interact to support the global system.

Processes That Shape the Earth

Standards: SC.6.E.6.1, SC.7.E.6.5, SC.7.E.6.7

A variety of landforms exist on Earth's surface. These include mountains, glaciers, lakes, rivers, coastlines, dunes and deltas. The FCAT is concerned with the internal and external sources of energy that form these landforms. These energy sources continuously alter Earth's surface by means of both constructive and destructive forces. Constructive and destructive forces help to build up and tear down Earth's surface. Geological processes involved include earthquakes, volcanic activity, plate tectonics, erosion, weathering, and deposition.

Earth's lithosphere is broken up into seven to eight major and several minor sections called **tectonic plates**. These rigid plates float on the hot, molten asthenosphere. Tectonic plates undergo some large scale motions which result in them always colliding or pulling apart. Although movement is only a few centimeters a year, the force it generates and the massive amounts of energy given off drastically changes the outward appearance of the Earth in many ways. For example, over millions of years continents have drifted apart. This has dramatically changed coastlines. Earlier maps of the world reveal how the east coasts of North and South America used to fit perfectly into the west coast of Africa and Europe. These continents have now drifted apart. **The Theory of Plate Tectonics** is the scientific theory which describes the large scale movement of tectonic plates. It is based on the **Theory of Continental Drift** proposed by Alfred Wegener in 1915, that continents have drifted apart significantly after having been a part of a large, single land mass (Pangea).

The movement of Earth's crustal plates causes both slow and rapid changes in Earth's surface. **_Earthquakes_** are a major consequence of this crustal movement.   As tectonic plates collide, strong vibrations cause the earth to shake (earthquakes).   When this occurs solid rock is broken and deformed by the great amount of energy that is produced. As a result, grounds are raised, lowered, and even separated. Earthquakes cause a lot of damage to property and buildings and loss of lives.

Most earthquakes and volcanic activity occur at **_plate boundaries_** (place where two plates meet). Mountain-building, ocean trenches, and volcanic activity also occur along **_plate boundaries_**. Three types of plate boundaries exist; **_divergent_**, **_convergent_** and **_transform_** boundaries.

1. **divergent boundaries** – are areas where plates move apart from each other. When they separate, they form a gap or rift between the two plates that allow molten lava underneath to flow upward. This happens in ocean crust as well. When the lava cools land formations such as volcanic islands and ocean ridges form. This spreading is also responsible for creating new sea floor as the lava cools and adds matter to the ocean crust. The expansion of the sea floor is known as sea floor spreading.   The Mid-Atlantic Ridge in the Atlantic Ocean was formed from diverging boundaries.

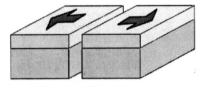

Divergent Boundary

2. **convergent boundaries** - are areas where two plates move towards one another.   The edges of the plates can be forced up in a rippling manner when the two plates are forced together. This rippling forms mountain ranges. Sometimes subduction occurs. This is when one plate moves beneath the other. Island arcs, ocean trenches, and mountains form in this manner. The world's largest mountain, Mt. Everest (located in Nepal) is an example. Volcanic mountains form from convergent boundaries when lava exits from the top of mountains.   Cooling lava can also form lava deltas, lava hills and other landforms.   Convergent boundaries also cause earthquakes.

Convergent Boundary

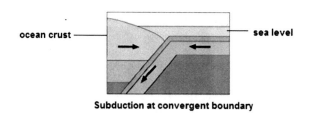

ocean crust ————— sea level

Subduction at convergent boundary

3. **transform boundaries**- are areas where two plates slide past each other sideways or horizontally. They are responsible for faults and earthquakes. The San Andreas Fault in California is the most popular transform boundary.

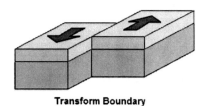

Transform Boundary

Convection currents in the upper mantle provide the energy plates need to move around. The convection currents are transmitted through the asthenosphere. Differences in density allow less dense, hotter portions of the mantle to rise while cooler, more dense material sinks. Massive heat flow and movement of material creates currents and motion which becomes the driving mechanism for the plates.

That mountains change size and shape over a long period of time provides evidence that destructive forces are also at play in shaping Earth's surface. A major force responsible for tearing down Earth's surface is _**erosion**_. Erosion is the force or process by which sediment and soil are transported from one place to another causing the surface of the Earth to be worn away. The process is at work every day and is constantly shaping the Earth. Erosion is due to the action of wind, water, glaciers, waves, etc. Erosion wears down mountains into hills. Avalanches and landslides cause big boulders to be broken up into smaller rocks and soil. Erosion caused by moving water is partly responsible for carving out and creating the Grand Canyon in Arizona.

In addition to erosion, _**weathering**_ is also a destructive force that breaks down Earth's surface. Weathering is the wearing away or breaking down of the Earth's surface (rocks, soils, minerals) or objects on the surface. Weathering involves no movement. It differs from erosion in that erosion involves agents such as wind or water that move objects. There are two types of weathering; ***chemical weathering*** and ***physical (mechanical) weathering***. Chemical weathering is the breaking down of structures by the use of atmospheric acids and other chemicals. The destruction of a park statue due to acid rain is an example of chemical weathering. Acid rain forms from the emission of compounds of carbon, ammonium, sulfur, and nitrogen into the air which reacts with water to produce acids.

Physical or mechanical weathering involves the breakdown of rock, soil, and minerals through direct contact with heat, pressure, water and ice. For example, water that seeps through cracks in rocks may freeze and expand when temperatures drop. When temperatures rise the ice melts. This constant cycle of water freezing, expanding and melting creates a force that breaks portions of rock apart. The breaking of the rock is mechanical weathering. Once the broken rock falls and is transported to another location that process is termed erosion.

Deposition is a force that works with erosion. Once erosion transports objects and sediments to other locations, deposition is responsible for the buildup of these materials in their new locations on land or water. This occurs when moving objects lose their kinetic energy and stop moving. Objects will accumulate wherever they stop.

Major Landforms of Florida

Standards: SC.6.E.6.2

Florida is rich in a variety of landforms. Visitors and residents can experience marshlands (i.e., Everglades), beaches (i.e., South Beach), gulfs (i.e., Florida's Gulf Coasts), bays (i.e., Apalachee Bay), sand dunes, lagoons, straits (i.e., Florida Straits), barrier islands, islands, ponds, rivers, lakes, streams, archipelagoes (i.e., Florida Keys), and peninsulas (i.e., Fairpoint Peninsula).

530 million years ago, before the super continent Pangea and before Florida drifted to its modern day location in North America, it was formed from a combination of volcanic activity and deposits of marine sediments (coral, shellfish, and fish skeletons) from the ocean. Several times in its history the Florida peninsula was submerged beneath ocean level. Increases in climate temperatures and melting of glaciers over the continent raised ocean levels and

flooded the Florida peninsula. As a result, a layer of limestone 100-1000 ft thick formed on the surface. Erosion of the Appalachian Mountains deposited clay and sand over the limestone layer. Quartz sand covering Florida today came from the erosion of these mountain rocks. Florida Keys formed from underwater coral reefs that formed in a chain-like fashion. The reef eventually raised above sea level as the flooded Florida peninsula emerged.

As Florida's limestone layer remained submerged below sea level certain areas dissolved and became porous. Cracks and passages formed in the limestone layer giving rise to several underground rivers. Where the underground rivers break through to the surface they form springs and sinkholes. Florida is honeycombed with underground rivers and streams. Above the surface there are many lakes and wetlands as well.

Florida is relatively flat with a few elevations ranging from 0-320 ft above sea level. Low-lying coastal areas and areas inland near rivers and lakes are more prone to flooding than other areas of the state. Erosion is constantly changing Florida's shoreline as sand is moved from one location to another by wind and waves.

Today, the state is considered geologically stable--volcanic and earthquake activity is nearly nonexistent (although certain sections of Florida do experience very weak tremors). The greatest threat to Florida is hurricane and tornado activity. For more detailed information on the geography of Florida please visit the US Geological Survey's website at **www.usgs.gov**

Rocks and Minerals
Standards: SC.7.E.6.2

There are 3 different types of rocks; **_sedimentary_**, **_igneous_**, and **_metamorphic_**. Each type is formed in a different way.

1. **_sedimentary rock_**-- is formed from the compacting and cementing of sediments (sand, pebbles, and rock fragments) over a period of time. Weathering and erosion on the surface of the Earth creates the sediments that form these types of rocks. Sedimentary rocks are deposited in layers.

2. ***igneous rock***-- ("fire rocks") is formed from the cooling and solidification of magma and lava. Igneous rock may form with or without crystals depending on how fast it cools. Rocks that cool quickly will have small or no crystals. The longer it takes for rocks to cool the larger the crystals will be. Plate tectonics is responsible for volcanic activity and mountain building. These activities cause magma within the Earth's interiors to be pushed up to the surface where it cools to form igneous rock.

3. ***metamorphic rock***-- is existing rock that has changed in form. A metamorphic rock could have originally been a sedimentary or igneous rock. The intense heat and pressure beneath the Earth's surface can cause these rock types to undergo a change to become metamorphic rock. Metamorphic rocks make up a large part of the Earth's crust. It is identified by its chemical and mineral composition as well as by its texture.

PART III EARTH SYSTEMS AND PATTERNS

The Rock Cycle

Standards: SC.7.E.6.2

The **rock cycle** is a pattern of cycling of matter on Earth as one rock type is changed into another. Erosion, weathering, heat and pressure, melting and cooling, compacting and cementing can change the identity of a rock as it goes through the rock cycle. Sedimentary rock can form igneous rock by intense melting and cooling. Sedimentary rock can change into metamorphic rock by applying heat and pressure. Processes such as plate tectonics and mountain building provide the energy and great pressure needed to transform rock into metamorphic rock.

Igneous rock can change into sedimentary rock when weathering and erosion breaks down the rock into sediments. Subsequent compacting and cementing of the pieces would create sedimentary rock. Igneous rock can be converted into metamorphic rock by the addition of heat and pressure.

Metamorphic rock can be changed into either igneous rock (by melting and cooling) or sedimentary rock (by erosion/weathering and compacting/cementing).

Igneous rock

Sedimentary rock

Metamorphic rock

Rock Cycle

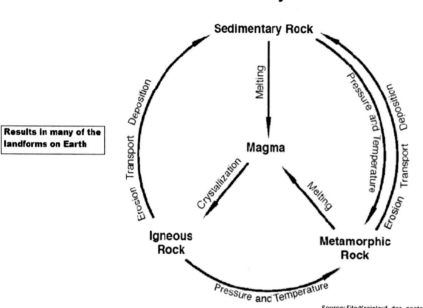

Source: File:Kreislauf_der_gesteine.png

Minerals are the materials that rocks are made up of. They are naturally occurring solid objects mostly made of inorganic matter. They have a definite composition and atomic structure. Minerals are identified based on their physical and chemical properties. Properties of minerals include **streak** (the color of its powder), **color**, **odor**, **hardness** (the strength of its chemical bonds), **density**, **luster** (the way it reflects light), **taste** (students should not test this property in the classroom as one should never put any mineral in the mouth), **shape**, **cleavage/fracture** (the way it breaks), **crystalline structure**, **specific gravity**, **transparency** (ability to allow light through), **tenacity** (ability of the particles to resist separation), **magnetism** (if it can attract a magnet) and its **response to acid** (whether it bubbles and fizzes when in contact with an acid). Minerals can be pure elements (on the periodic table) such as gold and silver. Minerals have multiple purposes. They can be used to make jewelry, copper pipes and wires, TV and electronic components (i.e., quartz), automotive and airplane components (i.e., bauxite), construction material (i.e., marble, granite, etc), paper and plastics (barite), and in food preservation (halite).

Weather
Standards: SC.5.E.7.3,   SC.5.E.7.4

Weather is defined as the current condition of the atmosphere at a given time and place. Descriptions of atmospheric conditions indicate whether it is hot or cold, clear or cloudy, stormy or calm, and wet or dry.   Weather involves daily temperature and **precipitation** activity. Precipitation includes all forms of water that fall from the sky (i.e., rain, snow, sleet and hail).

The difference between each type of precipitation has to do partly with temperature and the state of matter of the water in the atmosphere. You learned in chapter 2 that temperature influences states of matter. Lower temperatures cause water molecules to move slower which may lead to a change of state towards freezing. Likewise, low atmospheric temperatures in a given location affect the state of matter of atmospheric water vapor.   Combine this information with your knowledge of the water cycle and you will recall that it is condensation of water molecules in clouds that lead to precipitation.

Clouds may form initially when air moves upwards to higher elevations where air pressure is less. With less pressure the air expands and cools.   This cooling causes water vapor to condense. When clouds are full (**saturated**) the water will fall under the force of gravity. If the temperature is low enough the water may turn to ice crystals and fall as freezing rain, sleet or snow. If the temperature is warmer the water may fall as rain. Hail forms when strong winds repeatedly blow rain back into a cloud and it freezes in multiple layers. When clouds are saturated with these balls of ice they fall to the ground as hail.

Weather is a direct result of energy movement through air, land, and ocean (atmosphere, geosphere, and hydrosphere). Without energy from the Sun weather on Earth would not be possible. Solar energy is one of the primary drivers of our weather. Remember that solar radiation does not require a medium and can travel through a vacuum such as space.   The Sun's heat causes water to do two important things; to evaporate and to rise. These are basic tenets of weather. Most weather takes place in the lowest layer of the atmosphere (troposphere).

Weather Measurement

Standards: SC.6.E.7.2

Weather elements include temperature, wind, rainfall, and **_humidity_** (the amount of water vapor in the air). These elements are used when most people discuss weather. They may say it is hot, rainy, cold, or humid outside. **_Meteorologists_** (scientists who study and predict weather) measure and describe weather in terms of air pressure (barometric pressure), air temperature, humidity, wind direction, wind speed, the amount and type of precipitation, and the types of clouds. These parts all interact to influence weather.

As the Sun heats the atmospheric air it rises. A center of low barometric pressure is created because air molecules expand when heated and thus exert less of a force on the Earth beneath. This decreases the density of the air. Rising air brings along moisture which makes the air heavier. Air can hold more moisture at higher temperatures than it can at lower temperatures. Eventually, as the air continues to rise its temperature drops and it cools. Condensation of the accumulated water vapor will occur, along with precipitation. Low pressure centers generally bring rain or snow (depending on the temperature).

High barometric pressure centers tend to result in nicer weather since the air is denser (the air molecules are more compact) and contains less moisture. Instead of rising, the air sinks. Because of this the air molecules have greater capacity to hold water yet the air remains dryer.

Wind tends to move faster around low pressure centers and in a counter clockwise direction. Similar to gases, wind blows from areas of higher pressure to areas of lower pressure. As winds try to even out the differences between unequal pressures they inadvertently spread precipitation. Wind speed is a direct result of pressure differences between high and low pressure areas. The greater the difference the stronger the winds. Wind direction will often determine the type of weather that will occur in an area. Winds traveling from Canada may bring cool, dry air, while those traveling from the Caribbean may bring warm, moist air.

Relative humidity is a ratio of how much water vapor air is holding at a certain temperature as compared to how much it can hold at that particular temperature. It's a measure of saturation or how full the air is. The amount of humidity in the air affects how much more water can be absorbed. It affects how quickly water can be evaporated from your skin, road surfaces, lakes, etc. You feel hotter in humid weather because the air is holding so much water vapor that it cannot evaporate it from your skin fast enough. Your skin will then feel very hot and sticky.

Instruments can be used to collect weather data. Several examples of weather-measuring tools are listed in **Table 4-9** along with the weather elements they measure. These instruments mainly track current weather conditions.

Table 4-9 Weather Instruments

Weather Tools	What it Measures	Picture
barometer	air pressure	
rain gauge	the amount of rain fall	
hygrometer	humidity	
anemometer	wind speed and direction	
thermometers	air temperature	

Weather Forecasting
Standards: SC.5.E.7.3, SC.5.E.7.4

Weather forecasting is the application of science and technology to predict future weather conditions. More sophisticated instruments are utilized today than the tools described in **Table 4-9** on the previous page. Current weather technology includes computerized weather stations, radar, and satellites.   Once meteorologists collect weather data they use it to make observations and predictions. They form these predictions based on patterns of weather change and on predictable past behaviors. Meteorologists make assumptions that under similar conditions current weather will behave like similar atmospheric conditions of the past and as such they are able to predict the most likely events. They draw conclusions as to how the weather elements will interact to affect weather in a particular location.   With the data in hand and forecast models in mind, meteorologist predict what the weather will most likely be in the future.   Accuracy of weather forecasting is dependent on the amount of information received from computer models, observations, and knowledge of trends and patterns.

Influence of Global Patterns on Local Weather
Standards: SC.6.E.7.1 SC.6.E.7.3 SC.6.E.7.5

Weather changes each day. This is due to differences in density (moisture and temperature) from one location to another and the fact that the air in our atmosphere is always moving. Moving air is called **_wind_**. Wind distributes energy from the Sun to other parts of the Earth.

Earlier in the chapter we reviewed the flow of heat by convection currents as a method of heat transfer inside the Sun. Convection currents are responsible for heat transfer in the atmosphere as well. In addition, in chapter 2 we reviewed heat transfer by radiation and conduction as well. Solar energy travels from the Sun (which is the source of the heat) as radiation. This radiation transfers heat energy to the land, air, and water. As air heats up it warms other areas in contact by conduction.

Differences in temperatures between various surfaces including soil, air, and water create convection currents that transfer heat. This heat flow causes weather. Warm, less dense air rises while cold dense air sinks toward Earth's surface.   This continuous cycling of rising warm air and sinking cold air causes the movement of **_air masses_** in the atmosphere. An air mass is a large body of air having the same temperature and humidity throughout. Generally, the type of weather experienced in a particular area is due to the type of air mass present.

Table 4-10 Four Types of Air Masses

Continental Polar Air Mass	Continental Tropical Air Mass	Maritime Tropical Air Mass	Maritime Polar Air Mass
Cold, dry, stable air mass. High pressure air. In the U.S. it can bring bitter wintertime cold, even to Florida resulting in crop damage.	Warm, dry air. It is usually fairly stable. In areas of the Midwest, if it becomes stagnant it results in a drought.	Low air pressure, humid air. Has lots of moisture. The north-ward movement of tropical air masses transports warm moist air into the United States increasing the potential for precipitation.	Cold and moist air that brings mild weather to coastal locations.

When two different air masses meet a **_front_** is formed at their boundary. The air masses' temperature and water vapor content determines if the front will be classified as a cold or warm front. A cold front brings colder air into an area, while a warm front brings warmer air. These two fronts typically bring different types of weather. Changes in weather result from moving air masses. Storms often occur at the edges of air masses.

In a cold front fast moving cold air masses hit warm air masses. This pushes the warm air mass upwards quickly. The warm air mass contains a lot of moisture that condenses to form tall clouds. When the clouds become saturated, water droplets fall as precipitation. The resulting storm is often quick, violent with heavy rainfalls over a short period of time. The storm is typically accompanied by a lot of thunder and lightning.

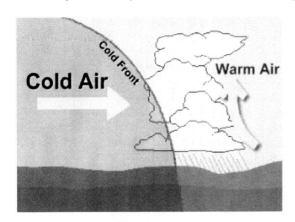

The events of a warm front are similar that of a cold front. Fast moving masses of warm air meet a cold air mass and rides up on top of it. Once again, the warm, humid air will form water droplets that will eventually be released from clouds as precipitation. Unlike the storms formed by cold fronts, the storms formed by warm fronts tend to last longer and are less violent. They produces steady precipitation for longer periods of time and may be accompanied by thunder and lightning.

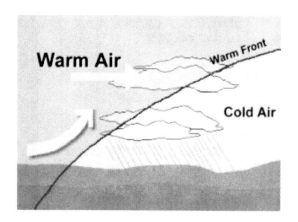

There are general patterns of weather that move around Earth. In the United States and the rest of North America most air masses typically move from west to east. Fronts will move in a similar patter (from west to east). Global wind patterns are shown in the diagram below.

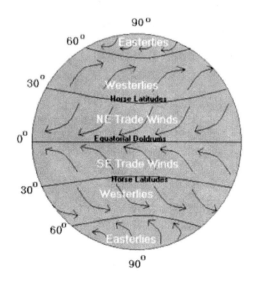

Global wind patterns

Drastic temperature difference between cold polar air masses and warm tropical air masses, along with the Earth's rotation creates _**jet streams.**_ These are fast flowing (greater than 57 mph), narrow air currents located at high altitudes (around 30,000 ft). They normally flow from west to east over the mid-latitudes.

Instabilities in jet stream flows create weather systems. They are related to weather patterns of high and low air pressure. Jet streams can change temperature, precipitation, and winds by affecting the movement of air. In fact, they influence and guide the direction of some air masses. For example, if the jet stream guides a northern air mass originating from a colder climate toward the central parts of the U.S., then the northerly winds will probably bring cold, dry air.

In addition to jet streams, ocean currents also affect local weather by affecting temperature and air pressure. Temperature differences in ocean waters create convection currents as warm water rises and cold water sinks. These temperature differences affect the pressure of the air above the oceans. Movement of air from high to low pressures creates winds that transfer heat energy and moisture to land areas. This affects the local weather in terms of temperature and often brings rain and violent weather such as hurricanes. Ocean currents can change the temperature of local regions. Warm winds from ocean currents bring warmer weather to an area. On the other hand, cold ocean currents can reduce the surrounding temperature of an area.

Local weather is also greatly influenced by geography. For example, coastal areas display different weather patterns than areas more inland. Coastal areas tend to be cooler in the day time (and in the summers) and warmer at night (and in the winters) due to the thermal properties of water. Water has a higher _**specific heat**_ than land (soil). This means that it takes more energy to change the temperature of water than it does to change the temperature of soil. Also, water holds on to energy a lot longer than soil. Soil is a better conductor of heat than water. The heat-holding ability of water warms the air above and affects weather. Soil heats up quickly and loses heat quickly as well. This causes the air above the land and water to have different temperatures. Differences in air temperature and pressure create winds and various types of weather such as storms.

Daily Wind Change in Coastal Areas

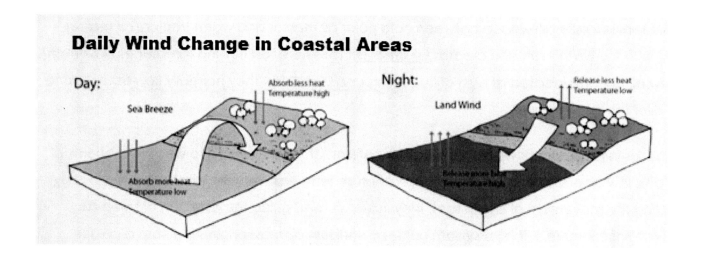

The effect of geography on weather is also seen at higher elevations. The air (and weather) on a mountain top tends to be cooler than on sea level. Air pressure is lower on the mountain top than at sea level. The air molecules are more spread out at these higher elevations and exert less of a force on the Earth below.

The Difference Between Weather and Climate

Standards: SC.6.E.7.6

Weather is the current atmospheric conditions, including temperature, rainfall, wind, and humidity for a given area. Weather changes very often. **Climate** is the general weather conditions over a longer amount of time. It is the expected weather patterns of a region. Climate includes things like the average temperature and amount of precipitation. Many of its changes are measured yearly, as opposed to daily as is the case of weather.

One of the main differences between weather and climate is simply the length of time involved. The climate of an area does not change as often as the weather. Climate is the "average weather" and it is long-term. It determines the kind of soil an area will have, the type of vegetation possible, and the types of animals that can live in an area.

As was mentioned previously, climate and weather are driven by energy differences as different parts of the Earth are heated differently by the Sun. Some areas receive more sun exposure than others depending on their latitudes and elevations. These differences can occur due to the angle of sunlight at any particular spot, which varies by latitude from the tropics. Regions near the equator receive direct sunlight (90 degrees). As distance above and below the equator increases the angle of incoming sunlight decreases. Latitudes above and below the equator receive less direct sunlight. In other words, the farther from the Equator you lie, the lower the sun angle is. Less direct sunlight results in cooler temperatures. Weather stations around the globe study the combined effects of moisture, air pressure, precipitation and temperature as they relate to the regular observation of weather and climate.

Small changes in one part of the system can have profound effects on other parts of the system. Interactions of the ocean and the atmosphere could result in adverse weather over the land, such as hurricanes. Atmospheric and geologic variables such as amount of solar radiation, volcanic eruptions, atmospheric composition, albedo (how much radiation is reflected back from the Earth's surface and clouds), soil moisture and vegetation all interact to influence climate. The global climate system can be seen as one huge interaction of the hydrosphere, atmosphere, cryosphere, biosphere, and geosphere. Any changes in these factors can result in local or global changes in climate due to exchanges in water vapor and heat through evaporation. There is a delicate balance.

The ability of glaciers and ice sheets (cryosphere) to reflect solar radiation back into space affects the warming of the oceans and the circulation of deep ocean currents. Ocean currents have an effect on weather/climate. Temperature variations cause differences in global circulation of warm and cold air and water currents. Changing water currents can lead to increased rainfall. Warm ocean currents bring forth moist air masses. As these warm air masses travel over land, thunderstorms and other forms of precipitation result. Jet streams also interact with ocean currents to influence weather/climate in measurable ways such as wind direction and speed, air pressure, temperature, humidity and precipitation.

Interactions between human activity and the biosphere also affect weather/climate. Soil and vegetation of the biosphere absorb solar radiation that warms the lower surface and also reflect heat back into the atmosphere. Vegetation influences water evaporation into the atmosphere. Human activities such as deforestation, erosion and the use of natural resources (i.e., burning of fossil fuels) affect how energy received from the Sun is returned to the atmosphere. These factors also lead to global warming which increases global temperatures and affect climate.

Table 4-11 The Climate of Florida

Physical Features	Most of Florida consists of a low, 400 mile long peninsula. Highest elevation is only 345 feet above sea level. Surface mostly covered by infertile sand or loam, often with a hardpan layer beneath which restricts water absorption. Surface sands and loams rest upon a thick layer of soluble limestone that has been greatly eroded. Numerous limestone features such as sinkholes, underground rivers, and large volume springs may be found.
Climate Zone	Most of the state lies within the extreme southern portion of the Northern Hemisphere's humid subtropical climate zone. Long hot and humid summers and mild and wet winter exists. Southernmost portion of the state is generally designated as belonging to the tropical savanna region (a climate that it shares with most of the Caribbean islands). This area is sometimes called the wet and dry tropics.
Factors that Affect Climate	Latitude, land and water distribution, prevailing winds, storms, pressure systems and ocean currents affect climate. Although no place in Florida is far from sea level, during the winter altitude can be a significant local factor in affecting temperature.
Temperature	Mean temperatures during Florida's coldest month (January) range from the lower 50s in the north to the upper 60s in the south. In the hottest month (usually July or August) it is almost the same throughout the entire State, between 27 and 28° C (81 and 83 ° F). Every day of the year the Sun reaches Florida at a higher angle than farther north, and consequently its power to heat is greater.
Precipitation	Florida is one of the wettest states in the nation. On average, approximately 54 inches of precipitation falls each year. Most precipitation is in the form of rain. The intensity of its precipitation exceeds other states. Snowfall occurs periodically (mostly in North Florida) with very little accumulation. Of the days in Florida when there is measurable precipitation, between 30 and 35 percent have accumulations of half an inch or more. The Panhandle and southeastern Florida are the wettest parts of the State. The driest portions are the Florida Keys and the offshore bar of Cape Canaveral.
Hazardous Weather	Florida experiences more tornadoes per 10,000 square miles than any state in the nation. These tornadoes are much lower in intensity than those in other states. Many are waterspouts that generally are both small and weak. More tropical systems of all kinds have made their first landfall in Florida. Hurricane season lasts from June to November. The northwestern coast experiences the most hurricanes, closely followed by the southeast and southwest. Very few hurricanes have entered Florida between Melbourne and Jacksonville.

Effect of the Water Cycle on Weather/Climate

Standards: SC.5.E.7.1, SC.5.E.7.2, SC.6.E.7.2

The **_water cycle_** is the continuous cycling of water in the hydrosphere, atmosphere, and geosphere. Changes in heat flow alter the state of water from liquid to gas (water vapor) and to solid (ice). It has an effect on weather patterns and climate. It involves the process of evaporation, transpiration, condensation, precipitation (rain, snow, sleet, and hail) and runoff. This circulation stores and transports a large amount of energy. The ocean is an integral part of the water cycle.

Oceans regulate climate on a longer time-scale and lead to natural climate variations due to their massive water stores and strong temperature changes. Water evaporates from the ocean, falls as precipitation and then goes back into the ocean. The process of evaporation and precipitation connects the oceans to all the Earth's water reservoirs.

Factors That Affect Characteristics of Different Climate Zones

Standards: SC.5.E.7.5 SC.5.E.7.6

Factors that affect characteristics (temperature and precipitation) of different climate zones include latitude, altitude (elevation), wind, proximity to bodies of water and geography (slope). Weather-related differences, such as temperature and humidity, can be found among different environments due to these factors. This explains the variation in weather among such environments as swamps, deserts, and mountains.

1. ***latitude*** -- latitude is the distance north and south of the equator. In general temperature decreases as you move away from the equator where more direct sunlight is received. Because the Earth's surface is curved solar radiation is dispersed unevenly. As latitude increases, so does the angle of inclination of solar rays resulting in less sunlight received at higher latitudes.

The Angle of The Sun's Rays and Earth

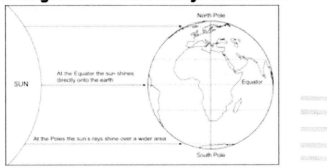

2. ***altitude*** --as elevation increases so does airflow, cloudiness and precipitation patterns. Higher altitudes have thinner atmospheres.   They gain and give off heat quickly because the air is less dense and cannot hold heat as easily.

3. ***wind*** --winds from warmer areas are warm winds and will raise temperatures. Winds from colder areas are cold and will lower temperatures.

4. ***distance from the ocean*** -- we have already mentioned that land heats and cools faster than water. Therefore, coastal areas have a smaller temperature range than those areas inland which tend to have more dramatic temperature changes. Coastal areas have milder winters and cooler summers than inland areas. Inland areas have hotter summers and colder winters.

5. ***geography***-- slope affects air movements. Mountain slopes that face the sun have different characteristics than those that do not. They tend to be warmer and have more moisture and vegetation. Mountain slopes facing away from the Sun tend to have colder and dryer climates.

Climate Variations on Mountain Ranges

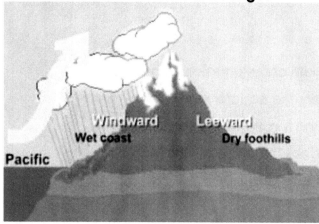

The five major climate zones based on the annual and monthly averages of temperature and precipitation are shown below:

Table 4-12 Characteristics of Different Climate Zones

Climate Zones	Characteristics (Temperature and Precipitation)	Latitude	Elevation	Proximity to Bodies of Water
Moist Tropical Climates	Year-round warm temperatures. Average monthly temperatures above 18 °C (64°F). Small seasonal temperature variations (less than 3°C). Abundant rainfall in all months. Total annual rainfall is often more than 250 cm. Humidity is between 77 and 88%. Very hot and humid summers.	Low latitude. Extend northward and southward from the equator to about 5° to 25° N and S of the equator	Low elevation. Close proximity to windward side of mountains.	Close proximity to oceans
Dry	Little rain. Huge daily and seasonal temperature range. High daytime	Low-latitude deserts.	High altitudes	Usually at great

Climates	temperatures and low nighttime temperatures (due to extremely low humidity). Daytime can reach 45°C/113°F or higher in the summer, and dip to 0°C/32°F or lower at nighttime in winter. Potential evaporation and transpiration exceed precipitation. Little to no vegetation. Annual precipitation is less than 25 cm. Associated with falling dry air masses.	Extend from 20° - 35° N and S of the equator.		distances oceans. Lack through-flowing streams.
Humid Middle Latitude Climates	Land/water differences play a large part. Warm, extremely dry summers and humid, cool, mild, wet winters. Distinct summer and winters. Average temperature of coldest month is below 18°C/ 64°C and above -3°C/ 27°F. Ample precipitation. Annual Precipitation is 42 cm (17 in). Located on the eastern and western sides of most continents.	Mid-latitudes Latitude Range: 25° - 40° N and S of the equator	Elevations of 1,200 to 2,100 m	Close proximity to oceans
Moist Continental	Warm to cool summers and severe, bitter cold winters with snow storms and blustery winds. Climate found in the interior regions of large land masses. Total precipitation is not very high and seasonal temperatures vary widely. Found only in northern hemisphere. Average temperature of coldest month must dip below -3°C/ 27°F. Annual temperature ranges can exceed 40°C/82°F. Daily temperatures change often. Evenly distributed precipitation during the year is around 20 -40 inches/year. This climate is in the polar front zone (where polar and tropical air masses meet). Being removed from the moderating influence of the oceans, the climate experience great swings in seasonal temperatures.	Mid-latitudes Found between 40° - 70° N latitudes	Low elevations	Not in close proximity to oceans
Polar	Polar and arctic air masses dominate. Long and severe winters. Short, mild season exists, but not a true summer season. Moderating ocean winds keep the temperatures from being as severe as interior regions. Average temperatures in the warmest months are below 10°C/50°F. Very cold temperatures and generally dry conditions. Low sun angle. Low temperatures reduce moisture content of the air. Precipitation is less than 250 mm a year. High pressure areas.	High latitudes Latitude Range: 60° - 75° N	1000 -4000 feet above sea level	Close proximity to ocean (arctic oceans)
Highland	Cool to cold climates. Snowy and windy. Climate change rapidly on mountains, becoming colder the higher the altitude gets. Have the same seasons and wet and dry periods as the biome they are located in. Temperature range is -18 °C to 10°C. In the summer average temperatures range from 10-15°C. In the winter temperatures are below freezing. Average precipitation is 23 cm.	Found all over the world	Found in mountains and high plateaus. Usually at an altitude of 10,000 ft or more.	Close proximity to ocean.

Natural Disasters and Their Effect on Human Life in Florida

Standards: SC.5.E.7.7, SC.6.E.7.7, SC.6.E.7.8

Florida is vulnerable to a broad range of natural disasters. These include hurricanes, tropical storms, tropical depressions, tornadoes, floods, and wildfires. These catastrophes regularly affect Florida's residents and visitors. Natural disasters have an economic, social and psychological effect on human life. Many lives are lost as a result of hazardous weather. In addition, housing and property damages and power outages can result in total losses exceeding millions or even billions of dollars. The extent of evacuations and the number of people forced out of their homes has a deep effect on human emotion and welfare and often result in homelessness. The devastation can be traumatizing.

Floridians can protect themselves from hazardous weather and sun exposure by educating themselves first on weather conditions. Watching or reading the daily weather report should be a part of every resident's routine. Outdoor activity should be planned according to weather conditions. For example, if a lightning storm has been predicted residents should remain indoors, keep blinds drawn, and plug out all electrical outlets to prevent lightening strikes and fire. Sun exposure can be minimized by wearing sunscreen with a high SPF level, wearing hats and sunglasses and refraining from outdoor activity when the sun is highest in the sky (early morning and late afternoon being more optimal times).

To prepare for a hurricane or other hazardous weather, basic provisions should be made that will minimize property losses and damage, prevent the loss of life, and create a more tolerable experience in the storm's aftermath. The suggestions are listed below:

1. Store food and water to last a few days
2. Board up windows or install permanent shutter on windows
3. Have flashlights, batteries and battery-powered radios available
4. Store valuables in plastic containers high off the ground
5. Unplug TVs and small appliances
6. Shut off gas and propane lines in the house
7. Lock windows and doors
8. Take cover under a table, stable object, a closet or hallway far away from windows and

doors with glass

9. Brace doors leading outside and close all interior doors
10. Secure and store outdoor furniture, equipment, yard decorations, etc. They could become deadly projectiles during strong winds
11. If your family has a boat or recreational vehicles secure them
12. Stay inside. If authorities call for an evacuation, leave immediately

It is very important for you and your family to design a family preparedness plan for natural disasters. Knowledge of such procedures will help you to safely escape disasters, thus increasing your survival rate. The plan should be made available to each member of the family and be rehearsed and drilled at regular intervals. While emergency plans may vary key elements should be common to all. These include:

1. Knowing the designated evacuation routes planned by your county
2. Making arrangements to stay with relatives outside the storm impact area
3. Letting other family members know of your destination
4. Creating an emergency evacuation kit that contains among other things financial and legal documents in the event you become homeless and require government assistance. Other items to be included in the evacuation kit includes cash, photos, medical records, medications, puzzles and activities for children, personal hygiene items, fire extinguisher, clothing, warm blankets, sleeping bags, paper and pencil, chlorine bleach and a medicine dropper for disinfecting, pet food, infant formula, diapers, cell phone with solar charger, maps, can opener, tools, garbage bags for personal sanitation, dust masks, and whistle to signal for help.
5. Planning for pets prior to the storm. Make a list of pet-friendly hotels, motels, and emergency shelters or other suitable shelter for your pet (animal shelter, boarding places or veterinarians).

SECTION REVIEW

CHAPTER 4 SAMPLE QUESTIONS

1. Scientists believe the universe began with a tremendous explosion of matter, bright lights, and intense energy. The desire for answers brought on the science of astronomy dating back to ancient times. Which of the following conclusions below can be made about the nature of scientific inquiry and space exploration?
    a. Man's need to explore has opened up windows of opportunities for the development of knowledge and understanding of our Solar System and the universe.
    b. Scientific inquiry into space is based on man's understanding of the natural world and only how it can be manipulated to serve his own needs.
    c. Man's need to explore space is based on a desire to plunder the riches of other galaxies.
    d. Scientific inquiry and investigation into space has had very little impact on developments in science.

2. Short wavelength X rays and UV radiation emitted by solar flares can be expected to
    a. Interfere with radar and other equipment operating under radio wave frequencies
    b. Be mostly filtered out by the Earth's atmosphere
    c. Have no effect on Earth
    d. Both (a) and (b)
    e. None of the above

3. A light-year is not only a measure of distance but it is also a measure of time. Based on this concept which of the following is a true statement?
    a. A star that is a million light-years way is visible to us on Earth only because its light was created and traveled a million years to reach Earth.
    b. When we look at stars that are light-years away we would be looking at how the star looked in the past and not how the star currently looks.
    c. Astronomers look at distant galaxies to get an idea of what early galaxies may have looked like and how they formed.
    d. All of the above

4. Which of the following correctly lists the size of the object in order from greatest to least in our solar system?
    a. Planet, comet, asteroid, meteorite
    b. Planet, asteroid, meteorite, comet
    c. Planet, asteroid, comet, meteorite
    d. Planet, meteorite, asteroid, comet

5. In the convection zone of the Sun, convection currents are responsible for the movement of gases from an area of higher temperature to an area of lower temperature in order to circulate thermal energy to the other layers of the Sun. This occurs to maintain the internal structure and overall functioning of the Sun. Which of the following cycles on Earth resembles this process?
   a. The water cycle
   b. The rock cycle
   c. The carbon cycle
   d. The nitrogen cycle

6.

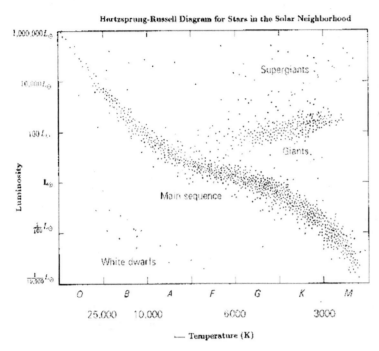

The H-R Diagram above compares stars at various stages of their lives using both the temperature and luminosity (brightness) of the star to show its age. Based on the diagram rank the following in order of increasing luminosity: blue supergiant, the Sun, red giant, white dwarf.
   a. The Sun, red giant, blue supergiant, white dwarf
   b. Red giant, blue supergiant, white dwarf, the Sun
   c. White dwarf, the Sun, red giant, blue supergiant
   d. Blue supergiant, white dwarf, the Sun, red giant

7. If Shannon, who is 15 years old, calculates her age in days based on the actual number of days in a year, which calculation below would provide the correct answer?
   a. Shannon has been alive for 5,475 days.
   b. Shannon has been alive for 5,478.75 days.
   c. Shannon has been alive for 5,400 days.
   d. Shannon has been alive for 380 days.

8. If spring tides occur when the Earth, Sun and Moon are aligned (are in line), and neap tides occur when the gravity of the Sun and Moon pull against each other, how would you know if the tide you see is a neap or spring tide?
    a. Spring tides occur in the Spring
    b. Neap Tides occur in the Fall
    c. Spring tides are usually stronger and neap tides are relatively weak tides
    d. You would not be able to tell the difference between the two

9. John and Corey planned to visit the local planetarium after school. They wanted to learn more about electromagnetic energy. Which facts about electromagnetic energy will they most likely encounter at the local planetarium?
    a. The Sun produces only short wavelength electromagnetic radiation.
    b. Electromagnetic energy is produced by the Earth, Moon and Sun.
    c. The electromagnetic spectrum includes only visible light and microwaves.
    d. Electromagnetic radiation travels through space in transverse waves that do not require a medium.

10. If air is heated it will rise due to its decreasing density.   As the Sun heats atmospheric air it rises as well. Which scenario below would most likely cause air to sink instead of rise?
    a. A global blackout resulting in another ice age.
    b. Several geysers shooting steam in the air all at once.
    c. A volcanic eruption poring lava into water creating superheated water vapor.
    d. An earthquake releasing hot gases that were trapped in the ground.

11. Comparatively speaking, how would you classify the inner planets versus the outer planets?
    a. The inner planets are primarily gaseous planets, while the outer planets are rocky or terrestrial.
    b. The inner planets are primarily rocky or terrestrial planets, while the outer planets are gaseous.
    c. The inner planets are much larger than the outer planets,
    d. The inner planets are equal in size to the outer planets.

12. A meteorologist would most likely measure wind speed and direction with a
    a. Barometer
    b. Rain gauge
    c. Anemometer
    d. Hygrometer

13. Which of the following associations concerning Earth's spheres is correct?
    a. Geosphere – polar ice caps
    b. Atmosphere – exosphere, troposphere, ozone layer
    c. Hydrosphere – rocks
    d. Biosphere – crust, mantle, inner core and outer core

14. The three main types of rocks are igneous, sedimentary, and metamorphic. Which type of rock would be affected most by the water cycle?
    a. Metamorphic
    b. Igneous rocks
    c. Sedimentary
    d. None of the above answers are correct because the water cycle involves the hydrosphere and does not affect the rock cycle.

15. All of the following characteristics of moist tropical climates are true **Except**
    a. Huge daily and seasonal temperature range
    b. Low latitudes
    c. Close proximity to oceans
    d. Abundant rainfall

16. How can Floridians protect themselves from natural disasters/hazardous weather conditions that are common to Florida?
    a. In a lightning storm residents should remain indoors, keep blinds drawn and plug out all electrical outlets to prevent lightening strikes and fire.
    b. They must educate themselves about the natural disasters that are more often associated with the area they live in so as to prevent unnecessary deaths.
    c. They should design a family preparedness plan for natural disasters that includes key provisions as water and food, first aid, and communication equipment.
    d. All of the above
    e. (b) and (c) only

17. Emma is wearing specially designed eyeglasses that allow her to look directly at the Sun's surface during a total eclipse. Identify the layers of the Sun Emma could possibly see.
    a. radiative zone
    b. chromosphere
    c. corona
    d. convection zone
    e. (b) and (c) only

ANSWERS TO CHAPTER 4 SECTION REVIEW

1. Feedback: Correct Answer: (A)
Reasoning: Of the four statements listed in this question the only one that is true is choice (A). Choices (B), (C), and (D) can all be eliminated since they are not factual.

2. Feedback: Correct Answer (D)
Reasoning: Shorter wavelength X rays and UV radiation emitted by solar flares can interfere with radar and other equipment operating under radio wave frequencies. Short wavelength ultraviolet radiation is mostly filtered out by the Earth's ozone layer. Based on these facts, both choice (A) and choice (B) would be true statements therefore, making choice (D) the correct answer. It has been shown that X rays and UV radiation emitted by solar flares do effect Earth therefore, choices (C) and (E) are both incorrect.

3. Feedback: Correct Answer (D)
Reasoning: A star that is 1 million light-years away is visible to us on Earth only because its light was created and traveled a million years to reach Earth. When we look at this star we would be looking at the past-- how the star looked one million years ago and not how the star currently looks. This is also true of distant galaxies. Astronomers look at distant galaxies to get an idea of what early galaxies may have looked like and how they formed. Choice (D) is the correct answer since all three statements choices (A, B, and C) are true statements concerning light-year being measure of distance as well as time.

4. Feedback: Correct Answer (C)
Reasoning: Based on the understanding of sizes of various space bodies, we can automatically exclude all choices except choice (C), since planets are larger than asteroids, which are larger than comets, which are larger than meteorites.

5. Feedback: Correct Answer (A)
Reasoning: This question requires an intricate understanding of the various cycles on Earth. Simply put, one should realize that the rock cycle does not involve convection so (B) is not correct. As for choice (C) and (D), convection does not drive these two cycles, only the plants that require these elements and the organisms that release carbon dioxide drive these cycles. This answer is also incorrect. The water cycle involves convection, which is the movement of heat or thermal energy through gases or liquids, thus making this answer correct.

6. Feedback: Correct Answer (C)
In order of increasing luminosity, from dimmest to most luminous would be: white dwarf, Sun, red giant, and blue supergiant. Choice (C) satisfies this order and is therefore the correct answer. All the other answer choices are incorrectly ranked.

7. Feedback: Correct Answer (B)
Reasoning: Since a year has exactly 365 1/4 days (365.25 days) in it, all you need to do to acquire the calculation is to multiply her age by the exact number of days in a year. All answer choices can be excluded with the exception of choice (B) which is the correct answer.

8. Feedback: Correct Answer (C)
Reasoning: Choices (A) and (B) are incorrect since spring or neap tides are not associated with the seasons. They occur during specific moon phases. As for Choice (D), both types of tides

FINAL EXAM

1. The following graph is of a chipmunk population that migrated into an environment where it had very little competition. Based on your knowledge of ecology which statement best explains the shape of the graph?

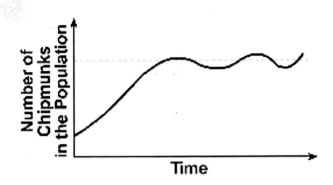

    a. The chipmunk population quickly increased but eventually stabilized as completion for limited resources occurred.
    b. The mutation rate of the chipmunks increased and they began to die off.
    c. The chipmunk population began to die off as the producers began competing with it for food.
    d. The chipmunk population was overrun by a squirrel population

2. Jacob and Anya would like to setup an experiment to test the affect of light on the rate of photosynthesis. What would be the best way for them to set up the control and experimental groups in their investigation?
    a. Jacob and Anya could take 80 plants and expose 40 to sunlight and the remaining 40 to carbon dioxide.
    b. Jacob and Anya could take 80 plants and expose them all to the same amount of sunlight so as to compare the type of plant.
    c. Jacob and Anya could take 80 plants and expose 20 to full sunlight, 20 to ½ sunlight, 20 to ¼ sunlight, and 20 to no sunlight.
    d. Jacob and Anya could take 80 plants and expose 40 to sunlight outdoors and 40 to darkness indoors.

3. The structure labeled 2 in the diagram below is classified as a
   a. Ribose sugar
   b. Deoxyribose sugar
   c. Nitrogen base
   d. Phosphate group

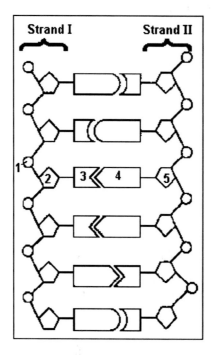

4. When a scientist has completed his/her research he/she should
   a. Keep the results a secret to prevent other scientist from benefitting from their hard work.
   b. Communicate his/her results and make recommendations based on them in order to add to the already vast scientific knowledge available.
   c. Analyze his/her results and then hoard the information to secure it.
   d. Communicate his/her results and immediately convert them into absolute law.

5. Under certain environmental conditions organisms with favorable variations reproduce more successfully than organisms with less favorable variations. This statement best describes the concept of
   a. Overproduction
   b. Ecological succession
   c. Natural selection
   d. Extinction

6. Asexual reproduction of organisms normally results in a new organism that contains cells with
   a. More chromosomes than found in the parent cell
   b. Less chromosomes than found in the parent cell
   c. The same number of chromosomes as the parent cell
   d. Exactly half the number of chromosomes as the parent cell

7. Phyllis has recorded her data on the effect of sodium hydroxide on bean plant leaf production. Below is a data table that documents her results. How could Phyllis convert this table to a more effective graph?

Plant Number	Amount of NaOH	Plant Leaf Count
1	1.0ml	9
2	2.0ml	5
3	3.0ml	3
4	4.0ml	2
Control	0ml	12

    a. Phyllis could have the dependent variable, which is the amount of NaOH on the x-axis, and the independent variable, which is the plant leaf count on the y-axis in a line graph.

    b. Phyllis could have the dependent variable, which is the amount of NaOH on the y-axis, and the independent variable, which is the plant leaf count on the x-axis in a line graph.

    c. Phyllis could have the independent variable, which is the amount of NaOH on the y-axis, and the dependent variable, which is the plant leaf count on the x-axis in a line graph.

    d. Phyllis could have the independent variable, which is the amount of NaOH on the x-axis, and the dependent variable, which is plant leaf count on the y-axis in a line graph.

8. Sean noticed that a large bowl of liquid that was cloudy one hour ago is now clear. He has arrived at the conclusion that

    a. The mixture is a suspension whose particles have settled out making the liquid clear.

    b. The liquid is a pure substance that has settled out and is now an even purer substance that is clear.

    c. The molecules inside the liquid have completely stopped moving.

    d. The mixture is a colloid whose particles have settled out making the liquid clear.

9. Which ecological term includes everything represented in the illustration below?

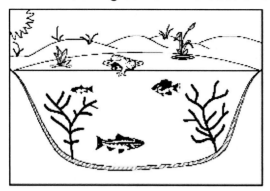

   a. Ecosystem
   b. Community
   c. Species
   d. Population

10. If a material has a density of 50 g/mL , what would the mass of the material be if the volume is 5 mL?
   a. 250g
   b. 10 g
   c. 0.1g
   d. More information is needed to solve this problem

11. Ernest Rutherford discovered through his gold-foil experiment that the atom was not a solid mass of positive and negative charges. He found that atoms were mostly made up of empty space surrounding a central nucleus. How was his discovery relevant to the development of scientific knowledge?
   a. It demonstrated that scientific knowledge builds upon itself.
   b. It demonstrated that scientific knowledge is modified as new information becomes available.
   c. It demonstrated that diversity in scientist's backgrounds, talents, and ethnicities, helped to successfully build scientific knowledge.
   d. All of the above
   e. None of the above

12. A student discovered a chemical in the lab that did not have an ionic charge. From reading the label he found two pieces of information; that the mass number was 23 and that it had 21 electrons. What knowledge does this information unknowingly provide to the student?
   a. That the liquid has 21 protons
   b. That the atomic number of the liquid is 21
   c. That the liquid has 2 neutrons
   d. All of the above
   e. None of the above

13. Samuel made a visit to his grandmother's house on a cool autumn day. He walked almost 2 miles to and from where his grandmother lived. Which type of energy transformation did Samuel demonstrate during his walk?
  a. Mechanical energy to sound energy when he crunched leaves beneath his feet.
  b. Potential energy to light energy when he glared at the Sun.
  c. Kinetic energy to nuclear energy which powered the nucleus of his cells.
  d. Choice b and c only.

14. Manette ran 1800 meters in 240 seconds northward towards the post office. Her velocity was
  a. 7.5 meters per second
  b. 0.13 meters per second
  c. 7.5 meters per seconds north
  d. Not enough information is given to solve the problem

15. A sports car jumps a highway divider at a speed of 50 mph and crashes head on into an SUV traveling in the opposite direction at 85 mph. The vehicles stick together after the crash and come to a complete stop 1000 meters in the same direction of travel as the SUV. Which conservation law was best demonstrated by the crash?
  a. The Law of Conservation of Chemical Energy
  b. The Law of Conservation of Crashes
  c. The Law of Conservation of Momentum
  d. None of the above

16. Which phrase best defines evolution?
  a. An adaptation of an organism to its environment
  b. A sudden replacement of one community by another
  c. A geographic relocation of organisms
  d. A process of change in a population over a period of time

17. All of the following life functions maintain homeostasis **Except**
  a. Respiration
  b. Growth
  c. Excretion
  d. Sexual reproduction

18. A change in the base sequence of DNA is known as
  a. A gene mutation
  b. Amino acid
  c. Pedigree
  d. A karyotype

19. Which Punnett square below demonstrates the cross between two heterozygous brown-eyed dogs that produces a blue-eyed offspring?

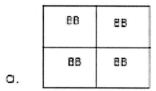
a.

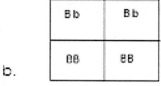
b.

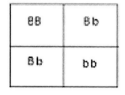
c.

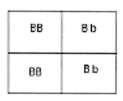
d.

20. Scientist study solar properties to expand their knowledge of life on Earth. Which statement below is true concerning the relationship between the Earth and solar properties?
   a. Electrons and neutrons emitted from the Sun disrupt Earth's magnetic field and cause it to have retrograde motion every leap year.
   b. Solar wind determines Earth's climate and is directly responsible for drastic changes in Earth's weather.
   c. Solar disturbances, such as sunspots, generate enormous electric currents that disrupt communication on Earth and damage equipment.
   d. The Sun's rotation is responsible for seasons on Earth.

21. How does natural selection operate to cause change in a population?
   a. The members of the population do not adapt to environmental changes.
   b. All the members of the population adapt to environmental changes.
   c. The members of the population differ so that the ones with favorable variations survive when the environment changes.
   d. The members of the population are equally able to survive any environmental change.

22. If strand 1 in a segment of a replicating DNA molecule has the bases **A-T-C-C-G-A-G-G-T**, the complementary DNA strand would contain the bases
   a. T-A-G-G-C-T-C-C-A
   b. T-U-G-G-C-T-C-C-G
   c. U-A-G-G-C-U-U-C-C
   d. A-T-G-G-C-T-C-C-A

23. We now say there are 8 known planets, a few dwarf planets and their natural satellites (moons). How are planets in our solar system distinguished from moons or other celestial bodies?
   a. Planets are always larger than any moon and smaller than stars.
   b. Planets and moons both have the same seasons.
   c. Planets all orbit the sun, while moons orbit the planets
   d. None of the above

24. How would you differentiate the outer planets of our solar system from the inner planets?
   a. The inner planets are much larger than the outer planets.
   b. The outer planets are primarily made of gases.
   c. The inner planets are primarily made of gases.
   d. The outer planets are closer to the sun than the inner planets.

25. Which of the following scenarios best demonstrates proper scientific methods for Adelina to follow in conducting an investigation?
   a. Adelina investigated an idea about solar radiation, decided to formulate a question about how solar radiation affects plastic, composed a conclusion that solar radiation reduces longevity of plastic, and shared her results with the scientific community.
   b. Adelina investigated an idea about solar radiation, decided to formulate a question about how solar radiation affects plastic, composed a hypothesis, conducted an experiment, analyzed her data, formulated a conclusion that solar radiation reduces longevity of plastic, and shared her results with the scientific community.
   c. Adelina investigated an idea about solar radiation, decided to formulate a question about how solar radiation affects plastic, formulated an experiment, composed a conclusion that solar radiation reduces longevity of plastic, decided on a hypothesis, and shared her results with the scientific community.
   d. Adelina investigated an idea about solar radiation, decided to formulate a question about how solar radiation affects plastic, composed a recommendation that solar radiation reduces longevity of plastic, and shared her results with the scientific community.

26. Why is it important for scientists to share the results of their research with the scientific community?
   a. Scientists need to share their results to get a complete answer since only half the experiment is ever done.
   b. Scientist share their results with the scientific community only to collect large profits from them.
   c. Scientists share their results to obtain knowledge of natural phenomena and to eliminate bias by having a system of checks and balances.
   d. Scientists share results only when they know the results are flawless and they hope to win a Nobel Peace prize.

27. The diagram below shows the Earth, the Sun's rays and the Moon at eight different positions on its orbit. What is the name of the moon phase for the position indicated by the letter?

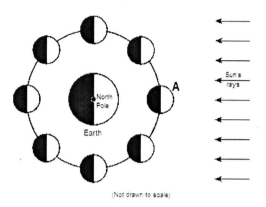

(Not drawn to scale)

    a. Waning Crescent
    b. Waxing Gibbous
    c. Full Moon
    d. New Moon

28. Under which conditions could igneous rock be converted to sedimentary rock?
    a. Heat and pressure
    b. Deposition
    c. Melting
    d. Weathering and erosion

29. The water cycle is depicted in the illustration below. Which letter represents the process of transpiration?

Water Cycle

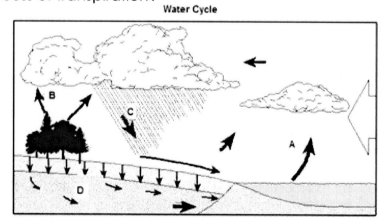

    a. A
    b. B
    c. C
    d. D

30. In the gas state of matter which of the following assumptions could be made regarding the levels of kinetic and potential energy of the atoms that compose that matter?

    a. The amount of kinetic energy of the molecules is quite less than that of the amount of potential energy being stored in the molecules.

    b. The amount of kinetic energy of the molecules is far more than that of the amount of potential energy being stored in the molecules.

    c. Gas molecules have a lot of kinetic energy and no potential energy.

    d. The amount of kinetic energy of the molecules is the same as the amount of potential energy being stored in the molecules.

31. The practice of science should proceed in ways that are not destructive and that adhere to the utmost standard of good behavior. Based on this premise which of the following scientific experiments should not be allowed for students to do?

    a. A student decided to find out how long it would take a potato plant that is nutrient starved to survive in cold temperatures.

    b. A student decided to find out how long it would take a human to starve by withholding food for several days.

    c. A student decided to find out how long it would take a beanstalk that is nutrient starved to survive in cold, warm, and hot temperatures.

    d. A student decided to find out how long it would take a sedimentary rock that is exposed to weathering to erode in cold temperatures.

32. Which of the following methods should a teacher stress in order for students to practice safety during and after science lab experiments?

    a. Allow students to eat only before lab activities and drink only purified water during lab activities to reduce exposure to dangerous chemicals that are used in the lab experiment.

    b. Make sure that the students pay close attention to the teacher only when the teacher is talking, mainly because this is the stage where all of the instructions are going to be given and then they can work at their own pace.

    c. Make sure that students follow directions and wear safety gear during the lab activity because it is critical that students follow directions and stay safe while dealing with any science lab materials or equipment.

    d. Make sure that students familiarize themselves with important safety symbols associated with the lab after the activity is finished.

33. Carlos conducted an experiment that followed an established scientific method. He sought to determine if the amount of sunlight exposure affected the diameter of a common tomato plant. What is one conclusion that can be drawn from the graph of his results below?

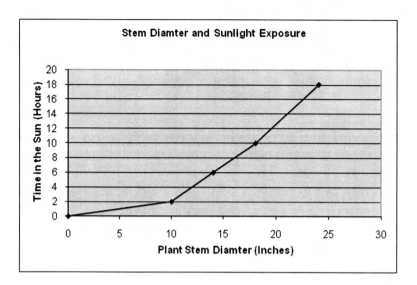

a. The amount of sunlight increases with a decrease in the diameter of the tomato plant.
b. The amount of sunlight has no impact on the diameter of the tomato plant since it did not increase.
c. The diameter of the tomato plant increased with a decrease in the amount of sunlight.
d. The diameter of the tomato plant increased with an increase in the amount of sunlight.

34. Latisha went through her entire science fair project and completed all of the parts in about three weeks. Towards the end of the science fair event at school she noticed that another student worked on the same project title as she did. If Latisha wants to repeat her experiment for next year's science fair how could knowledge of the other student's investigation help her?
a. Latisha should discuss her results with the other student and compare data. With the additional data she can either conduct further research if their results are different or draw conclusions based on similarities in both experimental results.
b. Since Latisha and the student has submitted the same research for the science fair it is ok for her to copy the students data and submit it along with her own.
c. Latisha already has enough data for her project and should just ignore the work of the other student.
d. Latisha should assume her results are incorrect, change her hypothesis and start over.

35. Connor conducted an experiment on the effects of sodium hydroxide on the growth of pumpkin plants. Based on the graph of Connor's results below, what is one conclusion that can be made regarding the results?

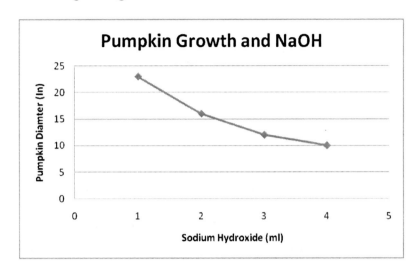

a. Connor can conclude that pumpkin diameter increases with increased levels of sodium hydroxide.
b. Connor can conclude that the greater the amount of sodium hydroxide the smaller the diameter of the pumpkin.
c. Connor can conclude that the level of sodium hydroxide had no effect on the diameter of pumpkins produced.
d. Not enough information is given to draw a conclusion to Connor's experiment.

36. The Milky Way Galaxy is shown in the picture below. This galaxy is classified as

a. Elliptical
b. Oval
c. Spiral
d. Irregular

37. Which statement below best identifies a human disorder and the body system it affects?
a. Polio/Reproductive system
b. Sickle Cell Anemia/ Circulatory system
c. Emphysema/Nervous system
d. Gout/Cardiovascular

38. A shopping cart full of groceries requires a much greater effort to push than an empty shopping cart. Which of Newton's Laws of Motion explains this?
   a. Force is equal to mass times acceleration.
   b. For every reaction there is an equal and opposite reaction.
   c. An object at rest remains at rest and an object in motion remains in motion unless an unbalanced force acts upon it.
   d. Energy is neither created nor destroyed.

39. All of the following are true statements about meiosis *Except*
   a. Meiosis results in genetic variation due to crossing over at prophase
   b. Meiosis results in two cell divisions (Meiosis 1 and 2)
   c. Meiosis occurs only in sex cells (gametes)
   d. Meiosis preserves the diploid number (2n)

40. The unit that is most appropriate for measuring the distance from the Sun to Earth is
   a. Light-minute
   b. Light-year
   c. Angstrom
   d. Miles

41. The diagram below shows a spectrum produced from a distant star compared to a standard spectrum. The distant star's spectral lines have shifted toward the infrared end of the spectrum.

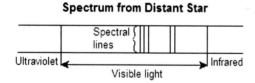

Which conclusion can be made by comparing the distant star's spectrum to the standard spectrum?
   a. The star is moving away from Earth
   b. The star is moving towards Earth
   c. The star is releasing helium at a rapid rate
   d. None of the above

42. Below is a model of a wave that was drawn but not labeled. The amount of time that this wave took to pass was 3 seconds. Which of the following statements correctly describes a property of this wave?

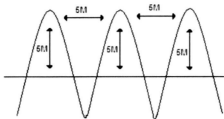

   a. The wavelength of this wave is 10m, because you would add up the two distances between the three crests to calculate wavelength.
   b. The frequency of the wave is 1 hertz, because three waves passed in three seconds.
   c. This amplitude of the wave is the distance from the crest of one wave to the crest of another.
   d. The trough of the wave is 5 times the height of the amplitude.

43. If it were possible to travel to the Sun, how would you expect your weight to change as you got closer to it?
   a. The Sun has the strongest gravitational pull of all of the celestial bodies in our solar system, so your weight would decrease as you got closer to the Sun.
   b. The Sun has the weakest gravitational pull of all of the celestial bodies in our solar system, so your weight would decrease as you got closer to the Sun.
   c. The Sun has the strongest chemical pull of all of the celestial bodies in our solar system, so your weight would decrease as you got closer to the sun.
   d. The Sun has the strongest gravitational pull of all of the celestial bodies in our solar system, so your weight would increase as you got closer to the Sun.

44. The electromagnetic spectrum provides many benefits to humans such as
   a. The ability to study hot bodies in space
   b. Improved ways to cook food
   c. Medical diagnostic equipment
   d. All of the above
   e. None of the above

45. Which process is represented by the series of diagrams below?

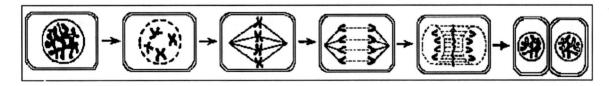

   a. Mitosis
   b. Meiosis
   c. Protein synthesis
   d. Gametogenesis

46. The length of time it takes for Earth to revolve around the Sun is
  a. 360 days
  b. 24 hours
  c. 1 day
  d. None of the above

47. Which statement illustrates an interaction between biotic and abiotic resources?
  a. Sharks transport remora fish to food
  b. Rainwater returns to the ocean as runoff
  c. A deer releases carbon dioxide, which is used by plants for photosynthesis
  d. Igneous rock undergoes intense heat and pressure to become metamorphic rock

48. A disease that disrupts the function of vacuoles in human cells would most likely affect which body system?
  a. Nervous system
  b. Digestive system
  c. Circulatory system
  d. Immune system

49. How is the Law of Conservation of Mass demonstrated when matter undergoes a change of state from a solid to a liquid?
  a. A change in the state of matter is a physical change which results in a small loss in the amount of matter when it changes to a liquid.
  b. A change in the state of matter is a chemical change that results in no loss in the amount of matter when it changes to a liquid.
  c. A change in the state of matter is a physical change that results in no loss or gain in the amount of matter when it changes to a liquid.
  d. A change in the state of matter is a chemical change that increases the amount of matter when it undergoes a change of state to a liquid.

50. Which of the following factors are responsible for the creation of seasons on Earth?
  a. Earth's revolution around the Sun
  b. The Earth's 23.5 degree tilt on its axis
  c. Both (a) and (b)
  d. Neither (a) nor (b)

51. How does the interaction between the geosphere and hydrosphere affect the physical structure of the Earth?
  a. The geosphere involves the movement of gases that force topographical changes in the mantle and crust of the hydrosphere.
  b. The geosphere involves the movement of liquid water that forces topographical changes in the crust and lithosphere of the hydrosphere.
  c. The hydrosphere involves the movement of liquid water that forces topographical changes in the crust and lithosphere of the geosphere.
  d. The hydrosphere involves the movement of molten lava that influences seismic changes in the crust and lithosphere of the geosphere.

52. The *least* favorable way to prepare for hurricanes and hazardous weather is to
   a. Familiarize yourself with evacuation routes
   b. Leave televisions plugged in so that you can monitor weather conditions on the news
   c. Store food and water to last a few days
   d. Secure and store outdoor furniture, equipment, etc

53. Florida's climate is *least* affected by
   a. Latitude
   b. Mountain ranges
   c. Altitude
   d. Distance from the ocean

54. The plate boundary shown in the diagram below would be most likely to cause

   a. Sea floor spreading
   b. Ocean ridges
   c. Mountain building
   d. Volcanic islands

55. How would a scientist use relative dating to determine the age of the organisms found in rock layers A - E below?

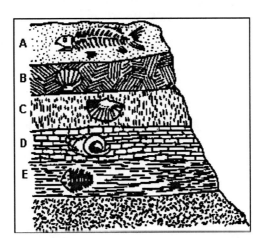

   a. It would be determined that layer A is the oldest since it is on top therefore, the fossil contained within must be the oldest organism.
   b. It would be determined that layer E is the oldest since it is the lowest layer of the four therefore; the fossil contained within must be the oldest organism.
   c. Layer C contains the most complex organism so it must be the oldest organism.
   d. Layer B contains the most complex organism so it must be the oldest.

56. The main difference between climate and weather is
     a. Climate is the current atmospheric condition and weather is the conditions over a longer amount of time.
     b. Climate changes more frequently than weather.
     c. Changes in weather are measured yearly, while changes in climate are measured daily.
     d. Weather is the current atmospheric conditions and climate is the conditions over a longer amount of time.

57. In order to reduce consumption of nonrenewable resources, humans could
     a. Build more cars that run on biofuels such as ethanol, instead of gasoline
     b. Commute to work in their own gasoline powered cars instead of commuting in hybrid buses
     c. Decrease the use of solar-powered buildings
     d. Use oil to heat homes instead of natural-gas

58. The diagram below represents a pyramid of energy in an ecosystem.

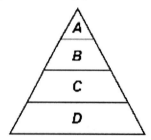

Under normal conditions, organisms at which level of the pyramid would have the *greatest* amount of stored energy?
     a. A
     b. B
     c. C
     d. D

59. Decomposers are important in the environment because they
     a. Can create oxygen from nitrogen that plants use in their respiration
     b. Hunt and eliminate dangerous predators from the environment
     c. Recycle nutrients from dead organisms back into the soil for plants to use
     d. Directly recycle water for the water cycle

60. The organelle below can be found inside both plant and animal cells.

If this organelle were to become defective these cells would not be able to
     a. Produce proteins
     b. Store water
     c. Produce energy
     d. Transport materials throughout the cell

FINAL EXAM ANSWER KEY

Question #	Correct Answer	Question #	Correct Answer
1	A	31	B
2	C	32	C
3	B	33	D
4	B	34	A
5	C	35	B
6	C	36	C
7	D	37	B
8	A	38	A
9	A	39	D
10	A	40	A
11	D	41	A
12	D	42	B
13	A	43	D
14	C	44	D
15	C	45	A
16	D	46	D
17	D	47	C
18	A	48	B
19	C	49	C
20	C	50	C
21	C	51	C
22	A	52	B
23	C	53	B
24	B	54	C
25	B	55	B
26	C	56	D
27	D	57	A
28	D	58	D
29	B	59	C
30	B	60	C

Calculations Section

1. Acceleration:

$$a = \Delta v / \Delta t = (v_{final} - v_{initial}) / (t_{final} - t_{initial})$$

or

$$a = \frac{\Delta v}{\Delta t} = \frac{Velocity \quad Change}{Ellapsed \quad Time}$$

Acceleration shows the change in velocity in a unit time. It is measured in (m/s)/s, or m/s^2, which can be both positive and negative depending on whether the object's velocity increases or decreases.

Example:

A car accelerates from 0 m/s to 60 m/s in 6 seconds. What is the car's acceleration?
Acceleration = (60 m/s) - (0 m/s) / (6 s)- (0 s) = (60 m/s)/ (6 s) = 10 m/s^2

---

2. Average Speed:

Average Speed = (distance traveled/ time taken to travel that distance)

The average speed of an object tells you the (average) rate at which it covers distance. It is the rate that position changes.

Example:

A car travels between 2 cities 80 miles apart in 8 hours. What is its average speed?
Answer:

Average speed = 80 miles/8 hours = 10 miles/hour.

---

3. Density:

$$D = m(g) / V (ml) \quad \text{or} \quad m(g) / V (cm^3)$$
Liquids   Solids

The density of a material is defined as its mass per unit volume. This means that density is equal to the amount of matter in an object in a certain amount of space or volume.

Example:

Calculate the density of a solid material that has a mass of 65.657 g and a volume of 23.5 cm^3.

Density = 65.657 g /23.5 cm^3.
Density = 2.7939 g/ cm^3 or 2.8 g/ cm^3 (the answer rounded to the nearest 10th place)

---

4. Percent Efficiency:

$$\text{Percent efficiency} = \frac{\text{Useful work done by the machine (output)}}{\text{Work done on the machine (input)}} \times 100\%$$

Percent efficiency basically tells how much of the energy that you put into a machine you can get back out. Work output and work input have to be in the same metric units before calculating.

Example:

If a machine puts out 200 J (Joules) of energy and takes in 400 J (Joules) of energy what is its efficiency?

% Efficiency = (200 J/400 J) X 100% = 0.5 X 100% = 50%

So the machine is 50% efficient and wastes the other 50% of its energy. Remember even though energy maybe wasted as heat it is never created nor destroyed.

---

5. Force:

Force (F) = mass (m) x acceleration (a)

Force is a push or a pull. It is measured in Newtons (N) or (kg $\bullet$ m/s^2).

Example:

Your motorcycle has a mass of 10.1 kilograms. You accelerate at a rate of 1.58 m/s^2. Calculate the force that is accelerating the motorcycle.

F = 10.1 kg X 1.58 m/s^2 = 15.958 N or 16.0 N (the answer rounded to the nearest 10th place).

---

6. Frequency:

$$\text{Frequency (f)} = \frac{\text{number of events (waves)}}{\text{time (s)}} \qquad \text{or} \qquad f = \frac{n \text{ of events}}{t}$$

Example:

A tuning fork is tapped against a table. If 6 beats are heard in 3 seconds, what is the frequency of the tuning fork?

f = 6waves /3seconds = 2Hz

---

7. Momentum:

Momentum = p = mass X velocity or p = m v   mass should be in units of kg and velocity in m/s

Momentum   is the product of an object's velocity and its mass.

Example:
A girl hits a 0.19-kg softball, giving it a velocity of 35 m/sec. What is the momentum of the ball?

p = 0.19 kg X 35 m/s = 6.65 kg•m/s

----

8. Wavelength:

$$\lambda = \frac{v}{f}$$ $$\text{Wavelength} (\lambda) = \frac{\text{velocity (m/s)}}{\text{frequency (Hz)}}$$

 Wavelength is defined as the distance between two points in the same phase in consecutive cycles of a wave.   The point can be from crest to crest, trough to trough, or two identical points on consecutive waves.

Example:

A ship is about to dock at shore near a lighthouse.   The frequency of the lighthouse's light waves is 350hertz, while the velocity of the light is 40 m/s.   What is the wavelength of the light?

λ = 40 m/s ÷ 350 Hz = 0.11 m

----

9. Work:

Work = Force x distance   W= F x d

Work is the movement of a object through force over a specific distance in meters or relative measurements. Work is the expenditure of energy.   It is measured in Joules (J).

Example:

Joseph uses 10N of force to push a large bucket of ice 5 meters across the floor towards the barbecue grill he is cooking on. How much work does he do?

Work = 10N x 5meters = 50 N/m or 50 J

CPSIA information can be obtained at www.ICGtesting.com
Printed in the USA
BVOW06s2155081214

378542BV00007B/37/P